PROCEDURES SUPPLEMENT

for

Fundamentals of Nursing

SIXTH EDITION

Barbara Kozier, RN, MN
Glenora Erb, RN, BSN
Sammie L. Justesen, RN

Prentice Hall Health
Upper Saddle River, New Jersey 07458

Publisher: Julie Alexander
Editor-in-Chief: Cheryl Mehalik
Project Editors: Virginia Simione Jutson, Grace Wong
Managing Editor: Wendy Earl
Associate Editor: Stephanie Kellogg
Publishing Assistants: Susan Teahan, Peggy Hammett
Production Supervisor: David Novak
Production Coordination: Sondra Kirkley Glider
Interior Design: The Left Coast Group, Inc.
Cover Design: Yvo Riezebos Design
Typesetting: The Left Coast Group, Inc.
Printer/Binder: Victor Graphics
Director of Manufacturing and Production: Bruce Johnson
Manufacturing Buyer: Ilene Sanford
Cover Illustration: The quilt is entitled *Summer's End*, © Joy Saville.
Photo by William Taylor.

Previously published by Addison-Wesley Nursing
A Division of the Benjamin/Cummings Publishing Company, Inc.
Redwood City, California 94065

10 9 8 7 6 5 4 3 2

ISBN 0–8053–8345–X

Prentice-Hall International (UK) Limited, London
Prentice-Hall of Australia Pty. Limited, Sydney
Prentice-Hall Canada Inc., Toronto
Prentice-Hall Hispanoamericana, S.A., Mexico
Prentice-Hall of India Private Limited, New Delhi
Prentice-Hall of Japan, Inc., Tokyo

Contents

Preface

When *Fundamentals of Nursing* was first published, instructors said they liked the combination of theory and procedures in a single comprehensive source. Their response led us to include more procedures in the subsequent editions. This *Procedures Supplement* has been developed to offer instructors an even more complete range of procedures.

This supplement does not duplicate any procedures in *Fundamentals of Nursing*. The chapter numbers of the supplement coincide with the corresponding chapter numbers of the main text. Several chapters do not have any supplementary procedures.

The procedures in this supplement are organized in the same framework as those in the text: Purposes, Assessment Focus, Equipment, Intervention, Evaluation Focus, and Sample Recording. The new features Lifespan Considerations and Home Care Considerations have been added to this new edition.

This book represents our continuing commitment and the commitment of the publisher to provide nurse educators with a variety of teaching materials in nursing fundamentals that can be adapted to almost any curriculum. We hope that the students and instructors using *Fundamentals of Nursing*, Sixth Edition, will find this supplement helpful and will continue to offer suggestions to improve its effectiveness.

Barbara Kozier
Glenora Erb
Sammie L. Justesen

Directions to the Student

Specific nursing actions have been omitted from each procedure to avoid repetition. These actions, which underlie safe, competent nursing, are as follows.

- Before implementing any procedure, refer to the agency's protocols for information and recommendations.

- Many agencies require a signed, informed consent for certain invasive procedures. Please refer to agency policies for this information.

- Some procedures refer to a physician performing diagnostic and therapeutic procedures, such as thoracentesis and paracentesis. In some agencies and settings, individuals practicing in expanded roles, including nurse practitioners and physician assistants, may be responsible for performing these procedures.

- Many of the procedures pertinent to intravenous therapy involve the use of needles. In many agencies use of a "needleless" system has replaced traditional needles for intravenous therapy. Please familiarize yourself with the agency's policies and practices.

- Recheck an abnormal reading or measurement (e.g., blood pressure) and if it is still abnormal, report and record it immediately.

- Carry out a hand wash before gathering any clean or sterile supplies or before implementing a procedure, and after contact with a client, to avoid transmission of microorganisms to clients, self, or others.

- Implement appropriate blood and body fluid precautions (see Appendix). Wear gloves for procedures that involve direct contact with any body fluid.

- Identify the client appropriately (for example, by reading the client's wrist band and asking the client her or his name).

- Explain the procedure to the client and, in some instances, to support persons, adjusting your explanation to their needs. Explaining what you plan to do reassures people by letting them know what to expect. Explanations are provided in some procedures.

- Provide privacy for the client when any aspect of the procedure could be embarrassing to the client or to other people and as an indication of respect for the client even when he or she is not conscious.

- Elevate the client's bed to a working level and lower the near side rail before starting a procedure. These actions help the nurse maintain good body mechanics.

- Following a procedure, lower the bed and raise the near side rail for clients requiring these precautions. These actions are taken for the client's safety.

- Ensure that the client is comfortable following the procedure.

- Dispose of used and unused supplies according to agency protocol. This step includes cleaning and/or disinfecting equipment as necessary.

15

Holistic Health Modalities

PROCEDURES

15–1 Teaching Progressive Relaxation

PURPOSES
- To reduce stress
- To control chronic pain
- To ease tension
- To obtain maximum benefits from rest and sleep periods
- To enable the client to gain control over body responses to stress and pain

ASSESSMENT FOCUS

> Willingness to participate in the relaxation exercises; the nature and location of any pain; vital signs; signs of stress.

INTERVENTION

1. **Ensure that the environment is quiet, peaceful, and at a temperature that promotes comfort to the client.** *Interruptions or distractions and a room that is too cool interfere with the client's ability to achieve full relaxation.*

2. **Tell the client how progressive relaxation works.**
   - Provide a rationale for the procedure. *This enables the client to understand how stress affects the body.*
   - Ask the client to identify the stressors operating in the client's life and the reactions to these stressors.
   - Demonstrate the method of tensing and relaxing the muscles. *Demonstration enables the client to understand the complete relaxation procedure clearly.*

3. **Assist the client to a comfortable position.**
   - Ensure that all body parts are supported and the joints slightly flexed, with no strain or pull on the muscles (e.g., arms and legs should not be crossed). *Assuming a position of comfort facilitates relaxation.*

4. **Encourage the client to rest the mind.**
   - Ask the client to gaze slowly around the room (e.g., across the ceiling, down the wall, along a window curtain, around the fabric pattern, and back up the wall). *This exercise focuses the mind outside the body, and creates a second center of concentration, facilitating relaxation.*

5. **Instruct the client to tense and then relax each muscle group.**
   - Progress through each muscle group in the following order, starting with the dominant side:
     a. Hand and forearm
     b. Upper arm
     c. Forehead
     d. Central face
     e. Lower face and jaw
     f. Neck
     g. Chest, shoulders, and upper back
     h. Abdomen
     i. Thigh
     j. Calf muscles
     k. Foot
   - Encourage the client to breathe slowly and deeply during the entire procedure. *Slow, deep breathing facilitates relaxation.*
   - Encourage the client to focus on each muscle group being tensed and relaxed.
   - Speak in a soothing voice that encourages relaxation, and coach the client to focus on each muscle group (e.g., "Make a tight fist," "Clench your fist tightly," "Hold the tension for 5 to 7 seconds," "Let all the tension go," and "Enjoy the feelings as your muscles become relaxed and loose.").

6. **Ask the client to state whether any tension remains after all muscle groups have been tensed and relaxed.**
   - Repeat the procedure for muscle groups that are not relaxed.

7. **Terminate the relaxation exercise slowly by counting backward from 4 to 1.**
   - Ask the client to move the body slowly: first the hands and feet; then arms and legs; and finally the head and neck.

8. **Document the client's response to the exercise.**

▶ **Procedure 15–1** *continued*

EVALUATION FOCUS

> Signs of relaxation (e.g., decreased muscle tension, slowed breathing); the client's feelings regarding success or problems with the technique.

SAMPLE RECORDING

Date	Time	Notes
9/10/04	1300	Instruction provided for progressive relaxation technique. States has difficulty relaxing and resting because of worries about recent diagnosis of cancer, work pressures, and financial concerns. During the technique respirations slowed to 14 and facial body tension not evident. Stated felt "more peaceful" following the technique.————————Sharon Stookey, RN

LIFESPAN CONSIDERATIONS

- Many older adults benefit from progressive relaxation techniques. *Older adults can develop depression and stress from chronic pain, isolation, and loss of control over their lives.*

- Positive mental attitudes help retard the aging process.

- Many older adults welcome new techniques for managing pain and stress. *It is a myth that older persons are closed-minded and set in their ways.*

HOME CARE CONSIDERATIONS

- Have the client choose a quiet, comfortable place in the home to perform the relaxation exercise.

- Eliminate noise and distractions, such as a television or loud conversation.

- The client may wish to play special music while performing the exercise at home.

- Teach the client to perform progressive relaxation at least once a day and as often as needed to cope with stress or pain.

- Clients who are able to leave the home often benefit from community classes in yoga or meditation.

15–2 Assisting with Guided Imagery

PURPOSES
- To improve the body's response to therapy
- To control acute and chronic pain
- To reduce muscle tension
- To augment other relaxation techniques

ASSESSMENT FOCUS

> Willingness to participate in imagery exercises.

INTERVENTION

1. **Provide a comfortable, quiet environment free of distractions.** *An environment free of distractions is necessary for the client to focus on the selected image.*

2. **Explain the rationale and benefits of imagery.** *The client is an active participant in an imagery exercise and must understand completely what to do and what the expected outcomes are.*

3. **Assist the client to a comfortable position.**

- Assist the client to a reclining position, and ask the client to close the eyes. *A position of comfort can enhance the client's focus during the imagery exercise.*

- Use touch only if this does not threaten the client. For some clients, physical touch may be disturbing because of cultural or religious beliefs.

4. **Implement actions to induce relaxation.**

- Use the client's preferred name. *During imagery exercises, the client is more likely to respond to the preferred name.*

- Speak clearly in a calming and neutral tone of voice. *Positive voice coaching can enhance the effect of imagery. A shrill or loud voice can distract the client from the image.*

- Ask the client to take slow, deep breaths and to relax all muscles.

- Use progressive relaxation exercises as needed to assist the client to achieve total relaxation (see Procedure 15–1).

- For pain or stress management, encourage the client to "go to a place where you have previously felt very peaceful."

  or

  For internal imagery, encourage the client to focus on a meaningful image of power and to use it to control the specific problem.

5. **Assist the client to elaborate on the description of the image.**

- Ask the client to use all the senses in describing the image and the environment of the image. Sometimes clients will think only of visual images. *Using all the senses enhances the client's benefit from imagery.*

6. **Ask the client to describe the physical and emotional feelings elicited by the image.**

- Direct the client to explore the response to the image. *This enables the client to modify the image. Negative responses can be redirected by the nurse to provide a more positive outcome. Positive responses can be enhanced by describing them in detail.*

7. **Provide the client with continuous feedback.**

- Comment on signs of relaxation and peacefulness.

8. **Take the client out of the image.**

- Slowly count backward from 5 to 1. Tell the client that he or she will feel rested when the eyes are opened.

- Remain until the client is alert.

9. **Following the experience, discuss the client's feelings about the experience.**

- Identify anything that could enhance the experience.

10. **Encourage the client to practice the imagery technique.**

- Imagery is a technique that can be done independently by the client once one knows how.

▶ **Procedure 15–2** *continued*

EVALUATION FOCUS

Signs of relaxation and/or decreased pain (e.g., decreased muscle tension; slow, restful breathing; and peaceful affect); the effectiveness of the image selected.

SAMPLE RECORDING

Date	Time	Notes
8/4/04	1000	States inability to get enough rest because of chronic back pain ("I wake up in the middle of the night and can't get back to sleep. During the day I can't sit in a chair for very long either so I have to walk and move to relieve the pain.") Assisted with guided imagery. Needed encouragement to use her senses of smell and hearing as well as the visual image. States would like to try imagery again this afternoon with assistance.——Marilyn Morrison, RN

LIFESPAN CONSIDERATIONS

- Children, adults, and older adults can benefit from guided imagery.

- Children especially enjoy using the imagination but may need help choosing an image at first.

- Younger children may have difficulty focusing. *Provide continuous positive feedback and support.*

HOME CARE CONSIDERATIONS

- Ask the client to choose a quiet, comfortable area of the home to practice guided imagery.

- Special music, a photograph, or a painting can help trigger positive images for the client.

- Teach the client to set a time and place for performing guided imagery at home. *Practicing the technique at least once a day can help control pain and reduce tension.*

- Clients who are able to leave home may benefit from classes in other therapies, such as yoga or meditation.

28

Vital Signs

PROCEDURES

Fetal Heart Assessment

The fetal heart rate (FHR) is audible as early as the tenth week of pregnancy, using the Doppler stethoscope with ultrasound. At about 18 to 20 weeks, the FHR can be heard by fetoscope or other stethoscope.

The FHR is usually about 140 beats per minute (RPM) with a normal range of 120 to 160 BPM. It can be detected during the early months of pregnancy at the midline of the abdomen over the mother's symphysis pubis (above the pubic hairline); later in the pregnancy, the location varies with the position of the fetus (Figure 28–1).

FHRs are taken under these circumstances:

- If there is any concern about the health of the fetus

- On the client's admission

- Every hour during the onset of regular contractions of the uterus

- During a contraction and for 30 seconds after a contraction

- Every 30 minutes during cervical dilation

- Every 5 minutes or continually during the second stage of labor

- Immediately after the rupture of the uterine membranes

Because fetal heartbeats are most clearly transmitted through the back of the fetus, locations of maximum FHR intensity vary according to the position of the fetus (Figure 28–2 on page 8).

The following kinds of stethoscopes are used in assessing FHRs:

- A fetal heart stethoscope (fetoscope) with a large weighted bell designed specifically for fetal heart auscultation (Figure 28–3 on page 8). The weighted bell negates the need to hold the stethoscope in place, thus avoiding the noise of finger movement, which can interfere with auscultation. Some fetal heart stethoscopes can be adapted to monitor the mother's heart rate and blood pressure by substituting a smaller bell.

- A head stethoscope, which augments the fetal heart sounds; sounds are transmitted not only to the nurse's eardrums but also by bone conduction through the headpiece the nurse wears.

- A Doppler ultrasound stethoscope with probe (transducer) and transmission gel. The DUS is a more sensitive and reliable instrument than other fetoscopes. The transducer is applied to the woman's abdomen in lieu of the bell of other fetoscopes.

Procedure 28–1 describes how to assess the fetal heart.

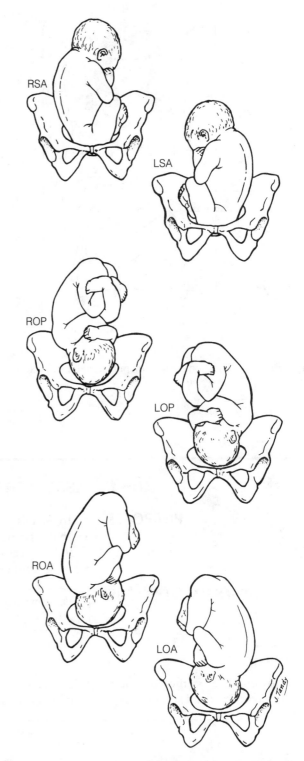

Figure 28–1 Six positions of the fetus: right sacrum anterior (RSA), right occiput posterior (ROP), right occiput anterior (ROA), left sacrum anterior (LSA), left occiput posterior (LOP), and left occiput anterior (LOA).

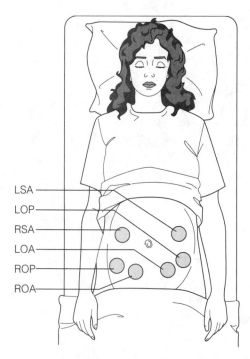

LSA
LOP
RSA
LOA
ROP
ROA

Figure 28–2   Locations of maximum FHR intensity according to the position of the fetus.

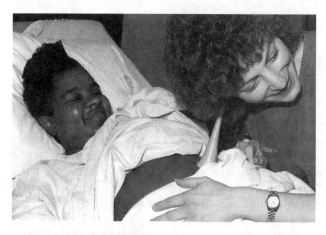

Figure 28–3   A fetoscope.

28–1   Assessing a Fetal Heart

PURPOSES
- To establish baseline data in the initial assessment of the client
- To determine whether the rate is within normal range, the rhythm regular, and the beat strong
- To determine any change from previous measurements

ASSESSMENT FOCUS

Varies with gestation period.

EQUIPMENT

- ❑ Fetoscope, head stethoscope, or a Doppler ultrasound stethoscope
- ❑ Soft tissues and aqueous solution, if Doppler equipment is used
- ❑ Watch with second hand

► **Procedure 28–1** *continued*

INTERVENTION

1. Position the client appropriately.

- Assist the woman to a supine position, and expose the abdomen.

2. Locate the maximum FHR intensity.

- Determine whether the area of maximum intensity is recorded on the client's chart or marked on the client's abdomen.

  or

  Perform Leopold's maneuvers to determine fetal position and locate its back.

3. Auscultate and count the FHR.

- Warm the hands and the head of the fetoscope before touching the client's abdomen.

- Place the bell of the fetoscope or the head stethoscope firmly on the maternal abdomen over the area of maximum intensity of the FHR in accordance with the identified fetal position: right sacrum anterior (RSA), right occiput posterior (ROP), right occiput anterior (ROA), left sacrum anterior (LSA), left occiput posterior (LOP), and left occiput anterior (LOA) (Figure 28–2). *The FHR is best heard when sounds are transmitted through the fetus's back.*

- Gently press the bell about 0.5 inches (1.3 cm) into the client's abdomen. Remove your hands to prevent extraneous noise.

- Listen to and identify the fetal heart tone.

- Differentiate the fetal heart tone from the uterine souffle by simultaneously taking the maternal radial pulse. The *uterine souffle* is the soft blowing sound made when the maternal heart propels the blood through the large blood vessels of the uterus. It synchronizes with the maternal heart rate and can be heard distinctly upon auscultation of the lower portion of the uterus.

- Differentiate the fetal heart tone from the *funic* (umbilical cord) *souffle*, a sharp hissing sound caused by blood rushing through the umbilical cord. It is equivalent to the fetal heart rate, that is, about 140 BPM.

- Count the FHR for at least 15 seconds whenever it is monitored during the gestation period before labor.

- During labor, count the FHR for 60 seconds during the relaxation period between contractions to determine the baseline FHR. Then count the FHR for 60 seconds during a contraction and for 30 seconds immediately following a contraction. *Signs of fetal distress may occur during a contraction but most often occur immediately after it. More than 160 or fewer than 120 BPM may indicate fetal distress.*

4. Assess the rhythm and the strength of the heartbeat.

- Assess the rhythm of the heartbeat by noting the pattern of intervals between the beats. A normal FHR has equal time periods between beats.

- Assess the strength (volume) of the heartbeat. Normally, the heartbeats are equal in strength and can be described as strong or weak.

- Encourage the mother and her support person to listen to the FHR.

5. Document and report pertinent assessment data.

- Record the FHR, including the rhythm and strength, on the appropriate record.

- If the fetal heart rate or strength is abnormal or marked changes occur, report this immediately to the nurse in charge or physician, and initiate electronic fetal monitoring if appropriate.

VARIATION: Using a Doppler Stethoscope

- Follow the manufacturer's instructions about attaching the headset to the audio unit and transducer.

- Apply transmission gel to the client's abdomen over the appropriate area. *Gel creates an airtight seal between the skin and the transducer and promotes optimal ultrasound wave transmission.*

- In the early months of pregnancy, ask the client to drink plenty of fluids before the procedure to fill the bladder and improve ultrasound transmission. Later in the pregnancy, this may cause discomfort to the client.

- Place the earpieces of the headset in your ears, adjust the volume of the audio unit, hold that unit in one hand, and place the transducer on the mother's abdomen.

- After determining the FHR, remove the excess gel from the mother's abdomen and from the transducer with soft tissues.

- Clean the transducer with aqueous solutions. *Alcohol or other disinfectants may damage the face of the transducer.*

▶Procedure 28–1 Assessing a Fetal Heart *continued*

EVALUATION FOCUS

> FHR in relation to baseline data and normal range; heartbeat rhythm and volume in relation to baseline data and health status.

SAMPLE RECORDING

Date	Time	Notes
9/14/04	1300	FHR 136 over right lower quadrant. Beats regular and strong.————————————————————————————Eva L. Mendez, SN

LIFESPAN CONSIDERATIONS

- Young mothers may need extra teaching and support.
- Promote a calm environment and take time to answer all questions.

HOME CARE CONSIDERATIONS

- Provide for privacy needs during the home visit.
- Keep the client informed of your findings and the importance of following any restrictions, such as decreased activity or a special diet. *Antepartal clients seen by the home care nurse usually have an associated medical problem, such as hypertension or diabetes.*
- Encourage the client to follow up as needed with her other health care providers.
- Assess the need for other services, such as a social worker or dietician.

An Infant's Blood Pressure

The blood pressure of an infant can be measured by auscultation, palpation, ultrasound (Doppler technique), or flush technique. Auscultation is often difficult on infants under age 3, because Korotkoff's sounds are relatively inaudible, but it is the method of choice for children over 3 years of age. When the blood pressure cannot be auscultated, it can be palpated or measured by the flush technique. Both of these methods reveal only a mean pressure between the systolic and diastolic pressures when the blood returns to the limb. The flush technique is largely being replaced by use of an ultrasound device. Some ultrasound models measure only systolic pressures; others measure both systolic and diastolic pressures.

When measuring an infant's blood pressure, the systolic pressure (phase 1) is noted when the first clear tapping sound is heard. Both phase 4 (muffling of sounds) and phase 5 (disappearance of sounds) are recorded for the diastolic pressure. They are recorded in the form "118/78/68." If only phases 1 and 4 can be identified, they are recorded "118/78/68." This indicates that sounds were heard to the 0 point on the manometer.

When a cuff of the appropriate size is not available for an infant or child, it is preferable (a) to use an oversized cuff rather than an undersized one (wide cuffs apparently do not cause the low readings noted in adults [Whaley and Wong 1989, p. 138]) or (b) to use a different site that will accommodate the cuff size. For example, a radial pressure may be taken if the cuff is too small, or a thigh blood pressure may be taken if only a large cuff is available. Systolic blood pressure in the radial artery is usually 10 mm Hg lower than in the brachial artery; it is usually 10 mm Hg higher in the popliteal artery than in the brachial artery in children over age 1. Arm and thigh pressures are equal in children under age 1.

28–2   Assessing an Infant's Blood Pressure

PURPOSES
- To establish a baseline in the initial assessment of the infant
- To determine any change from previous measurements
- To determine the adequacy of the arterial blood pressure

ASSESSMENT FOCUS

> Signs and symptoms of hypertension and hypotension; factors affecting blood pressure.

EQUIPMENT
- ❏ Blood pressure cuff of a suitable size
- ❏ Sphygmomanometer (auscultatory method)
- ❏ Stethoscope (auscultatory method) or DUS
- ❏ Elastic bandage of suitable width to cover the limb distal to the cuff (flush method)

INTERVENTION

1. **Prepare the infant or child appropriately.**

- Explain each step of the procedure to children of preschool age and above. Tell them how the cuff will feel (tight or like an arm hug) and to "watch the silver rise in the tube." When possible, demonstrate the procedure on a toy or your own arm.

- Be sure that the environment in which the blood pressure measurement is to take place is quiet and reassuring to the infant. *Frightening sounds or sights can contribute to error in measurement since anxiety and restlessness increase the blood pressure.*

- Allow time for the infant to recover from any activity or apprehension.

- Assist the child to a comfortable position. Infants and small children may be more quiet if placed in a sitting position on the parent's lap.

- Expose the arm fully, if used, and then support it comfortably at the child's heart level.

2. **Use the auscultation method for a child over 3 years of age.**

- The auscultatory method is essentially the same for children as for adults. (See Procedure 28–6 in *Fundamentals of Nursing.*)

►Procedure 28–2 Assessing an Infant's Blood Pressure *continued*

- Identify the manometer reading at phases 1, 4, and 5 of Korotkoff's sounds. Phase 1 is the systolic pressure and phases 4 and 5 the diastolic pressures.

3. **Use the palpation method, the flush technique, or a Doppler stethoscope when the blood pressure cannot be auscultated.**

Palpation Method

- Place the cuff around the limb so that the lower edge is about 1 cm (0.4 in) above the antecubital space (Figure 28–4).

- Palpate the brachial pulse.

- Inflate the cuff to about 30 mm Hg beyond the point where the brachial pulse disappears.

- Release the cuff at the rate of 2 to 3 mm Hg per second, and identify the manometer reading at the point where the pulse returns in the brachial artery. This pressure is a mean pressure between the systolic and diastolic pressures.

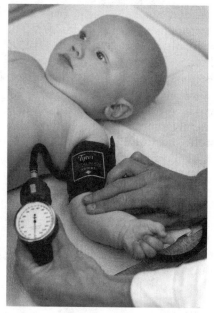

Figure 28–4   Taking an infant's blood pressure by palpation.

Flush Technique

This procedure requires two people and a well-lighted room, so that the pressure at which the flush appears can be accurately determined.

- Place the cuff on the infant's wrist or ankle.

- Elevate the limb. *This promotes venous blood flow to the heart.*

- Wrap the limb distal to the cuff with an elastic bandage. Wrap firmly, starting at the fingers or toes and working up to the blood pressure cuff. *The bandage will force venous blood into the upper part of the limb and restrict arterial blood flow into the lower part of the limb.*

- Lower the extremity to the heart level.

- Inflate the bladder of the cuff rapidly to about 200 mm Hg. *This stops arterial blood flow to the limb.*

- Remove the bandage. The limb should appear pale because of the absence of blood.

- Gradually release the pressure at no more than 5 mm Hg per second.

- Record the pressure at the appearance of a flush as the blood returns in the extremity distal to the cuff. This pressure is a mean blood pressure between the systolic and diastolic pressures.

EVALUATION FOCUS

The blood pressure in relation to baseline data, normal range for age, and heart status; relationship to pulse and respiration.

SAMPLE RECORDING

Date	Time	Notes
3/23/04	1600	BP 116/64 by ultrasound. AP-120.————————Nancy Lopez, SN

LIFESPAN CONSIDERATIONS

- Arm and thigh pressures are equal in children under age 1.

- Ask the parent to hold the infant during the examination. *Infants between 6 and 12 months of age are most likely to be upset if separated from the parent.*

- Expect the infant to respond to voice by exhibiting the blink or startle reflex, turning the head toward the sound, or lying still as though listening.

HOME CARE CONSIDERATIONS

- If possible, find a private, quiet place in the home for your examination of the infant.

- Determine the caregiver's learning needs and establish a teaching plan.

- Listen to the mother and include the parents and siblings in care plan responsibilities. *The family is an integral part of the success of the home treatment plan.*

- Assess the home environment and family dynamics.

29

Health Assessment

PROCEDURES

Lumbar Puncture

In a **lumbar puncture** (LP, or spinal tap), cerebrospinal fluid (CSF) is withdrawn through a needle inserted into the **subarachnoid space** of the spinal canal between the third and fourth lumbar vertebrae or between the fourth and fifth lumbar vertebrae. At this level the needle avoids damaging the spinal cord and major nerve roots (Figure 29–1). During a lumbar puncture, the physician frequently takes CSF pressure readings using a **manometer,** a glass or plastic tube calibrated in millimeters. A Queckenstedt-Stookey test may also be done while the manometer is in place. When the veins of the neck are compressed on one or both sides, cerebrospinal pressure rises rapidly in healthy persons, but

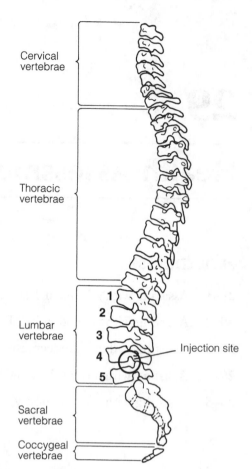

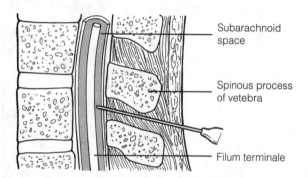

Figure 29–1   A diagram of the vertebral column, indicating a site for insertion of the lumbar puncture needle into the subarachnoid space of the spinal canal.

quickly returns to normal when pressure is removed from the neck. If pressure of the cerebral spinal fluid remains unchanged, rises only slightly, or takes longer than 20 seconds to return to baseline, blockage is present in the vertebral canal. The nurse may be asked to exert digital (finger) pressure on one or both of the internal jugular veins for this test (Figure 29–2).

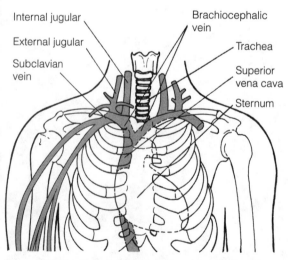

Figure 29–2   Location of the internal jugular vein for the Queckenstedt-Stookey test.

29–1 Assisting with a Lumbar Puncture

PURPOSES
- To obtain a CSF specimen
- To take CSF pressure readings
- To administer drugs or anesthetics
- As treatment to lower the pressure of spinal fluid
- To inject dye or gas for contrast during radiologic studies

ASSESSMENT FOCUS

Baseline vital signs; neurologic status; presence of headache; allergies to skin antiseptics or anesthetic agents.

EQUIPMENT

- Sterile lumbar puncture set containing:
  Sterile sponges or gauze squares
  Skin antiseptic
  Drapes (one may be fenestrated)
  Syringe and needle to administer the local anesthetic (A 2-mL syringe and #24 and #22 needles are often provided)
  Spinal needle 5 to 12.5 cm (2 to 5 in) long, with stylet. The shorter needles are used for infants.
  Manometer
  Three-way stopcock (a valve between the spinal needle and the manometer that regulates the flow of CSF by shutting off the CSF drainage, allowing the CSF to flow either into the manometer or out into a receptacle)
  Specimen containers and labels

  Local anesthetic, e.g., 1% procaine (if not included in preassembled set, a vial or ampule of it must be obtained)
  Small dressing
- Face masks (optional)
- Sterile gloves
- Examining light, if needed

INTERVENTION

Preprocedure

1. **Explain the procedure to the client and support persons.**

- Tell the client
  a. That the physician will be taking a small sample of spinal fluid from the lower spine.
  b. That a local anesthetic will be given to minimize discomfort.
  c. When and where the procedure will occur, e.g., at the bedside or in the treatment room.
  d. Who will be present, e.g., the physician and the nurse.
  e. That it will be necessary to lie in a certain position without moving for about 15 minutes.

- In addition, tell the client he may feel a slight pinprick when the local anesthetic is injected and a

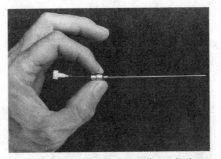

Figure 29–3 A spinal needle with the stylet protruding from the hub.

sensation of pressure as the spinal needle (Figure 29–3) is inserted.

2. **Prepare the client.**

- Have the client empty the bladder and bowels prior to the procedure. *This prevents unnecessary discomfort.*

- Position the client laterally with the head bent toward the chest, the knees flexed onto the abdomen, and the back at the edge of the bed or examining table (Figure 29–4 on page 16). Place a small pillow under the client's head to maintain the alignment of the spine. *In this position the back is arched, increasing the spaces between the vertebrae so that the spinal needle can be inserted readily.*

- Drape the client to expose only the lumbar spine.

- Open the lumbar puncture set (Figure 29–5 on page 16) if requested to do so by the physician.

During the Procedure

3. **Support and monitor the client throughout.**

- Stand in front of the client, and support the back of the neck and knees if the client needs help remaining still (Figure 29–4 on page 16).

- Reassure the client throughout the procedure by explaining what is happening. Encourage normal

▶ Procedure 29–1 Assisting with a Lumbar Puncture *continued*

Figure 29–4   Supporting the client for a lumbar puncture.

breathing and relaxation. *Excessive muscle tension, coughing, or changes in breathing can increase CSF pressure, giving a false reading.*

- Observe the client's color, respirations, and pulse during the lumbar procedure. Ask the client to report headache or persistent pain at the insertion site.

4. Handle specimen tubes appropriately.

- Wear gloves to prevent contact with the CSF when handling test tubes.

- Label the specimen tubes in sequence if they are not already labeled. Take care not to contaminate the physician's sterile gloves, the sterile field, or yourself while handling the tubes. *The CSF may contain virulent microorganisms, e.g., organisms that cause meningitis.*

- Send the CSF specimens to the laboratory immediately.

5. Place a small sterile dressing over the puncture site. *This helps prevent infection after the needle is removed.*

Postprocedure

6. Ensure the client's comfort and safety.

- Assist the client to a dorsal recumbent position with only one head pillow. The client remains in this position for 1 to 12 hours, depending on the physician's orders. *Some clients experience a headache following a lumbar puncture, and the dorsal recumbent position helps prevent this.*

- Determine whether analgesics are ordered and can be given for headaches.

- Offer oral fluids frequently, unless contraindicated. *Extra fluid helps restore the volume of CSF.*

7. Monitor the client.

- Observe for swelling or bleeding at the puncture site.

- Determine whether the client feels faint.

- Monitor changes in neurologic status, such as pupillary response, level of consciousness, and muscle strength.

- Determine whether the client is experiencing any numbness, tingling, or pain radiating down the legs. *This may be due to nerve irritation.*

8. Document the procedure on the client's chart. Include the date and time performed; the physician's name; the color, character, and amount of CSF; and the number of specimens obtained. Also document CSF pressure readings and the nurse's assessments and interventions.

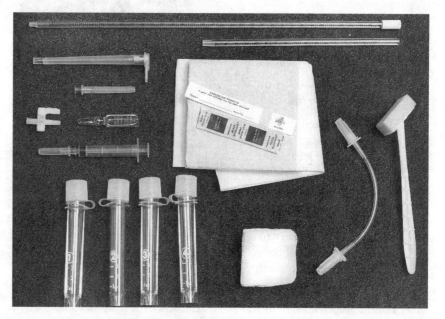

Figure 29–5   A preassembled lumbar puncture set. Note the manometer at the top of the set.

▶ **Procedure 29–1** *continued*

EVALUATION FOCUS

Vital signs; neurologic status; status of puncture site; complaints of discomfort or feelings of numbness or tingling in the lower extremities.

SAMPLE RECORDING

Date	Time	Notes
5/24/04	1500	Lumbar puncture performed by Dr Guido. Four 2 mL specimens of cloudy serous CSF sent to lab. Initial pressure 130 mm. Closing pressure 100 mm. Neurological status unchanged. Denies discomfort or numbness to lower extremities. BP 120/66, RR 18, RP 74. Resting.————Sarah 0. Nicols, NS

LIFESPAN CONSIDERATIONS

Younger Clients

- Briefly demonstrate the procedure on a doll or stuffed animal. Allow time to answer questions.

- One member of the health care team should maintain eye contact with the young client and provide reassurance during the procedure.

Older Clients

- Some clients need help maintaining the flexed position due to arthritis, weakness, or tremors.

- Provide an extra blanket to keep the client warm during the procedure. *Older adults have a decreased metabolism and less subcutaneous fat.*

- If the client has a hearing loss, speak slowly and distinctly, especially when unable to make eye contact.

Abdominal Paracentesis

Normally the body creates just enough peritoneal fluid for lubrication. The fluid is continuously formed and absorbed into the lymphatic system. However, in some disease processes, a large amount of fluid accumulates in the cavity; this condition is called **ascites.** Normal ascitic fluid is serous, clear, and light yellow in color. An **abdominal paracentesis** is carried out to obtain a fluid specimen for laboratory study and to relieve pressure on the abdominal organs due to the presence of excess fluid.

The procedure is carried out by a physician with the assistance of a nurse. Strict sterile technique is followed. A common site for abdominal paracentesis is midway between the umbilicus and the symphysis pubis on the midline (Figure 29–6). The physician makes a small in-

cision with a scalpel, inserts the **trocar** (a sharp, pointed instrument) and **cannula** (tube), and then withdraws the trocar, which is inside the cannula (Figure 29–7). Tubing is attached to the cannula and the fluid flows through the tubing into a receptacle. If the purpose of the paracentesis is to obtain a specimen, the physician may use a long aspirating needle attached to a syringe rather than making an incision and using a trocar and cannula. Normally about 1500 mL is the maximum amount of fluid drained at one time to avoid hypovolemic shock. The fluid is drained very slowly for the same reason. Some fluid is placed in the specimen container before the cannula is withdrawn. The small incision may or may not be sutured; in either case, it is covered with a small sterile bandage.

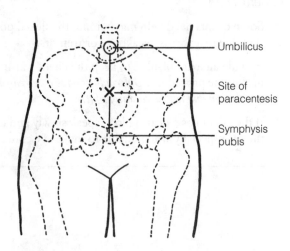

Figure 29–6   A common site for an abdominal paracentesis

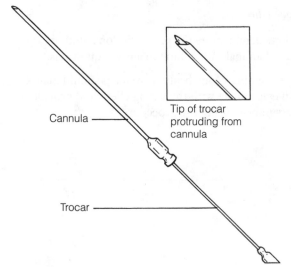

Figure 29–7   A trocar and cannula may be used for an abdominal paracentesis.

29–2 Assisting with an Abdominal Paracentesis

PURPOSES
- To obtain a fluid specimen
- To relieve abdominal pressure due to excess fluid

ASSESSMENT FOCUS

> Baseline vital signs; degree of ascites in the abdomen (weigh the client and measure the abdominal girth at the level of the umbilicus); general appearance and health status; allergies to skin antiseptic or anesthetic agents.

▶ **Procedure 29–2** *continued*

EQUIPMENT

- ❏ Sterile set containing:
  Sterile sponges or gauze squares with an antiseptic solution
  Drape or drapes (one may be fenestrated)
  Trocar, cannuls, three-way stop-cock 50-mL syringe

- 2-mL syringe and #24 and #22 needles
  Small scalpel, needle holder, and sutures
  Aspirating set or aspirating needle
  Local anesthetic
- ❏ Vacutainer bottles for the fluid

- ❏ Specimen containers and labels
- ❏ Masks (optional)
- ❏ Sterile gloves
- ❏ Nonsterile disposable gloves for the nurse
- ❏ Goggles and protective gowns for the nurse and physician

INTERVENTION

Preprocedure

1. **Prepare the client.**

- Explain the procedure to the client. Normally, the procedure isn't painful and can relieve discomfort caused by excess fluid. The procedure to remove ascitic fluid usually takes 30 to 60 minutes. Obtaining a specimen usually takes about 15 minutes. Emphasize the importance of remaining still during the procedure. Tell the client when and where the procedure will occur and who will be present.

- Have the client void just before the paracentesis. *This lessens the possibility of puncturing the urinary bladder.* Notify the physician if the client cannot void.

- Help the client assume a sitting position in bed, in a chair, or on the edge of the bed supported by pillows. This allows fluid to accumulate in the lower abdominal cavity. Gravity and pressure from the abdominal organs will help move fluid from the cavity.

- If a fenestrated drape is used, place the opening at the site where fluid will be removed. Maintain the client's privacy and provide blankets for warmth.

During the Procedure

2. **Assist and monitor the client.**

- Support the client verbally, and describe the steps of the procedure as needed.

- Observe the client closely for signs of distress, e.g., abnormal pulse rate, skin color, and blood pressure. Observe for signs of hypovolemic shock induced by the loss of fluid: pallor, dyspnea, diaphoresis (profuse perspiration), a drop in blood pressure, and restlessness or increased anxiety.

- Place a small sterile dressing over the site of the incision after the cannula or aspirating needle is withdrawn. *This prevents bleeding or leakage of fluid.*

Postprocedure

3. **Monitor the client closely.**

- Observe for hypovolemic shock (see step 2).

- Observe for scrotal edema with male clients.

- Monitor vital signs, urine output, and drainage from the puncture site every 15 minutes for at least 2 hours and every hour for 4 hours thereafter, or as the client's condition indicates.

- Measure the abdominal girth at the level of the umbilicus.

4. **Document all relevant information.**

- Document the procedure on the client's chart, including date and time; the physician's name; abdominal girth before and after; the color, clarity, and amount of drained fluid; and the nurse's assessments and interventions.

5. **Transport the correctly labeled specimens to the laboratory.**

▶ **Procedure 29–2 Assisting with an Abdominal Paracentesis** *continued*

EVALUATION FOCUS

Abdominal girth; weight; vital signs; urine output; drainage from puncture area; signs of infection (elevated body temperature); signs of internal hemorrhage (lowered blood pressure, accelerated pulse, hard, boardlike abdomen).

SAMPLE RECORDING

Date	Time	Notes
7/18/04	1400	Paracentesis performed by Dr Johnson, 300 mL clear serosanguinous fluid obtained. Abdominal girth at umbilical level 114 cm before, 109 cm after. Specimen sent to laboratory. P 72, BP 120/85. Slight pallor. Resting comfortably. Sterile dressing applied to puncture site.——————————————————Roxanne J. Tuttle, NS

LIFESPAN CONSIDERATIONS

- Provide pillows and blankets to help older adults remain comfortable during the procedure.

- Ask the client to empty the bladder just before the procedure. *Older adults may need to void more frequently and in smaller amounts.*

- Remove ascitic fluid slowly and monitor the client for signs of hypovolemia. *Older adults have less tolerance for fluid loss and may develop hypovelemia if a large volume of fluid is drained rapidly.*

Thoracentesis

Normally, only sufficient fluid to lubricate the pleura is present in the pleural cavity. However, excessive fluid can accumulate as a result of injury, infection, or other pathology. In such a case or in a case of pneumothorax, a physician may perform a **thoracentesis** to remove the excess fluid or air to ease breathing. Thoracentesis is also performed to introduce chemotherapeutic drugs intrapleurally.

The physician and the assisting nurse follow strict sterile technique. The physician attaches a syringe and/or stopcock to the aspirating needle. The stopcock must be in the closed position so that no air will enter the pleural space. The physician inserts the needle through the intercostal space to the pleural cavity. In some instances, the physician threads a small plastic tube through the needle and then withdraws the needle. (The tubing is less likely to puncture the pleura.)

If a syringe is used to receive the fluid, the plunger is pulled out to withdraw the pleural fluid as the stopcock is opened. If a large container is used to receive the fluid, the tubing is attached from the stopcock to the adapter on the receiving bottle. When the adapter and stopcock are opened, gravity allows fluid to drain from the pleural cavity into the container, which should be kept below the level of the client's lungs. After the fluid has been withdrawn, the physician removes the needle or plastic tubing.

29–3 Assisting with a Thoracentesis

Before the thoracentesis, note any orders for medication. A cough suppressant is sometimes ordered to be given 30 minutes before the procedure. An analgesic may also be ordered.

PURPOSES
- To remove excess fluid or air from the pleural cavity
- To introduce chemotherapeutic drugs intrapleurally
- To relieve respiratory distress caused by pulmonary compression

ASSESSMENT FOCUS

> Baseline vital signs; respirations for bilateral depth and chest movement during inspiration; any differences in chest expansion between the sides; dyspnea, abnormal breath sounds, coughing, or chest pain; character and amount of sputum if cough is productive; allergies to skin antiseptics or anesthetic agents; presence of a bleeding disorder.

EQUIPMENT

❑ Sterile set containing:
  Sterile sponges or gauze squares
  Skin antiseptic
  Drape or drapes (one may be fenestrated)
  2-mL syringe and #24 and #22 needles
  Receptacle for the fluid (50-mL syringe and #16 needle or an airtight container)

  Three-way stopcock
  Two-way stopcock with connecting tubing
  Thoracentesis needle, usually a #15 needle about 5 to 7.5 cm (2 to 3 in) long

  Local anesthetic
  Specimen containers and labels
❑ Sterile gloves
❑ Disposable gloves for the nurse
❑ Masks (optional)

▶ **Procedure 29–3 Assisting with a Thoracentesis** *continued*

INTERVENTION

Preprocedure

1. Prepare the client.

- Explain the procedure to the client. Normally, the client may experience some discomfort and a feeling of pressure when the needle is inserted. The procedure may bring considerable relief if breathing has been difficult. The procedure takes only a few minutes, depending primarily on the time it takes for the fluid to drain from the pleural cavity. To avoid puncturing the lungs, it is important for the client not to cough while the needle is inserted. Explain when and where the procedure will occur and who will be present.

- Help the client assume a position that allows easy access to the intracostal spaces. This is usually a sitting position with the arms above the head, which spreads the ribs and enlarges the intercostal space. Two positions commonly used are one in which the arm is elevated and stretched forward (Figure 29–8, A) and one in which the client leans forward over a pillow (Figure 29–8, B). To make sure that the needle is inserted below the fluid level when fluid is to be removed (or above any fluid if air is to be removed), the physi-

cian will palpate the chest and select the exact site for insertion of the needle. A site on the lower posterior chest is often used to remove fluid, and a site on the upper anterior chest is used to remove air. A chest x-ray prior to the procedure will help pinpoint the best insertion site.

- Cover the client as needed with a bath blanket. If using a fenestrated drape, place the opening at the site of the thoracentesis.

- Open the sterile thoracentesis tray and assist the physician as needed.

During the Procedure

2. Support and monitor the client throughout.

- Support the client verbally, and describe the steps of the procedure as needed.

- Observe the client for signs of distress, such as dyspnea, pallor, and coughing. If the client becomes distressed or has to cough, the procedure is halted briefly.

3. Collect drainage and laboratory specimens.

4. Place a small sterile dressing over the site of the puncture.

Postprocedure

5. Monitor the client.

- Assess pulse rate and respiratory rate and skin color. *A shift in the mediastinum (e.g., heart and large blood vessels) can occur with removal of large amounts of fluid.* Signs of mediastinal shift include pallor, accelerated pulse rate, dyspnea, accelerated respiration rate, and dizziness.

- Don't remove more than 1000 mL of fluid from the pleural cavity within the first 30 minutes. *Removing fluid too quickly can lead to pulmonary edema and hypovolemic shock.*

- Observe changes in the client's cough, sputum, respiratory depth, breath sounds, and note complaints of chest pain.

- A postprocedure chest x-ray is often performed to evaluate the results of the thoracentesis.

6. Position the client appropriately.

- Some agency protocols recommend that the client lie on the unaffected side with the head of the bed elevated 30 degrees for at least 30 minutes: *This position facilitates expansion of the affected lung and eases respirations.*

7. Document all relevant information.

- Record the thoracentesis on the client's chart, including the date and time; the name of the physician; the amount, color, and clarity of fluid drained; and nursing assessments and interventions provided.

8. Transport the specimens to the laboratory.

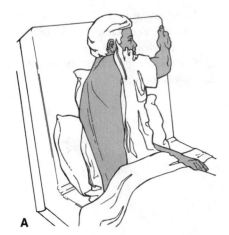
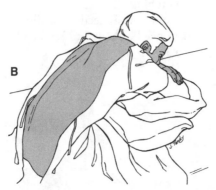

Figure 29–8 Two positions commonly used for a thoracentesis: *A,* sitting on one side with the arm held to the front and up; *B,* sitting and leaning forward over a pillow.

▶ **Procedure 29–3** *continued*

EVALUATION FOCUS

> Respiratory rate, depth, and bilateral chest movement; bilateral breath sounds; vital signs; evidence of cyanosis or dyspnea; complaints of chest pain.

SAMPLE RECORDING

Date	Time	Notes
4/18/04	1500	Thoracentesis performed by Dr Sargent. 275 mL of cloudy serosanguineous fluid removed. Specimen sent to laboratory. R 32, shallow and wet. P 76. Skin pale. Coughing occasionally. Small amount of thick white sputum. Resting more comfortably. BP 110/68. Sterile dressing applied to left mid-axillary thoracentesis site. Specimen sent to lab for culture and sensitivity and Gram stain.————————————————————Ron L. Landry, NS

LIFESPAN CONSIDERATIONS

- Some older clients will need help maintaining the proper position due to arthritis, tremors, or weakness.

- Provide support with pillows during the procedure.

- Absence of body fat in older adults can help the physician locate the intercostal spaces.

- Provide an extra blanket to keep your client warm during the procedure. *Older adults have a decreased metabolism and less subcutaneous fat.*

Bone Marrow Biopsy

A bone marrow biopsy is the removal of a specimen of bone marrow for laboratory study. The biopsy is used to detect specific diseases of the blood, such as pernicious anemia and leukemia. The bones of the body commonly used for a bone marrow biopsy are the sternum and the iliac crests. The posterior superior iliac crest is the preferred site (Figure 29–9).

After injecting a local anesthetic, a small incision may be made with a scalpel to avoid tearing the skin or pushing skin into the bone marrow with the needle. The physician introduces a bone marrow needle with stylet into the red marrow of the spongy bone (Figure 29–10). Once the needle is in the marrow space, the stylet is removed and a 10-mL syringe is attached to the needle. The plunger is withdrawn until 1 to 2 mL of marrow has been obtained. The physician replaces the stylet in the needle, withdraws the needle, and places the specimen in test tubes and/or on glass slides.

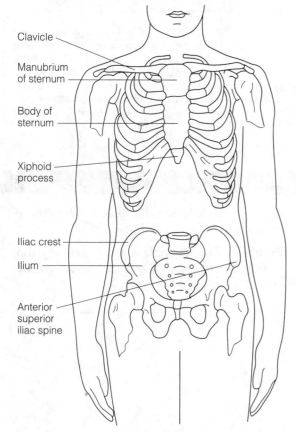

Figure 29–9 The sternum and the iliac crests are common sites for a bone marrow biopsy.

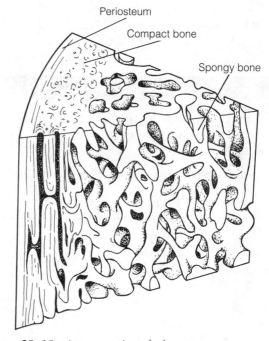

Figure 29–10 A cross section of a bone.

29–4 Assisting with a Bone Marrow Biopsy

PURPOSES
- To obtain a bone marrow sample to check for abnormal blood cell development
- To evaluate response to cancer therapy

ASSESSMENT FOCUS

Baseline vital signs; allergies to skin antiseptics or anesthetic agents.

EQUIPMENT

- ❑ A sterile set containing:
  Drape or drapes (one is often fenestrated)
  Antiseptic
  Local anesthetic
  2-mL syringe and #25 needle

- 10-mL syringe
  Bone marrow needle with stylet
  Sterile gauze squares
  Test tubes and/or glass slides
  Scalpel

- ❑ Masks (optional)
- ❑ Sterile gloves
- ❑ Disposable, nonsterile gloves for the nurse
- ❑ Specimen containers and labels

▶ **Procedure 29–4** *continued*

INTERVENTION

Preprocedure

1. Prepare the client.

- Explain the procedure. The client may experience pain when the marrow is aspirated and hear a crunching sound as the needle is pushed through the cortex of the bone. The procedure usually takes 15 to 30 minutes. Explain when and where the procedure will occur, who will be present, and which site will be used.

- Help the client assume a supine position (with one pillow if desired) for a biopsy of the sternum (sternal puncture) or a prone position for a biopsy of either iliac crest. Fold the bedclothes back or drape the client to expose the area.

- Administer a sedative as ordered.

During the Procedure

2. Monitor and support the client throughout.

- Describe the steps of the procedure as needed, and provide verbal support.

- Observe the client for pallor, diaphoresis, and faintness due to bleeding or pain.

3. Place a small dressing over the site of the puncture after the needle is withdrawn.

- Some agency protocols recommend direct pressure over the site for 5 to 10 minutes to prevent bleeding.

4. Assist with preparing specimens as needed.

Postprocedure

5. Monitor the client.

- Assess for discomfort and bleeding from the site. The client may experience some tenderness in the area. Bleeding and hematoma formation need to be assessed for several days. Report bleeding or pain to the nurse in charge.

- Provide an analgesic as needed and ordered.

6. Document all relevant information.

- Record the procedure, including the date and time of the procedure, the name of the physician, and any nursing assessments and interventions. Document any specimens obtained.

7. Transport the specimens to the laboratory.

EVALUATION FOCUS

Vital signs and puncture site for bleeding.

SAMPLE RECORDING

Date	Time	Notes
8/19/04	0900	Bone marrow biopsy from right iliac crest performed by Dr Rosenthal. Site dry, no apparent bleeding. No complaints of discomfort. Specimen sent to the laboratory. Sterile dressing applied to site.———Donna S. Lambert, NS

LIFESPAN CONSIDERATIONS

Younger Clients

- Young clients need emotional support due to the pain and pressure associated with this procedure.

- Young clients may require gentle restraint to prevent movement during the procedure.

Older Clients

- Older adults with osteoporosis will experience less needle pressure.

- Ask the client to empty the bladder for comfort before the procedure.

- Provide pillows and blankets to help older clients remain comfortable during the procedure.

Liver Biopsy

A liver biopsy is a short procedure, generally performed at the client's bedside, in which a sample of liver tissue is aspirated. A physician inserts a needle in the intercostal space between two of the right lower ribs and into the liver (Figure 29–11), or through the abdomen below the right rib cage (subcostally). The client exhales and stops breathing while the physician inserts the biopsy needle, injects a small amount of sterile normal saline to clear the needle of blood or particles of tissue picked up during insertion, and aspirates liver tissue by drawing back on the plunger of the syringe. After the needle is withdrawn, the nurse applies pressure to the site to prevent bleeding, often by positioning the client on the biopsy site.

Because many clients with liver disease have blood clotting defects and are prone to bleeding, prothrombin time and platelet count are normally taken well in advance of the test. If the test results are abnormal, the biopsy may be contraindicated.

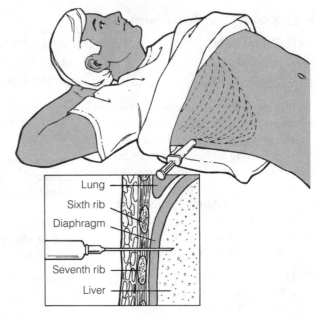

Lung
Sixth rib
Diaphragm
Seventh rib
Liver

Figure 29–11   A common site for a liver biopsy.

29–5 Assisting with a Liver Biopsy

PURPOSES
- To obtain data about the nature of liver disease
- To facilitate diagnosis
- To gain information about specific changes in liver tissue

ASSESSMENT FOCUS

> Client's ability to hold the breath for up to 10 seconds and remain still while the biopsy needle is inserted; prothrombin time and platelet count; allergies to skin antiseptics and anesthetic agents.

EQUIPMENT

- ❑ Sterile liver biopsy set containing:
  Sterile sponges or gauze squares
  with an antiseptic solution
  2-mL syringe and a #22 and #25
  needle (6 in)

Large biopsy syringe and needle
Drapes
Local anesthetic
Sterile normal saline
Specimen container with formalin

- ❑ Face masks (optional)
- ❑ Sterile gloves
- ❑ Disposable gloves for the nurse
- ❑ Specimen containers and labels

INTERVENTION

Preprocedure

1. **Prepare the client.**

- Give preprocedural medications as ordered. *Vitamin K may be given for several days before the biopsy to reduce the risk of hemorrhage. Vitamin K may be lacking in some clients with liver disease. It is essential for the production of prothrombin, which is required for blood clotting.*

- Explain the procedure. Tell the client

  a. That the physician will take a small sample of liver tissue by putting a needle into the client's side or abdomen.

  b. That a sedative and local anesthetic will be given, so the client will feel no pain.

  c. When and where the procedure will occur, who will be present, and the time required.

  d. What to expect as the procedure is being performed; for example, the client may expe-

▶ **Procedure 29–5** *continued*

rience mild discomfort when the local anesthetic is injected and slight pressure when the biopsy needle is inserted.

- Ensure that the client fasts for at least 2 hours before the procedure.

- Administer the appropriate sedative about 30 minutes beforehand or at the specified time.

- Help the client assume a supine position, with the upper right quadrant of the abdomen exposed. Cover the client with the bedclothes so that only the abdominal area is exposed.

During the Procedure

2. Monitor and support the client throughout.

- Support the client in a supine position.

- Instruct the client to take a few deep inhalations and exhalations and to hold the breath after the final exhalation for up to 10 seconds as the needle is inserted, the biopsy obtained, and the needle withdrawn. *Holding the breath after exhalation immobilizes the chest wall and liver and keeps the diaphragm in its highest position, avoiding injury to the lung and laceration of the liver.*

- Instruct the client to resume breathing when the needle is withdrawn.

- Apply pressure to the site of the puncture. *Pressure will help stop any bleeding.*

3. Apply a small dressing to the site of the puncture.

Postprocedure

4. Position the client appropriately.

- Assist the client to a right side-lying position with a small pillow or folded towel under the biopsy site (Figure 29–12). Instruct the client to remain in this position for several hours. *The right lateral position compresses the biopsy site of the liver against the chest wall and minimizes the escape of blood or bile through the puncture site by applying pressure to the area.*

5. Monitor the client.

- Assess the client's vital signs—pulse, respirations, blood pressure—every 15 minutes for the first hour following the test or until the signs are stable. Then monitor vital signs every hour for 24 hours or as needed. *Complications of a liver biopsy are rare, but hemor-*

rhage from a perforated blood vessel can occur.

- Determine whether the client is experiencing abdominal pain. Severe abdominal pain may indicate bile peritonitis *(an inflammation of the peritoneal lining of the abdomen caused by bile leaking from a perforated bile duct).*

- Check the biopsy site for localized bleeding. Pressure dressings may be required if bleeding does occur.

6. Document all relevant information.

- Record the procedure, including the date and time it was performed, the name of the physician, and all nursing assessments and interventions.

7. Transport the specimens to the laboratory.

Figure 29–12 The position to provide pressure on a liver biopsy site.

▶ **Procedure 29–5 Assisting with a Liver Biopsy** *continued*

EVALUATION FOCUS

> Vital signs; bleeding from puncture site; complaints of abdominal pain.

SAMPLE RECORDING

Date	Time	Notes
2/13/04	1000	Liver biopsy performed by Dr Martinez. Specimen sent to laboratory. P 86, R 16 and regular, BP 110/76/70. Sterile dressing applied to site. Small amount bleeding at site (0.3 cm diameter). Resting comfortably in right lateral position.————————————————————Theresa A. Milligan, NS

LIFESPAN CONSIDERATIONS

- Observe for skin irritation from tape applied to the sterile dressing. *Older adults often have fragile skin.*

- Ask the client to empty the bladder before the procedure. *Older adults may need to void more often and in smaller amounts.*

30

Asepsis

PROCEDURE

30–1 Performing a Surgical Hand Scrub

PURPOSES
- To render the hands and forearms as free as possible of microorganisms
- To apply an antimicrobial residue on the skin and reduce the growth of microorganisms for several hours

EQUIPMENT

❑ Antimicrobial solution
❑ Deep sink with foot, knee, or elbow controls

❑ Sterile towels for drying the hands
❑ Nail-cleaning tool, such as a file or orange stick

❑ Two surgical scrub brushes
❑ Mask and cap

INTERVENTION

1. **Prepare for the surgical hand scrub.**

- Remove wristwatch and all rings, unless plain bands are allowed by agency protocol. Ensure that fingernails are trimmed. *A wristwatch and rings can harbor microorganisms and be damaged by water.*

- Check hands and arms for abnormal skin conditions. *Inflamed skin can harbor microorganisms.*

- Make sure that sleeves are above the elbows and ensure that the uniform is well-tucked in at the waist. *A loose-fitting uniform can contaminate the hands if it touches them.*

- Apply cap and face mask.

- Turn on the water, and adjust the temperature to lukewarm. *Warm water removes less protective oil from the skin than hot water. Soap irritates the skin more when hot water is used.*

Figure 30–1 The hands are held higher than the elbows during a hand wash before sterile technique.

2. **Scrub the hands.**

- Wet the hands and forearms under running water, holding the hands above the level of the elbows so that the water runs from the fingertips to the elbows (Figure 30–1). *The hands will become cleaner than the elbows. The water should run from the least contaminated to the most contaminated area.*

- Apply 2 to 4 mL (1 tsp) antimicrobial solution to the hands. Most agencies supply a liquid antimicrobial beside the sink. In some agencies, antimicrobial soap wafers are available.

- Use firm rubbing and circular movements to wash the palms and backs of the hands, the wrists, and the forearms. Interlace the fingers and thumbs, and move the hands back and forth. Continue washing for 20 to 25 seconds. *Circular strokes clean most effectively, and rubbing ensures a thorough and mechanical cleaning action. (Other areas of the hands still need to be cleaned, however.)*

- Hold the hands and arms under the running water to rinse thoroughly, keeping the hands higher than the elbows. *The nurse rinses from the cleanest to the least clean area.*

- Check the nails, and clean them with a file or orange stick if necessary. Rinse the nail tool after each nail is cleaned. *Sediment under the nails is removed more readily when the hands are moist. Rinsing the nail tool prevents the transmission of sediment from one nail to another.*

- Apply antimicrobial solution and lather the hands again. Using a scrub brush, scrub each hand for 45 seconds. Scrub each side of all fingers, including the skin between each of the fingers and the thumb, and the back and the palm of the hand. *Scrubbing loosens bacteria, including those in the creases of the hands.*

- Using the scrub brush, scrub from the wrists to 5 cm (2 in) above each elbow. Scrub all parts of the arms: lower forearm (15 seconds), upper forearm (15 seconds), and antecubital space to marginal area above elbows (15 seconds). Continue to hold the hands higher than the elbows. *Scrubbing thus proceeds from the cleanest area (hands) to the least clean area (upper arm).*

- Discard the brush.

- Rinse hands and arms thoroughly so that the water flows from the hands to the elbows. *Rinsing removes resident and transient bacteria and sediment.*

- If a longer scrub is required, use a second brush and scrub each hand and arm with soap for the recommended time (e.g., each hand for 30 seconds, forearms for 45 seconds).

- Discard second brush, and rinse hands and arms thoroughly.

- Turn off the water with the foot or knee pedal.

► **Procedure 30–1** *continued*

- If the hands or arms inadvertently touch the sink, use an extra 10 strokes to decontaminate the skin in that area.

3. **Dry the hands and arms.**

- Use a sterile towel to dry one hand thoroughly from the fingers to the elbow. Use a rotating motion. Use a second sterile towel to dry the second hand in the same manner. In some agencies towels are of a sufficient size that one half can be used to dry one hand and arm and the second half for the second hand and arm. *Moist skin readily becomes chapped and subject to open sores. Thorough drying also makes it easier to don sterile gloves. The nurse dries the hands from the cleanest to the least clean area.*

- Discard the towels.

- Keep the hands in front and above the waist. *This position maintains the cleanliness of the hands and prevents accidental contamination.*

32

Hygiene

PROCEDURES

Infant Hygiene Care

Practices in the hygienic care of infants vary considerably. For example, in some agencies the nurse bathes the newborn when it is first admitted to the nursery; in others, the nurse simply removes any birth debris from the infant's face, for aesthetic reasons, and then diapers and wraps the baby warmly in a blanket. Some agencies require that the nurse remove the **vernix caseosa** (the whitish, cheesy, greasy protective material found on the skin at birth), whereas others do not. When the newborn's status is stabilized, daily hygienic care often includes a sponge bath until the umbilical cord stump falls off. Cord care and, for some male infants, circumcision care are also required. The cord stump usually falls off spontaneously in 5 to 8 days, but it may remain up to 2 weeks. Procedure 32–1 explains how to give an infant sponge bath.

After the cord stump has separated and the umbilicus is healed, the infant's body can be immersed in a tub of water. New parents need information from the nurse about this basic hygienic care. Many agencies provide bath demonstrations and opportunities for new parents to ask questions before they leave the hospital. Procedure 32–2 describes how to give an infant tub bath. Procedure 32–3 describes how to change a diaper.

32–1 Giving an Infant Sponge Bath

Before commencing the infant's sponge bath, determine (a) whether the infant requires a complete or partial bath, (b) whether the baby's weight is to be taken in conjunction with the bath; and (c) whether the infant's temperature is to be taken after the bath. Wear gloves when having contact with a baby's mucous membranes, non-intact skin, body fluids, and blood. Also wear gloves during the period after delivery until the first bath is completed and during diapering.

PURPOSES
- To remove the vernix caseosa that covers the skin of the fetus, particularly from creases and folds, such as under the foreskin of the glans penis in male babies and between the labia in female babies, if required
- To clean the skin, including the scalp, genitals, and buttocks
- To provide care for the umbilical cord stump
- To assess the skin, healing of the cord stump, and circumcision incision, and general physical growth and functioning

ASSESSMENT FOCUS

Dry, cracked, or peeling skin areas; cradle cap on the scalp; signs of redness at the cord stump or a foul-smelling discharge around the umbilicus; diaper rash, healing of circumcision, overall color of skin.

EQUIPMENT

- Basin with water at 38C to 40C (100F to 105F)
- Gloves
- Towel to place under the baby during the bath
- Disposable cups
- Soft washcloth or absorbent pad
- Cotton balls
- Moisture-resistant bag
- Mild, nonperfumed soap in a container
- Soft-bristled brush or baby comb
- Isopropyl alcohol
- Bath blanket or towel to cover the infant
- Mild lotion or baby oil if needed for dry skin
- Shirt and/or nightgown
- Diaper

▶ Procedure 32–1 Giving an Infant Sponge Bath *continued*

INTERVENTION

1. Prepare the environment.

- Wash hands before handling a newborn, because infants have few defenses against unfamiliar microorganisms.

- Ensure that the room is warm and free of drafts. *This is particularly important when caring for newborns, because their temperature-regulating mechanisms are not completely developed.*

- Measure the temperature of the water with a bath thermometer, or test it against the inside of your wrist or elbow.

- Don gloves, if necessary.

2. Prepare the infant.

- Remove the infants diaper, and wipe away any feces on the baby's perineum with tissues.

- Reassure the infant before and during the bath by talking in soothing tones, and hold the infant firmly but gently.

- Undress the infant, and bundle it in a supine position in a towel.

- Place small articles such as safety pins out of the infant's reach.

- Ascertain the infant's weight and vital signs. They are often measured in conjunction with a bath.

3. Wash the infant's head.

- Clean the baby's eyes with water only, using a washcloth or cotton balls. Use a separate corner of the washcloth or a separate ball for each eye. Wipe from the inner to the outer canthus. Some nurses prefer to wash the infants eyes, face, and scalp *before* the infant is undressed. Dispose of cotton balls in moisture-resistant bag. *Using a separate corner or ball prevents the transmission of microorganisms from one eye to the other. Wiping away from the inner canthus avoids wiping debris into the nasolacrimal duct.*

- Wash and dry the baby's face using water only. Soap may be used to clean the ears. *Soap can be very irritating to the eyes.*

- Pick the baby up using the football hold; that is, hold the baby against your side, supporting the body with your forearm and the head with the palm of your hand (Figure 32–1). Position the baby's head over the washbasin, and lather the scalp with a mild soap. Massage the lather over the scalp using the soft-bristled brush, the baby comb, or your fingertips. *This loosens any dry scales from the scalp and helps to prevent cradle cap.* If cradle cap is present, it may be treated with baby oil, a dandruff shampoo, or ointment prescribed by the physician.

- Rinse and dry the scalp well. Place the baby supine again.

4. Wash the infant's body.

- Wash, rinse, and dry each arm and hand, paying particular attention to the axilla. Avoid excessive rubbing. Dry thoroughly. *Rubbing can cause skin irritation, and moisture can cause excoriation of the skin.*

- Wash, rinse, and dry the baby's chest and abdomen.

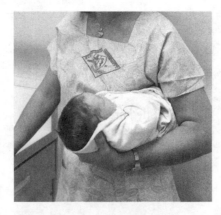

Figure 32–1   Using a football hold to carry an infant.

- Keep the baby covered with the bath blanket or towel between washing and rinsing. *Covering the infant prevents chilling.*

- Clean the base of the umbilical cord with a cotton ball dipped in 70 percent isopropyl alcohol. Other antiseptics, such as povidone-iodine (Betadine) are also used. *Using alcohol promotes drying and prevents infection.*

- Wash, rinse, and dry the baby's legs and feet. Expose only one leg and foot at a time. Give special attention to the areas between the toes. *Keeping exposure to a minimum maintains the baby's warmth.*

- Turn the baby on the stomach or side. Wash, rinse, and dry the back.

5. Clean the genitals and anterior perineum.

- Place the baby on the back. Clean and dry the genitals and anterior perineal area from front to back. *The rectal area is cleaned last because it is the most contaminated.*

- Clean the folds of the groin.

- For females, separate the labia, and clean between them. Clean the genital area from front to back, using moistened cotton balls. Use a clean swab for each stroke. *The smegma that collects between the folds of the labia (and under the foreskin in males) facilitates bacterial growth and should be removed. Lotions, powders, and so on, can also accumulate between the labia and need to be removed. Clean swabs are used to avoid spreading microorganisms from the rectal area to the urethra.*

- If a male infant is uncircumcised, retract the foreskin if possible, and clean the glans penis, using a moistened cotton ball. If the foreskin is tight, do not forcibly retract it. Gentle pressure on a tight foreskin over a period of days or

▶ **Procedure 32–1** *continued*

weeks may accomplish eventual retraction. **Phimosis** (narrowness of the opening of the foreskin) may require correction by circumcision. After swabbing, replace the foreskin to prevent edema (swelling) of the glans penis. Clean the shaft of the penis and the scrotum. In some agencies, the foreskin is not retracted.

- If a male infant has been recently circumcised, clean the glans penis by gently squeezing a cotton ball moistened with clear water over the site. Note any signs of bleeding or infection. In some agencies, petroleum jelly or a bactericidal ointment is applied to the circumcision site. Avoid applying excessive quantities of ointment. *Excess ointment may obstruct the urinary meatus.*

- Apply A and D ointment (lanolin and petrolatum) to the perineum according to agency protocol. *This helps prevent diaper rash.*

6. **Clean the posterior perineum and buttocks.**

- Grasp both of the baby's ankles, raise the feet, and elevate the buttocks.

- Wash and rinse the area with the washcloth.

- Dry the area, and apply ointment, according to agency policy. Do not apply powder. *The baby may inhale particles of powder, which can irritate the respiratory tract.*

7. **Check for dry, cracked, or peeling skin, and apply a mild baby oil or lotion as required.**

8. **Dress and position the infant.**

- Clothe the baby in a shirt (if the temperature of the environment warrants it) and/or nightgown and a diaper. Place the diaper below the cord site. *Exposing the cord site to the air will promote healing.*

- Until the umbilicus and circumcision are healed, position the baby on its side in the crib with a rolled towel or diaper behind the back for support. *This position allows more air to circulate around the cord site, facilitates drainage of mucus from the mouth, and is more comfortable for circumcised babies.*

- After the umbilicus and circumcision are healed, place the baby in a safe position.

- Cover and bundle the baby with a blanket, if the environmental temperature permits. *This gives the baby a sense of security as well as providing warmth.*

9. **Record any significant assessments.**

EVALUATION FOCUS

Reddened areas or skin rashes; color and consistency of stool; state of cord stump; state of circumcision incision.

SAMPLE RECORDING

Date	Time	Notes
03/3/04	0900	Bathed infant. Skin moist, slightly jaundiced. Umbilicus healing well, no discharge. Responsive to tactile stimulation.————————Laurie Law, SN

HOME CARE CONSIDERATIONS

- Use the bath as an opportunity to teach infant care and assessment skills to the caregiver. Listen to the mother and encourage questions.

- Emphasize the importance of giving the bath in an environment free of distractions. *Distractions to the caregiver, such as other children, a ringing telephone, or pets in the immediate area, can place the infant at risk for injury.*

- Evaluate the home environment and family dynamics to determine bonding and infant safety.

32–2 Giving an Infant Tub Bath

Before commencing an infant tub bath, determine (a) whether the baby's weight and temperature are to be measured in conjunction with the bath, and (b) any skin problems and other progress assessments that need to be made.

PURPOSES

- To clean and deodorize the skin
- To stimulate circulation to the skin
- To provide a sense of well-being
- To assess the skin, reflexes, and so on

ASSESSMENT FOCUS

> Skin color, texture, turgor, and temperature; presence of lesions or skin breakdown.

EQUIPMENT

- Tub with bath water at 38C to 40C (100F to 105F)
- Towel to place under the baby before and after the bath and to dry the infant
- Soft washcloth or absorbent pad
- Cotton balls
- Bag in which to dispose of used cotton balls
- Mild, nonperfumed soap in a container
- Soft-bristled brush
- Bath blanket or towel to cover the infant before and after the bath
- Mild lotion or baby oil if needed for dry skin
- Shirt and/or nightgown
- Diaper
- Gloves if indicated

INTERVENTION

1. Prepare the bath area.

- Prepare a flat, padded surface in the bath area on which to dress and undress the infant. It should be high enough so that you or the parent can avoid stooping, which can produce back strain. Usually parents use a counter or table top in the bathroom or kitchen, unless a bathinette is available. Cover the surface with a towel.

- Assemble all supplies needed so that they are within easy reach. *A baby left unattended or out of sight for even a few seconds can move or fall from the bath area.* Keep supplies out of reach of the infant, however. *Small articles, such as safety pins, can be hazardous to an active and curious infant.*

- For small infants, use a wash basin.

- Place the tub or basin near the dressing surface to prevent exposure and chilling when transfer-

ring the baby in and out of the tub. Be sure the room is warm and free from drafts.

- Measure the temperature of the water with a bath thermometer, or test it against the inside of your wrist or elbow.

2. Clean the infant's eyes and face before placing the infant in the tub.

- Follow Procedure 32–1, step 3.

3. Pick up and place the infant in the tub.

- Pick up and hold the baby securely, with the head and shoulders supported on one forearm and the hips and buttocks supported on the other hand (Figure 32–2). *Young infants have not developed sufficiently to hold their heads up alone.*

- Gradually immerse the baby into the tub. *This gives the infant time to adjust to the water.*

Figure 32–2 Holding an infant while placing him in a tub.

4. Wash the infant.

- Keeping the baby's head and back supported on your forearm (Figure 32–3), lather the scalp with a mild soap. Massage the lather over the scalp, using the soft-bristled brush or your fingertips. Rinse the scalp well. *This loosens any dry scales from the scalp and helps prevent cradle cap.* If cradle cap is present, it may be treated with mineral oil, a dandruff

▶ **Procedure 32–2** *continued*

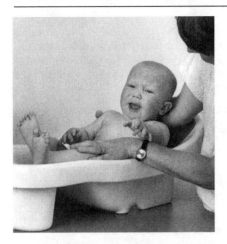

Figure 32–3 Keeping the infant's head and back supported during a tub bath.

shampoo, or ointment prescribed by the physician.

- Soap and rinse the baby's trunk, extremities, genitals, and perineal area with your free hand. Hold the baby as shown in Figure 32–3 throughout. If the baby enjoys the bath, this can be done in a leisurely manner.

5. **Remove the infant from the tub, and dry the infant well.**

- Remove the baby from the tub by the hold shown in Figure 32–2, and quickly bundle the baby in a towel. *It is important to avoid chilling the infant.*

- Gently pat the baby dry, giving special attention to the body creases and folds. *Rubbing can cause skin irritation.*

- Apply baby oil or lotion to dry, cracked, or peeling areas.

6. **Ensure the infant's comfort and safety.**

- Clothe the baby in a shirt (if the temperature of the environment warrants it) and/or a nightgown and a diaper.

- Place the baby in a side-lying position in the crib. *This position facilitates the drainage of mucus from the mouth.*

- Cover and bundle the baby with a blanket, if the environmental temperature permits. *This gives the baby a sense of security as well as providing warmth.*

7. **Document all pertinent information.**

- Record any significant observations, such as reddened areas or skin rashes, and the color and consistency of the stool.

EVALUATION FOCUS

See Assessment Focus.

SAMPLE RECORDING

Date	Time	Notes
03/5/04	1010	Tub bath given. Skin clear, moist, warm. No reddened areas.————————————————————————————————————Laurie Law, SN

HOME CARE CONSIDERATIONS

For home safety, teach the caregiver

- To perform the bath in a warm, private area of the home.

- The importance of not leaving the baby unattended or out of sight for even a few moments.

- The importance of checking the water temperature before placing the baby in the basin.

- How to hold the baby securely during transfers.

- How to make the bath a pleasant experience for the baby.

32–3 Changing a Diaper

When a diaper becomes soiled with either urine or feces, it should be changed promptly so that the baby's skin does not become irritated by the waste products. The infant's perineal—genital area is washed and thoroughly dried before a clean diaper is applied.

Before changing the diaper, determine the type of diaper required and any special precautions, such as not elevating the buttocks by lifting the legs or the need for a stool specimen.

PURPOSES
- To maintain the infant's comfort and cleanliness
- To maintain the integrity of the skin by preventing irritation from urine and/or feces

ASSESSMENT FOCUS

> Condition of the skin around the perineum and buttocks; amount, color, and odor of the urine and feces; state and progress of circumcision and cord stump.

EQUIPMENT

- Clean disposable diaper or cloth diaper
- Receptacle for the soiled diaper
- Commercially prepared wipes or a basin with warm water, 38C to 40C (100F to 105F)
- Soap
- Washcloth
- Towel
- Mild lotion or protective ointment (e.g., zinc oxide)
- Gloves

INTERVENTION

1. **Fold a clean diaper, if using a cloth diaper.**

- Three methods can be used to fold diapers: rectangular, triangular, or kite (Figures 32–4 to 32–6). When using the rectangular method, provide an extra thickness of material either at the front (for boys) or the back (for girls) for additional absorbency. It may also be placed at the front for girls who are positioned on their stomachs for sleep (so that the urine runs to the front).

2. **Position and handle the infant appropriately.**

- Place the infant in a supine position on a clean, flat surface near the assembled supplies.

- Handle the infant slowly and securely, and speak in soothing tones. *Slow movements and sooth-ing voice tones will help calm any of the infant's fears.*

3. **Remove the soiled diaper.**

- Place your fingers between the baby's skin and the diaper, and unpin the diaper on each side. Close the pins, and place them out of reach of the infant. *The fingers protect the baby from being pricked as the pins are removed. Babies may grab the pins and place them in their mouths if the pins are within reach.*

- Pull the front of the diaper down between the infant's legs.

- Grasp the infant's ankles with one hand, and lift the buttocks (Figure 32–7 on page 40).

- Use the clean portion of the diaper to wipe any excess urine or feces from the buttocks. Wipe from anterior to posterior. *Wiping toward the posterior of the infant moves soiled material away from the urethral orifice and decreases the possibility of transferring microorganisms to the urinary tract.*

- Remove the diaper. Lower the baby's buttocks. Dispose of the diaper. Do not let the infant out of your sight or reach. *The infant could roll over and off the changing surface.*

4. **Clean the buttocks and anal-genital area.**

- Use warm water and soap or commercial cleansing tissues.

- Clean toward the posterior as in step 3. *Cleaning removes remaining urine and feces, which can irritate the skin.*

- Rinse and dry the area well with the towel. *Drying well prevents irritation of the skin by moisture.*

- Apply a protective ointment or lotion to the perineum and

▶ **Procedure 32–3** *continued*

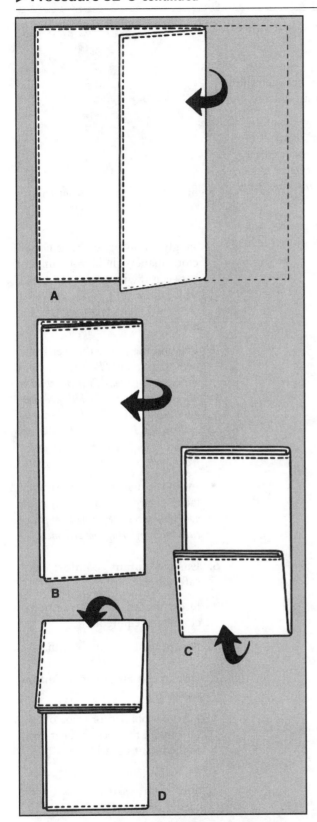

Figure 32–4 The rectangular method of folding a diaper. *A, B,* Fold the diaper into a rectangle by bringing the sides over; *C,* fold the bottom edge up to provide the thickness in front; or *D,* fold the top edge down to provide the thickness at the back.

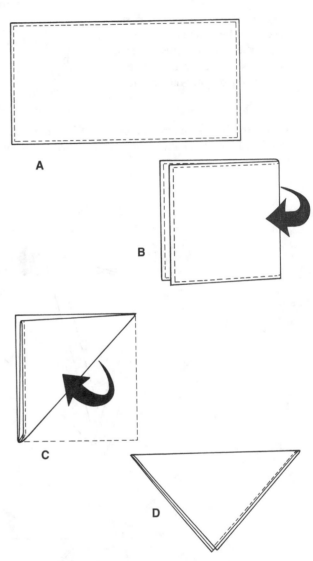

Figure 32–5 The triangular method of folding a diaper: *A,* Fold a square cloth to a rectangular shape; *B,* fold the cloth again to form a square; *C,* bring opposite corners together to form a triangle; *D,* apply the triangle with the fold at the waist.

▶ Procedure 32–3 Changing a Diaper *continued*

buttocks, especially to the skin creases.

5. Apply the clean diaper, and fasten it securely.

- Lay the diaper flat on a clean surface with the folded edges up, and place the baby on the center of the diaper width so that the back edge of the diaper is at waist level.

or

Grasp the baby's ankles with one hand and raise the baby's legs and

buttocks. Place the diaper under the baby so that the back edge is at waist level.

- Draw the diaper up between the baby's legs to the waist in front.

- Fold the diaper below the umbilicus until the infant's cord stump has healed. *This promotes drying and healing of the stump site and minimizes possible infection from wet diapers.*

- Fasten the diaper at the waist with tape provided so that it fits

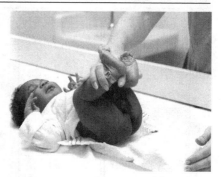

Figure 32–7   Lifting the infant's buttocks to remove a soiled diaper.

snugly. If using safety pins for cloth diapers, hold your fingers between the baby and the diaper while pinning. *The fingers protect the baby from being pricked with the pins.*

- Position the pins either vertically or horizontally. *The horizontal position is suggested when the child is old enough to sit. The pins are then less likely to poke the body. The vertical position is suggested for diapers pinned at the sides rather than at the front, if the infant does not yet sit up.*

- Insert the diaper pins so that they face upward or outward. *If a pin opens inadvertently, it will not puncture the baby's thigh or abdomen.*

6. Ensure infant comfort and safety.

- Dress the infant with additional clothes as required.

- Return the infant to the crib.

7. Document all pertinent information.

- Record stool and/or urine observations on the record sheet and/or the infant's chart.

- Record other pertinent observations, such as skin redness, on the client's record.

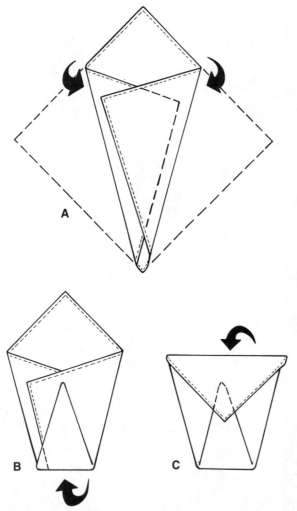

Figure 32–6   The kite method of folding a diaper: *A,* Make a triangle by folding the side corners to the center; *B,* bring the bottom corner up to the center; *C,* fold down the top corner.

▶ **Procedure 32–3** *continued*

EVALUATION FOCUS

See Assessment Focus.

SAMPLE RECORDING

Date	Time	Notes
10/3/04	1800	Father assisted with diaper change. Demonstrated procedure without difficulty. Small amount of yellow stool noted.————————Amy Mulcahay, RN

HOME CARE CONSIDERATIONS

- Assess the home environment and family dynamics to determine bonding and infant safety.

- Listen to the mother and encourage questions.

Teach the caregiver

- To change the diaper promptly when it becomes soiled. *This prevents the baby's skin from becoming irritated by waste products.*

- To perform the diaper change in a warm, private area of the home.

- Not to leave the baby unattended for even a few moments. *The infant could roll over and off the changing surface.*

- The importance of wiping soiled material from anterior to posterior. *This helps prevent microorganisms from entering the urinary tract.*

32–4 Care of the Client with Pediculosis

PURPOSE • To destroy and remove lice

ASSESSMENT FOCUS

Presence of skin abrasions from scratching; location of lice (head, body, or pubic area); presence of lice on other family members or other close contacts.

EQUIPMENT

For Head Lice

❑ Shampoo containing gamma benzene hexachloride (or lindane) or similar acting medications (e.g., Kwell, GBH, Scabine)
❑ Fine-toothed comb and brush

For Body and Pubic Lice

❑ Cream, lotion, or powder containing a medication (e.g., Kwell)
❑ Topical ointment for the skin as ordered (e.g., antibiotic, antipruritic, or steroid cream)

For All Types

❑ Gown and gloves
❑ Surgical cap (as recommended by agency)
❑ Bath towels
❑ Impervious isolation bag
❑ Clean gown and bed linens

INTERVENTION

1. Remove head lice.

• Don gown, gloves, and (if agency recommends) surgical cap before the procedure. *These prevent spread to the nurse's clothing and skin, and subsequent transmission to others.*

• Place a small damp or dry washcloth over the client's eyes to protect them from the shampoo. *The medication in the shampoo is irritating to the eyes.*

• Check the scalp for rawness or excoriation. Don't apply shampoo if excoriated or inflamed areas of skin are present. Notify the physician. *The shampoo can be painful to irritated skin and cause further excoriation.*

• Apply the medicated shampoo according to the manufacturer's directions. Some shampoos may be left in place for 5 minutes.

• Shampoo the hair and scalp thoroughly. Be careful to keep the medicated shampoo out of the client's eyes.

• Rinse the hair and scalp thoroughly. *Thorough rinsing removes dead lice and the medicated shampoo and prevents scalp irritation.*

• If necessary, remove dead lice and nits with a fine-toothed comb or brush dipped in hot vinegar (optional). *A comb or brush dipped in hot vinegar tends to loosen nit cement and facilitates removal of nits.*

• Disinfect the comb and brush with the medicated shampoo. Repeat the shampoo if indicated.

2. Remove body and pubic lice.

• Have the client bathe in soap and water.

• Don gown and gloves.

• Apply medicated topical cream or lotion to infested areas—for example, axillae, chest, and pubic areas—and allow it to remain for the prescribed time period, according to the manufacturer's directions.

• Clean the treated areas with soap and water to remove dead lice

and medication and prevent skin irritation.

• If eyelashes are involved, use a prescribed ophthalmic ointment as ordered and directed. Remove nits manually.

3. Dispose of linens and clothing appropriately.

• Place any used towels and the client's soiled gown and bed linen into a labeled isolation bag.

• Provide a clean gown and bed linens for the client.

• Dispose of your gown and gloves appropriately, and wash your hands.

4. Document any pertinent information.

• Include the date and time of treatment, area of the body treated, and all nursing assessments and interventions.

▶ **Procedure 32–4** *continued*

EVALUATION FOCUS

Client's knowledge of preventive and control measures and presence of pediculi.

SAMPLE RECORDING

Date	Time	Notes
11/9/04	1030	Hair shampooed with Kwell soap as ordered for pediculosis. Pustules present behind ears and at hairline. Instructed to shower and apply Kwell lotion. Infested clothing bagged for family to clean at home. Family instructed on how to clean the home and prevent further infestation.———————————Michelle M. Nutter, RN

LIFESPAN CONSIDERATIONS

- Pediculosis is common among children in schools or day care centers. *Crowded buildings provide ideal conditions for lice to migrate.*

- Teach children not to share articles such as combs, hair brushes, hats, towels, coats, and sweaters. *The parasites spread through direct contact with clothing and toilet articles.*

- Instruct parents to frequently inspect the child for pediculosis, especially if an outbreak occurs at school.

- Instruct parents not to use the shampoo more than once a week without permission from the physician. *Repeated or prolonged use can cause skin irritation or systemic toxicity.*

HOME CARE CONSIDERATIONS

Teach the client to prevent pediculosis in the home by

- Dry-cleaning or washing linens, towels, and clothing with detergent and hot water.

- Treating carpet and upholstery with specially formulated sprays if needed.

- Not sharing clothing or toilet articles.

- Checking all family members and close contacts of the infested person for pediculosis.

- Recognizing the signs of pediculosis.

32–5   Inserting Contact Lenses (Hard and Soft)

Before inserting contact lenses, determine (a) the client's own practices regarding cleaning and inserting the lenses, and (b) any reasons for not inserting the lenses.

PURPOSE

- To enhance the client's visual acuity

ASSESSMENT FOCUS

> Presence of eye inflammation, infection, discomfort, or excessive tearing; when lenses were last worn and cleaned; cleanliness of the lenses; any scratches on the lenses.

EQUIPMENT

- ❑ Client's lens storage case
- ❑ Gloves (optional)
- ❑ Wetting agent

INTERVENTION

1. **Take the client's lens storage case and select the correct lens for the eye.** *Each lens is ground to fit the individual eye and correct its visual defect.*

- Start with the right eye. *Always starting with the right eye establishes a habit so that incorrect placement of each lens is avoided.*

- Don gloves, if desired.

To Insert Hard Lenses

2. **Lubricate the lens.**

- Put a few drops of sterile wetting solution on the right lens. Solutions of saline, methyl cellulose, or polyvinyl alcohol are frequently used. *Wetting solution helps the lens to glide over the cornea, thus reducing the risk of injury.*

- Spread the wetting solution on both surfaces of the lens by using your thumb and index finger or an absorbent applicator, or place the lens in the palm of your hand and spread the solution with your index finger.

3. **Insert the lens.**

- Ask the client to tilt the head backward.

Figure 32–8   Inserting a hard contact lens.

- Place the lens convex side down on the tip of your dominant index finger (the right, if you are righthanded; Figure 32–8).

- Instruct the client to gaze slightly upward.

- Separate the upper and lower eyelids of the right eye with the thumb and index finger of your nondominant hand (Figure 32–8). Separate the eyelids by exerting gentle pressure with your fingers over the supraorbital and infraorbital bony prominences. *This prevents direct pressure, discomfort, and injury to the eyeball.*

- Place the lens as gently as possible on the cornea, directly over the iris and the pupil.

- Repeat the above steps for the other lens.

4. **If the lens is off center, center the lens.**

- Separate the eyelids, using the index or middle finger of the left hand to lift the upper lid, and the index or middle finger of the right hand to depress the lower lid.

- Locate the lens, and ask the client to gaze in the opposite direction (Figure 32–9).

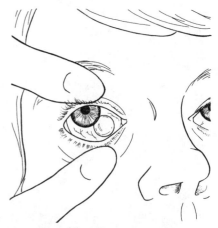

Figure 32–9   Locating a lens that is off center by separating the eyelids and asking the client to gaze in the opposite direction.

▶ **Procedure 32–5** *continued*

• Gently push the lens in the direction of the cornea, using a finger or the eyelid margins.

• Ask the client to look slowly toward the lens. The lens will slide easily onto the cornea as the client looks toward it.

To Insert Soft Lenses

5. Keep the dominant finger dry for insertion.

• Remove the lens from its saline-filled storage case with your non-dominant hand. *Because "waterloving" soft contact lenses have a natural attraction to wet surfaces, the lens will adhere more readily to the moist eye if the finger is dry.*

6. Position the lens correctly for insertion.

For a Regular Soft Lens

• Hold the lens at the edge between your thumb and your index finger.

• Flex the lens slightly. The lens is in the correct position if the edges point inward. If the edges point outward, it is in the wrong position (inside out) and must be reversed (Figure 32–10). *A lens placed on the eye inside out is less comfortable (an edge sensation may be felt), tends to fold on the eye, can drop to a lower position on the eye, and may move excessively on blinking.*

For an Ultrathin Soft Lens

• Do not flex an ultrathin lens. Instead, put the lens on your placement finger and allow it to dry slightly for a few seconds.

• Closely inspect the lens to see whether the edges turn upward (Figure 32–11, *A*). If they turn downward (Figure 32–11, *B*), the lens is inside out and must be reversed. *Flexing an ultrathin lens may cause the lens to fold and stick together.*

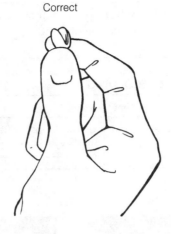
Correct

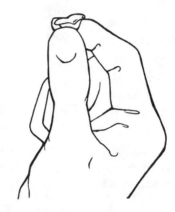
Inside out

Figure 32–10 Checking the position of a soft contact lens before insertion.

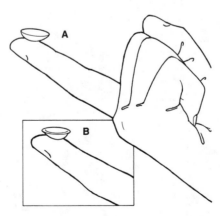

Figure 32–11 Checking the position of an ultrathin contact lens before insertion: *A*, position is correct, i.e., edges are turned upward; *B* lens is inside out and must be reversed.

7. Wet the lens with saline solution using your nondominant fingers.

• See step 2 for hard lenses.

8. Insert the lens.

• Ensure that your placement finger is dry. This is particularly important for ultrathin soft lenses.

• Place the lens convex side down on the tip of your dominant index finger.

• Insert the lens in the same manner as a hard contact lens.

9. Store lens equipment appropriately.

• Replace the lens container, lens cleaner, and wetting solution in the drawer of the bedside table.

10. Document pertinent information.

• Record insertion of the contact lenses if a nurse is required to remove them; otherwise, this is not normally recorded (consult agency protocol).

• Record all assessments, and report to the nurse in charge any problems observed in the eyes or the lenses.

• Record on the nursing care plan the time for the lenses to be removed.

▶**Procedure 32–5 Inserting Contact Lenses** *continued*

EVALUATION FOCUS

Discharge from eyes; color and clarity of conjunctiva; discomfort; tearing; client's perception of sight.

SAMPLE RECORDING

Date	Time	Notes
10/10/04	2100	Contact lenses inserted in both eyes. Slight white discharge from inner canthus R eye. Upper eyelid R eye reddened. No discomfort. States can read now.————————————————————————Marilyn S. McLean, SN

LIFESPAN CONSIDERATIONS

- Older adults often wear contact lenses after cataract surgery.

- Older adults are more likely to have dry eyes, which can cause discomfort from contact lenses.

- Lack of manual dexterity can be a problem for older adults who wear contact lenses. *Arthritis or hand tremors are more common in older adults.* Extended wear lenses can help alleviate this difficulty.

- The corneas tend to become less sensitive with aging, making it easier to adjust to contact lenses. *However, the client may overlook signs of corneal abrasion or a foreign object under one of the lenses.*

- Periodically assess the client's ability to wear contact lenses. *Changes in alertness, orientation, or manual dexterity might mean glasses are a more practical alternative.*

HOME CARE CONSIDERATIONS

- Insert contact lenses in a private area of the home without distractions.

- Emphasize the importance of a clean environment and washing the hands before handling contact lenses. *This reduces the risk of contamination by microorganisms.*

- Teach the client to identify signs of infection, such as reddened eyes, excessive tearing, or pain.

- Teach the client how to examine the contact lenses for scratches, tears, or other damage.

32–6 Removing Contact Lenses (Hard and Soft)

PURPOSES
- To prevent eye damage from prolonged lens wearing
- To prevent loss of the lenses

ASSESSMENT FOCUS

> Any eye irritation; length of time lens has been in place; the client's usual practice for removing the lenses.

EQUIPMENT

- ❑ Gloves (optional)
- ❑ Flashlight (optional)
- ❑ Cotton applicator dipped in saline (optional)
- ❑ Lens storage case; or, if not available, two small medicine cups or specimen containers partially filled with normal saline solution and marked "L lens" and "R lens."

INTERVENTION

1. **Locate the position of the lens.** *The lens must be positioned directly over the cornea for proper removal.*

- Don gloves, if needed.
- Ask the client to tilt the head backward.
- Retract the upper eyelid with your index finger, and ask the client to look up, down, and from side to side.
- Retract the lower eyelid with your index finger, and ask the client to look up and down and from side to side.
- Use a flashlight if necessary to find a colorless soft lens.

2. **Reposition a displaced lens.**

- Ask the client to look straight ahead.
- Using your index fingers, gently exert pressure on the inner margins of the upper and lower lids, and move the lens back onto the cornea.

or

- Using a cotton-tipped applicator dipped in saline, gently move the lens into place.

To Remove Hard Lenses:

The lens may pop out on its own if the nurse or client pulls the eyelid up and outward toward the ear. Ask the client to blink to release the lens from the cornea. Cup one hand under the eye to catch the lens.

3. **Separate the upper and lower eyelids.**

- Use both thumbs or index fingers to separate the upper and lower eyelids of one eye until they are beyond the edges of the lens (Figure 32–12). Exert pressure toward the bony orbit above and below the eye. *Retraction of the eyelids against the bony orbit*

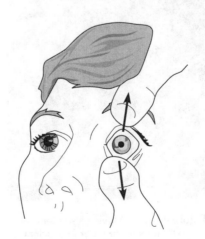

Figure 32–12 Separating the eyelids until they are beyond the edges of a hard lens.

prevents direct pressure, discomfort, and injury to the eyeball.

or

Use the middle finger to retract the upper eyelid and the thumb of the same hand to retract the lower lid. *Using one hand for retraction keeps the other hand free to receive the lens.*

4. **Remove the lens.**

- Gently move the margins of both the lower eyelid and the upper eyelid toward the lens. *The margins of the lids trap the edges of the lens.*

- Hold the top eyelid stationary at the edge of the lens, and lift the bottom edge of the contact lens by pressing the lower lid at its margin firmly under the lens (Figure 32–13 on page 48). *Pressure exerted under the edge of the lens interrupts the suction of the lens on the cornea.*

- After the lens is slightly tipped, slide the lens off and out of the eye by moving both eyelids toward each other (Figure 32–14 on page 48).

- Grasp the lens with your index finger and thumb, and place it in the palm of your hand.

▶ Procedure 32–6 Removing Contact Lenses *continued*

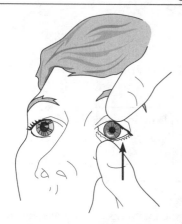

Figure 32–13   Holding the top lid stationary at the edge of a hard lens and lifting the bottom edge of the lens by pressing the lower lid at its margin.

- To avoid lens mixups, place the first lens in its designated cup in the storage case before removing the second lens.

- Repeat the above steps for the other lens.

To Remove Soft Lenses:

5. Separate the eyelids.

- Ask the client to look upward at the ceiling and keep the eye opened wide.

- Retract the lower or upper lid with one or two fingers of your *nondominant* hand.

- Using the index finger of your dominant hand, move the lens down to the inferior part of the sclera (Figure 32–15). *Moving the lens onto the sclera reduces the risk of damage to the cornea.*

6. Remove the lens.

- Gently pinch the lens between the pads of the thumb and index finger of your dominant hand (Figure 32–16). *Pinching causes the lens to double up, so that air enters underneath the lens, breaking the suction and allowing removal. The pads of the fingers are used to prevent scratching the eye or the lens with the fingernails.*

- Place the lens in the palm of your hand.

- For *ultrathin* lenses, open the lens with the thumb and index finger *immediately* on removal. *This keeps the edges from sticking together.*

- Repeat the above steps for the other lens.

7. Clean and store the lenses appropriately.

- Clean the lenses according to manufacturer's instructions.

- Place the lens in the correct slot in its storage case. The slots are labeled for right and left lenses.

- Be sure each lens is centered in the storage case. *If the lens is not centered, it may crack, chip, or tear.* Tighten or close the cover.

- Place the contact lens container in the drawer of the bedside table. *The lenses and the case should never be exposed to direct sunlight or extreme heat, because these can dry or warp them.*

8. Document all relevant information.

- Document the removal of the lenses prior to surgery or when this is a nursing responsibility.

- Document all assessments and problems, such as redness of the conjunctiva, and report problems to the nurse in charge.

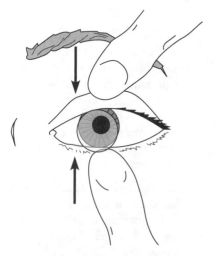

Figure 32–14   Sliding a hard lens out of the eye by moving both eyelids toward each other.

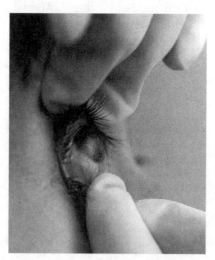

Figure 32–15   Moving a soft lens down to the inferior part of the sclera.

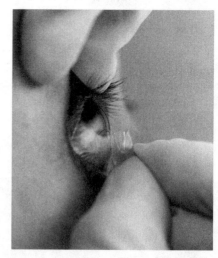

Figure 32–16   Removing a soft lens by pinching it between the pads of the thumb and index finger.

▶ **Procedure 32–6** *continued*

EVALUATION FOCUS

> Absence of eye inflammation; adequacy of visual acuity with lenses inserted; integrity of lenses; eye comfort.

SAMPLE RECORDING

Date	Time	Notes
03/22/04	2100	Contact lenses removed. No redness of eyelids or conjunctiva noted. Both lenses intact.————————————————————Anita R. Rodriguez, SN

LIFESPAN CONSIDERATIONS

- Older clients often wear contact lenses after cataract surgery.

- Older clients are more likely to have dry eyes, which can cause discomfort and make lenses more difficult to remove.

- The corneas tend to become less sensitive with aging. *The client may overlook signs of corneal abrasion or a foreign object under one of the lenses.*

HOME CARE CONSIDERATIONS

- Remove the lenses in a clean, private area of the home without distractions.

- Evaluate the client's ability to properly care for his lenses at home.

- Emphasize the importance of a clean environment and washing the hands before removing contact lenses. *This reduces the risk of contamination by microorganisms.*

- Teach the client to identify signs of infection or abrasion, such as reddened eyes, excess tearing, or pain.

- Teach the client how to examine the contact lenses for scratches, tears, or other damage.

32–7   Removing, Cleaning, and Inserting an Artificial Eye

Before removing, cleaning, and inserting an artificial eye, determine the client's routine eye care practices.

PURPOSES
- To maintain the integrity of the eye socket and eyelids
- To prevent infection of the eye socket and surrounding tissues
- To assess the tissues and sockets for irritation or infection
- To maintain the client's self-esteem

ASSESSMENT FOCUS

Client's care regimen; inflammation of surrounding tissues; drainage from the eye socket; crusting of the eyelashes.

EQUIPMENT

- ❏ Small labeled storage container, such as a denture or specimen container
- ❏ Gloves (optional)

- ❏ Small rubber bulb, a syringe bulb, or a medicine dropper bulb (optional)

- ❏ Soft gauze or cotton wipe
- ❏ Bowl of warm normal saline
- ❏ Eye irrigation solution

INTERVENTION

1. Remove the eye.

- Make sure that the container in which the prosthesis will be stored has been lined to cushion the eye and prevent scratches. Also, be sure to use sterile supplies. (This is not a sterile procedure, however.)

- Assist the client to a sitting or supine position, if the client's health permits. If the client's prosthesis is glass, the supine position on a soft surface is preferred. *This helps prevent accidental breakage of the prosthesis.*

- Identify the eye to be removed, and don gloves, if indicated.

- If the client has an effective method for removing the eye, follow that method. *Most people can remove their own eyes under normal circumstances, and they may have a convenient method.*

- Otherwise:

  a. Pull the lower eyelid down over the infraorbital bone with your dominant thumb,

and exert slight pressure below the eyelid (Figure 32–17).

or

  b. Compress a small rubber bulb, and apply the tip directly on the eye. Gradually decrease the finger pressure on the bulb, and draw the eye out of the socket. Compression squeezes air from the bulb and creates negative pressure. Releasing finger pressure counteracts the

Figure 32–17   Removing an artificial eye by retracting the lower eyelid, and exerting slight pressure below the eyelid.

suction holding the eye in the socket.

- Receive the eye with the other hand, and place it carefully in the container. Do not scratch or drop the eye.

- Place a folded tissue or cotton wipe against the lower eyelid to catch any fluid that may appear when the prosthesis is removed.

2. Clean the eye and the socket.

- Expose the socket by raising the upper lid with the index finger and pulling the lower lid down with the thumb.

- Clean the socket with soft gauze or cotton wipes and normal saline. Pat dry.

- Wash the tissue around the eye, stroking from the inner to the outer canthus using a fresh gauze for each wipe. *This avoids washing any debris down the lacrimal canaliculi, if they are still intact.* Be sure to wash crusts off the upper and lower lids and eyelashes.

▶ **Procedure 32–7** *continued*

- Dry the tissues gently, in the direction described in the step above, using dry wipes.

- Wash the artificial eye gently with the warm normal saline, and dry it with dry wipes. *Never use alcohol to clean a prosthetic eye.*

- If the eye is not to be inserted, place it in the lined container filled with water or saline solution, close the lid, label the container with the client's name and room number, and place it in the drawer of the bedside table.

3. **Reinsert the eye.**

- Ensure that the eye is moistened with water or saline. *Moisture facilitates insertion by reducing friction.*

- Using the thumb and index finger of one hand, retract the eyelids, exerting pressure on the supraorbital and infraorbital bones (Figure 32–18).

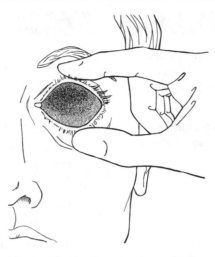

Figure 32–18 Exposing the socket by retracting the upper and lower eyelids.

- With the thumb and index finger of the other hand, hold the eye so that the front of it is toward the palm of your hand (Figure 32–19). Slip the eye gently into the socket, and release the lids. The eye should fit securely under the lids.

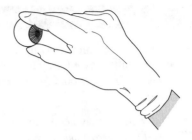

Figure 32–19 Holding an artificial eye between the thumb and index finger for insertion.

- Moisten the prosthesis with an eye irrigation solution once it is in place.

4. **Document pertinent information.**

- Record the removal, cleaning, and/or insertion of an artificial eye prior to surgery or for a helpless person. Otherwise, these procedures are not usually recorded.

- Document any assessments and problems, and report them to the nurse in charge.

EVALUATION FOCUS

Clean appearance and uniform pale pink color of tissues in the eye socket; absence of encrustations on the eyelids; scratches or rough areas on eye.

SAMPLE RECORDING

Date	Time	Notes
01/8/04	1200	Client safely and correctly replaced artificial eye. No redness or drainage noted in socket.————————————————————Elizabeth Corwin, SN

▶**Procedure 32–7 Artificial Eyes** *continued*

LIFESPAN CONSIDERATIONS

- Arthritis or tremors may make it difficult for the older adult to care for a prosthetic eye without assistance. *A caregiver can learn to perform the procedure at home.*

- Older adults may need extra time to perform activities. *Depth perception and peripheral vision are diminished when one eye isn't functioning.*

HOME CARE CONSIDERATIONS

- Perform the procedure in a clean, private area of the home and provide teaching for the client and caregiver.

- Assess the client or caregiver's ability to care for the prosthetic eye.

- Stress the importance of hand washing and a clean environment when handling the prosthesis.

- Ask the client to report pain, drainage, or redness of the affected eye. *A properly fitted prosthesis should be comfortable, and the eye free of signs of infection.*

- Teach the client to wear the prosthesis day and night. *Removal for cleaning may be needed only once every few months.*

33

Medications

PROCEDURES

33–1 Administering Dermatologic Medications

PURPOSES
- To decrease itching (pruritus)
- To lubricate and soften the skin
- To cause local vasoconstriction or vasodilation
- To increase or decrease secretions from the skin
- To provide a protective coating to the skin
- To apply an antibiotic or antiseptic to treat or prevent infection
- To reduce inflammation
- To administer sustained-action transdermal medications
- To debride necrotic tissue

ASSESSMENT FOCUS

Discomfort; pruritus; color of affected and surrounding area (e.g., redness, rash); swelling; discharge; amount of hair on affected area (excessive hair may need to be removed before the medication is applied).

EQUIPMENT

Use sterile supplies for all open skin lesions.
- ❑ Gloves (disposable and sterile if required)
- ❑ Solution to wash area as ordered
- ❑ 2 × 2 gauze pads for cleaning
- ❑ Medication container or tube
- ❑ Tongue blades (sterile if required)
- ❑ Gauze to cover area (if required)

INTERVENTION

1. Verify the order.

- Compare the medication record with the most recent order.
- Compare the label on the medication tube or jar with the medication record.
- Determine whether area is to be washed before applying the medication.

2. Prepare the client.

- Provide privacy.
- Expose the area of the skin to be treated.

3. Prepare the area for the medication.

- Wash hands and don gloves.
- Determine that the body part to be treated is clean; if not, wash it gently as directed, and pat it dry with gauze pads.

4. Apply the medication and dressing as ordered.

- Place a small amount of cream (e.g., emollient) on the tongue blade, and spread it evenly on the skin.

  or

  Pour some lotion on the gauze, and pat the skin area with it.

  or

  If a liniment is used, rub it into the skin with the hands using long, smooth strokes.

- Repeat the application until the area is completely covered. *For complete coverage, no skin should show through cream or ointment. However, applying too much of the preparation can cause skin to become softened (macerated) from prolonged exposure to moisture.*

- Apply medicated products only to the area being treated. *Some medications can irritate the surrounding skin.*

- Apply a sterile dressing as necessary.

  or

- Apply a prepackaged transdermal patch as directed.

5. Ensure client comfort.

- Provide a clean gown or pajamas after the application if the medication will come in contact with the clothing. *Agency clothes can be washed more easily than the client's own clothes.*

- Remove and discard the gloves.

6. Document all assessments and interventions.

- Record the type of preparation used; the site to which it was applied; the time; and the response of the client, including data about

▶ **Procedure 33–1** *continued*

the appearance of the site, discomfort, itching, and so on.

- Return at a time by which the preparation should have acted to assess the reaction, such as redness (for a rubefacient, e.g., an agent that reddens the skin), and/or relief of itching, burning, swelling, or discomfort.

EVALUATION FOCUS

Presence of redness or discharge; increased or decreased comfort.

SAMPLE RECORDING

Date	Time	Notes
8/7/04	2100	Thin film of 0.5% Topicort cream applied to affected areas as ordered. Area is dry and has flaky patches (2.5 cm in diameter) scattered on chest, back, and abdomen. States no itching or pain.————Lawrence Campbell, RN

LIFESPAN CONSIDERATIONS

- Elderly clients benefit from moisturizing lotion and extra attention to the skin. *Skin becomes dry and thin with aging and loses elasticity.*

- Children (and some adults) may scratch or rub the affected area of skin. To prevent this, apply a cotton stockingette or rolled gauze dressing to the area. *Some skin conditions, such as poison ivy, are spread by contact.*

HOME CARE CONSIDERATIONS

- Teach the client or caregiver how to apply the medication.

- Assess the home environment for causes of the client's skin disorder. *Insect bites, allergies, and poor hygiene can contribute to skin problems.*

- Ensure that the client can obtain refills of the medication as needed. *Financial concerns or lack of transportation can prevent the client from getting medication.*

33–2 Administering Nasal Instillations

PURPOSES
- To decrease nasal congestion and improve nasal breathing
- To treat infections, inflammations, or allergies of the nasal cavity or facial sinuses
- To administer local anesthetic prior to a rhinolaryngolic examination or procedure

ASSESSMENT FOCUS

Appearance of nasal cavities; congestion of the mucous membranes and any obstruction to breathing; facial discomfort with or without palpation (see Intervention, step 3).

EQUIPMENT

❑ Disposable tissues   ❑ Correct medication   ❑ Dropper

INTERVENTION

1. **Verify the medication or irrigation order.**

- Carefully check the physician's order for the solution to be used, its strength, the number of drops, the frequency of the instillation, and the area to receive the instillation (e.g., the eustachian [auditory] tube or specific sinuses).

2. **Prepare the client.**

- If secretions are excessive, ask the client to blow the nose to clear the nasal passages.

- Inspect the discharge on the tissues for color, odor, and thickness.

3. **Assess the client.**

- Assess congestion of the mucous membranes and any obstruction to breathing. Ask the client to hold one nostril closed and blow out gently through the other nostril. Listen for the sound of any obstruction to the air. Repeat for the other nostril.

- Assess signs of distress when nares are occluded. Block each naris of an infant or young child and observe the child for signs of greater distress when the naris is obstructed.

- Assess facial discomfort. An infected or congested sinus can cause an aching, full feeling over the area of the sinus and facial tenderness on palpation.

- Assess any crusting, redness, bleeding, or discharge of the mucous membranes of the nostrils. Use a nasal speculum. The membrane normally appears moist, pink, and shiny.

4. **Position the client appropriately.**

- To treat the opening of the eustachian tube, have the client assume a back-lying position. *The drops will flow into the nasopharynx, where the eustachian tube opens.*

- To treat the ethmoid and sphenoid sinuses, have the client take a back-lying position with the head over the edge of the bed or a pillow under the shoulders so that the head is tipped backward. This is called the *Proetz position* (Figure 33–1).

- To treat the maxillary and frontal sinuses, have the client assume the same back-lying position, with the head turned toward the side to be treated. This position is called the *Parkinson position*. (Figure 33–2). If only one side is to be

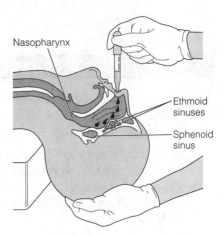

Figure 33–1   The Proetz position

treated, be sure the person is positioned so that the correct side is accessible. If the client's head is over the edge of the bed, support it with your hand so that the neck muscles are not strained.

5. **Administer the medication.**

- Draw up the required amount of solution into the dropper.

- Hold the tip of the dropper just above the nostril, and direct the solution laterally toward the middle of the nose as the client breathes through the mouth. Do not touch the mucous membrane

▶ **Procedure 33–2** *continued*

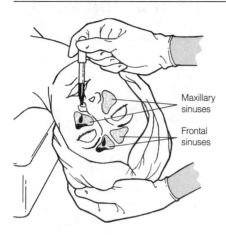

Figure 33–2 The Parkinson position.

of the nares. *If the solution is directed toward the base of the nasal cavity, it will run down the eustachian tube. Touching the mucous membrane with the dropper could contaminate the dropper and cause the client to sneeze.*

- Repeat for the other nostril if indicated.

- Ask the client to remain with the head tilted back for 5 minutes and breathe through the mouth. *This position will allow the solution to reach all of the nasal surface or flow into the desired area.*

- Wipe excess medication from the client's face and provide tissues for the client to expectorate any medication that flows into the mouth.

- Discard any remaining solution in the dropper, clean the dropper with warm water, and dispose of soiled supplies appropriately.

6. **Document all relevant information.**

- Document nursing assessments and interventions.

EVALUATION FOCUS

Relief of complaints (for example, nasal congestion, difficulty breathing, and discomfort); amount and character of secretions; appearance of nasal mucosa; adverse reactions or side effects of medication.

SAMPLE RECORDING

Date	Time	Notes
12/6/04	2250	Moderate amount clear secretions cleared from nose by blowing. Neosynephrine 2 gtts administered in both nares. No nasal or facial discomfort. Mucosa is pink.————————Sharona Von Stachenberg, RN

LIFESPAN CONSIDERATIONS

- Infants with nasal congestion may receive nasal drops 20 to 30 minutes before each feeding. *Nasal congestion impairs the sucking reflex.*

- Watch for signs of aspiration when giving nasal drops to infants or children. If coughing occurs, immediately sit the child up.

- Pushing gently on the tip of a child or an infant's nose will help open the nostrils.

- Attach a small piece of tubing to the end of the dropper when administering nasal drops to a young child. *The tubing helps prevent damage to mucous membranes.*

HOME CARE CONSIDERATIONS

- Teach the client or caregiver how to administer nasal drops at home. Explain possible side effects of the medication.

- Ensure that the client has the proper medication and can obtain refills if needed. *Financial concerns or lack of transportation can prevent the client from getting medication.*

- Caution the client not to use the medication more often than prescribed or longer than prescribed. *Certain medications can have a rebound effect, which worsens the condition.*

33–3 Administering an Intradermal Injection

PURPOSES
- To administer a medication for sensitivity and allergy testing
- To administer some types of immunizations

ASSESSMENT FOCUS

Appearance of injection site; specific drug action and expected response; client's knowledge of drug action and response; agency protocol about sites to use for skin tests.

EQUIPMENT

- Vial or ampule of the correct medication
- Sterile 1 mL syringe calibrated into hundredths of a milliliter and a needle 1/4 to 5/8 inch long with #25, #26, or #27 gauge
- Acetone and 2 × 2 sterile gauze square (optional)
- Swab moistened with alcohol or other colorless antiseptic
- Nonsterile gloves (according to agency protocol)
- Band-Aid (optional)
- Epinephrine, a bronchodilator, and antihistamine on hand

INTERVENTION

1. **Verify the order.**

- Check the physician's orders carefully for the medication, dosage, and route.

2. **Prepare the medication from the vial or ampule.**

- See Procedure 33–2 in *Fundamentals of Nursing*.

3. **Identify and prepare the client for the injection.**

- Check the client's arm band, and ask the client to tell you his or her name.

- Explain that the medication will produce a small bleb, like a blister. The client will feel a slight prick as the needle enters the skin. Some medications are absorbed slowly through the capillaries into the general circulation, and the bleb gradually disappears. Other drugs remain in the area and interact with the body tissues to produce redness and induration (hardening), which will need to be interpreted at a particular time (e.g., in 24 or 48 hours).

This reaction will also gradually disappear.

- Restrain a confused client or an infant or small child. *This prevents accidental injury from sudden movement.*

4. **Select and clean the site.**

- Select a site (e.g., the forearm about a hand's breadth above the wrist and three or four fingerwidths below the antecubital space).

- Avoid using sites that are tender, inflamed, or swollen and those that have lesions.

- Don gloves as agency protocol indicates.

- Defat the skin if agency protocol dictates, using a gauze square or swab moistened with acetone. Start at the center and widen the circle outward.

- Using the same method, clean the site with a swab moistened with alcohol or other colorless antiseptic, according to agency protocol. Allow the area to dry thoroughly. *A colorless antiseptic*

does not hinder the reading of the test.

5. **Prepare the syringe for the injection.**

- Remove the needle cap while waiting for the antiseptic to dry.

- Expel any air bubbles from the syringe. Small bubbles that adhere to the plunger are of no consequence. *A small amount of air will not harm the tissues.*

- Grasp the syringe in your dominant hand, holding it between thumb and four fingers, with your palm upward. Hold the needle at a 15° angle to the skin surface, with the bevel of the needle up.

6. **Inject the fluid.**

- With the nondominant hand, pull the skin at the site until it is taut, and thrust the tip of the needle firmly through the epidermis into the dermis (Figure 33–3, *A*). Do *not* aspirate.

- Inject the medication carefully so that it produces a small bleb on the skin (Figure 33–3, *B*).

▶ **Procedure 33–3** *continued*

- Withdraw the needle quickly while providing countertraction on the skin, and apply a Band-Aid if indicated.

- Do not massage the area. *Massage can disperse the medication into the tissue or out through the needle insertion site.*

- Dispose of the syringe and needle safely.

- Remove gloves, if worn.

7. **Document all relevant information.**

- Record the testing material given, the time, dosage, route, site, and nursing assessments.

8. **Assess the client.**

- Evaluate the client's response to the testing substance. *Some medications used in testing may cause allergic reactions.* An antidote drug

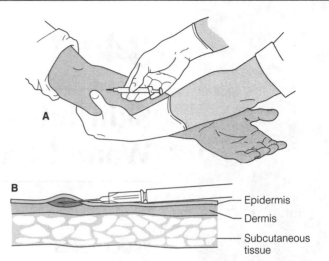

Figure 33–3   For an intradermal injection: *A,* the needle enters the skin at a 15° angle; and *B,* the medication forms a bleb under the epidermis.

(e.g., epinephrine hydra chloride) may need to be given.

- Evaluate the condition of the site in 24 or 48 hours, depending on the test. Measure the area of redness and induration in millimeters at the largest diameter and document findings.

EVALUATION FOCUS

Client's response; size of induration and redness at the injection site. See step 8.

SAMPLE RECORDING

Date	Time	Notes
02/26/04	1500	Tuberculin skin test (0.1 mL) administered intradermally in inner aspect of L forearm. No adverse systemic or local response.————————————————————Maureen Kirkpatrick, RN
02/28/04	1500	Small wheal (4 mm in diameter) formed.————Maureen Kirkpatrick, RN

LIFESPAN CONSIDERATIONS

- A small child or infant will need to be gently restrained during the procedure. *This prevents injury from sudden movement.*

- Make sure the child understands that the procedure is not a punishment.

- Ask the child not to rub or scratch the injection site. Place a stockingette or gauze dressing over the site if needed. *Rubbing the site can interfere with test results by irritating the underlying tissue.*

HOME CARE CONSIDERATIONS

- Be certain the client understands the need for a follow-up visit to examine the injection site. Set up an appointment for the visit.

- Instruct the client not to wash, rub, or scratch the injection site.

34

Skin Integrity and Wound Care

PROCEDURES

34–1 Basic Bandaging

PURPOSES
- To provide comfort
- To prevent further injury
- To promote healing
- To promote venous return in the extremities

ASSESSMENT FOCUS

Status of the skin area to which the bandage is to be applied; presence of an open wound; adequacy of circulation to the part; degree of pain.

EQUIPMENT
- ❏ Clean bandage of the appropriate material and width
- ❏ Padding, such as ABD pads or gauze squares
- ❏ Tape or a safety pin
- ❏ Nonsterile gloves, if an open wound is present

INTERVENTION

1. **Position and prepare the client appropriately.**

- Provide the client with a chair or bed, and arrange support for the area to be bandaged. For example, if a hand needs to be bandaged, ask the client to place the elbow on a table, so that the hand does not have to be held up unsupported. *Because bandaging takes a little time, holding up a body part without support can fatigue the client.*

- Make sure that the area to be bandaged is clean and dry. Wash and dry the area if necessary. *Washing and drying remove microorganisms, which flourish in dark, warm, moist areas.*

- Align the part to be bandaged with slight flexion of the joints, unless this is contraindicated. *Slight flexion places less strain on the ligaments and muscles of the joint.*

2. **Apply the bandage.**

Circular Turns

- Hold the bandage in your dominant hand, keeping the roll uppermost, and unroll the bandage about 8 cm (3 in). *This length of unrolled bandage allows good control for placement and tension.*

- Apply the end of the bandage to the part of the body to be bandaged. Hold the end down with the thumb of the other hand (Figure 34–1).

- Encircle the body part a few times or as often as needed, making sure that each layer overlaps one-half to two-thirds of the previous layer. *This provides even support to the area.*

- The bandage should be firm, but not too tight. Ask the client if the bandage feels comfortable. *A tight bandage can interfere with blood circulation, while a loose bandage doesn't provide adequate protection.*

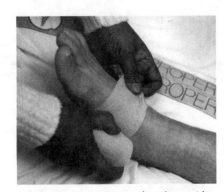

Figure 34–1 Starting a bandage with two circular turns.

- Secure the end of the bandage with tape or a safety pin over an uninjured area. *Pins can cause discomfort when situated over an injured area.*

Spiral Turns

- Make two circular turns. *Two circular turns anchor the bandage.*

- Continue spiral turns at about a 30° angle, each turn overlapping the preceding one by two-thirds the width of the bandage (Figure 34–2).

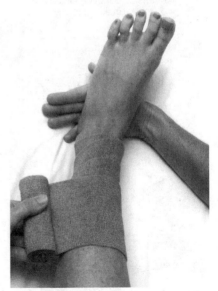

Figure 34–2 Applying spiral turns.

▶ Procedure 34–1 Basic Bandaging *continued*

- Terminate the bandage with two circular turns, and secure the end as described for circular turns.

Spiral Reverse Turns

- Anchor the bandage with two circular turns, and bring the bandage upward at about a 30° angle.

- Place the thumb of your free hand on the upper edge of the bandage (Figure 34–3, *A*). *The thumb will hold the bandage while it is folded on itself.*

- Unroll the bandage about 15 cm (6 in), then turn your hand so that the bandage falls over itself (Figure 34–3, *B*).

- Continue the bandage around the limb, overlapping each previous turn by two-thirds the width of the bandage. Make each bandage turn at the same position on the limb so that the turns of the bandage will be aligned (Figure 34–3, *C*).

- Terminate the bandage with two circular turns, and secure the end as described for circular turns.

Recurrent Turns

- Anchor the bandage with two circular turns.

- Fold the bandage back on itself, and bring it centrally over the distal end to be bandaged (Figure 34–4).

- Holding it with the other hand, bring the bandage back over the end to the right of the center

bandage but overlapping it by two-thirds the width of the bandage.

- Bring the bandage back on the left side, also overlapping the first turn by two-thirds the width of the bandage.

- Continue this pattern of alternating right and left until the area is covered. Overlap the preceding turn by two-thirds the bandage width each time.

- Terminate the bandage with two circular turns (Figure 34–5). Secure the end appropriately.

Figure-Eight Turns

- Anchor the bandage with two circular turns.

- Carry the bandage above the joint, around it, and then below it, making a figure eight (Figure 34–6).

- Continue above and below the joint, overlapping the previous turn by two-thirds the width of the bandage.

- Terminate the bandage above the joint with two circular turns, and then secure the end appropriately.

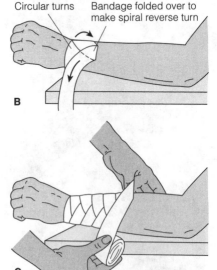

A

Circular turns   Bandage folded over to make spiral reverse turn

B

C

Figure 34–3A Applying spiral reverse turns.

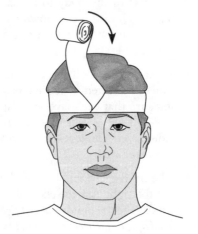

Figure 34–4 Starting a recurrent bandage with two circular turns.

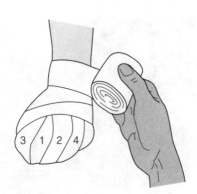

3 1 2 4

Figure 34–5 Completing a recurrent bandage with two circular turns.

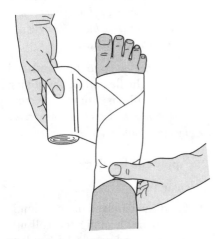

Figure 34–6 Applying a figure-eight bandage.

► **Procedure 34–1** *continued*

Thumb Spica

- Anchor the bandage with two circular turns around the wrist.

- Bring the bandage down to the distal aspect of the thumb, and encircle the thumb. Leave the tip of the thumb exposed if possible. *This allows you to check blood circulation to the thumb.*

- Bring the bandage back up and around the wrist, then back down and around the thumb, overlapping the previous turn by two-thirds the width of the bandage.

- Repeat the above two steps, working up the thumb and hand until the thumb is covered (Figure 34–7).

- Anchor the bandage with two circular turns around the wrist, and secure the end appropriately.

3. Document all relevant information.

- Record the type of bandage applied, the area to which it is applied, and nursing assessments, including skin problems or neurovascular problems.

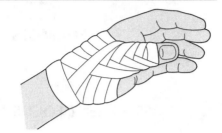

Figure 34–7   A thumb spica bandage.

EVALUATION FOCUS

Adequacy of distal circulation to bandaged part (e.g., skin color for pallor or cyanosis, skin temperature, strength of pulse, presence of numbness or tingling); client's ability to reapply the bandage when needed; client's ability to perform ADLs and assistance required.

SAMPLE RECORDING

Date	Time	Notes
04/07/04	0700	Elastic spiral bandage applied to right leg. Toes warm and pink. No numbness. Rt pedal pulse 60 beats per mm strong.———Laura R. Stenhouse, NS

LIFESPAN CONSIDERATIONS

- Older clients may need extra support during the procedure, especially if arthritis, contractures, or tremors are present.

- Avoid constricting the client's circulation with a tight bandage and observe bony prominences for signs of impaired circulation. *The risk for skin breakdown increases with age.*

- If a young client is apprehensive, demonstrate the procedure on a doll or stuffed animal.

- Encourage the child to decorate his bandage.

- Allow the child to help with the procedure by holding supplies or opening boxes.

HOME CARE CONSIDERATIONS

- Assess the client or caregiver's ability and willingness to perform the bandaging procedure.

- Ensure that the client has the proper supplies and knows how to obtain replacement supplies.

- Instruct the client's caregiver to:

  a. Wash hands thoroughly prior to handling dressing supplies and applying the bandage.

  b. Report skin breakdown, redness, pain, or pallor of the affected area.

  c. Check for adequate peripheral circulation after applying the bandage.

34–2 Applying a Stump Bandage

PURPOSES
- To support the return flow of venous blood
- To apply pressure and minimize bleeding and/or swelling
- To retain a surgical dressing
- To help shape a stump in preparation for a prosthesis

ASSESSMENT FOCUS

> The amount of any drainage on the dressing; the color, temperature, and swelling of the skin near the dressing to provide baseline data for evaluating the blood circulation to and from the area after the bandage has been applied; any discomfort, such as "phantom" pain (pain or irritation perceived to be in the removed part of the limb).

EQUIPMENT

- ❏ Clean bandage
- ❏ Tape or safety pins
- ❏ Sterile or nonsterile gloves, if drainage or an open wound is present

INTERVENTION

1. **Position the client appropriately.**

- Assist the client to a semi-Fowler's position in bed or to a sitting position on the edge of the bed.

- Clean the skin or stump wound and apply a sterile dressing as needed.

2. **Apply the bandage.**

Figure-Eight Bandage

- Anchor the bandage with two circular turns around the hips.

- Bring the bandage down over the stump and then back up and around the hips (Figure 34–8).

- Bring the bandage down again, overlapping the previous turn and make a figure eight around the stump and back up around the hips.

- Repeat, working the bandage up the stump (Figure 34–9).

- Anchor the bandage around the hips with two circular turns.

- Secure the bandage with tape *or* safety pins.

- Place the end of the elastic bandage at the top of the anterior surface of the leg, and have the client hold it in place. Bring the bandage diagonally down toward the end of the stump.

- Then, applying even pressure, bring the bandage diagonally upward toward the groin area (Figure 34–10).

- Make a figure-eight turn behind the top of the leg, downward again over and under the stump, and back up to the groin area (Figure 34–11).

- Repeat these figure-eight turns at least twice.

- Anchor the bandage around the hips with two circular turns.

- Secure the bandage with tape, safety pins, or clips.

Recurrent Bandage

- Anchor the bandage with two circular turns around the stump.

- Cover the stump with recurrent turns.

- Anchor the recurrent bandage with two circular turns (Figure 34–12).

- Secure the bandage with tape or safety pins.

Spiral Bandage

- Make recurrent turns to cover the end of the stump.

- Apply spiral turns from the distal aspect of the stump toward the body (Figure 34–13).

- Anchor the bandage with two circular turns around the hips.

- Secure the bandage with tape, safety pins, or clips.

3. **Document all relevant information.**

- Record the application of the bandage, all nursing assessments, and the client's response.

▶ **Procedure 34–2** *continued*

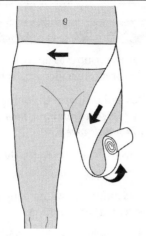

Figure 34–8 One way of beginning a figure-eight stump bandage.

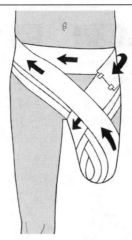

Figure 34–9 Figure-eight stump bandage applied around stump and waist.

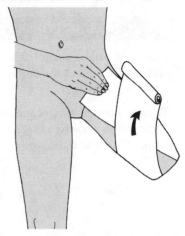

Figure 34–10 A second way to begin a figure-eight stump bandage.

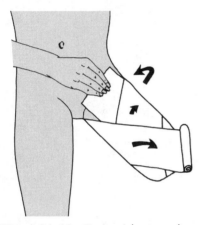

Figure 34–11 Figure-eight stump bandage applied around stump only.

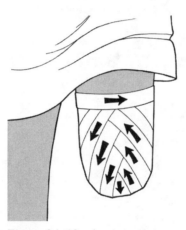

Figure 34–12 A recurrent stump bandage.

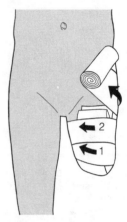

Figure 34–13 A spiral stump bandage.

EVALUATION FOCUS

> Adequacy of circulation to the stump (e.g., skin color for pallor or cyanosis; skin temperature; strength of pulses; presence of numbness or tingling).

SAMPLE RECORDING

Date	Time	Notes
07/11/04	0930	Figure-eight stump bandage removed as ordered. Slight serosanguineous drainage on one 4 × 4 gauze. Sterile dressing applied and figure-eight stump bandage reapplied. Wound is clean with minimal inflammation; stump skin color pink, feels warm to touch. No complaints of numbness or tingling.————————————————————Sam Fields, RN

▶ **Procedure 34–2 Applying a Stump Bandage** *continued*

LIFESPAN CONSIDERATIONS

- Instruct the older client to exercise both the affected and unaffected limbs. *Aging increases loss of muscle tone and muscle atrophy.*

- Provide ambulation aids and encourage the older client to remain active after a lower extremity amputation. *Older clients can lose muscle tone quickly.*

HOME CARE CONSIDERATIONS

- Teach the client or caregiver how to apply the stump dressing at home. Ask for a return demonstration.

- Demonstrate exercises and proper positioning for the affected extremity. *This prevents muscle contractures and helps maintain muscle tone.*

- Teach the client how to bathe and care for the stump.

- Instruct the client to examine the stump daily and report any redness, swelling, or irritation.

Infant Radiant Warmer

An *infant radiant warmer* or similar device is an open heating unit. A row of long lights is positioned at a stationary height from a bedding pad below. The radiant warmer is used to prevent the loss of body heat from the newborn infant. This warming process is crucial to the immature infant who has difficulty maintaining body temperature because of insufficient subcutaneous body fat and inadequate temperature self-regulation mechanisms. If the environmental temperature is not maintained with a radiant warmer or some similar thermal device, the infant will expend significant metabolic energy, with a resultant increase in oxygen and caloric needs. Procedure 34–3 describes how to apply an infant radiant warmer.

34–3 Applying an Infant Radiant Warmer

Before applying the radiant warmer, determine (a) that the equipment is in proper working order and (b) the manufacturer's operating instructions and institutional policy regarding the temperature control process and alarm setting protocols.

PURPOSE

- To assist the newborn or immature infant in establishing and maintaining a stable body temperature.

ASSESSMENT FOCUS

> The infant's initial body temperature; parental knowledge of the warmer function.

EQUIPMENT

- ❏ Radiant warmer with appropriate skin temperature sensors and reflective sensor covers (according to institutional policy)
- ❏ Prewarmed towels and infant blankets
- ❏ Infant head cover and diaper (according to institutional policy)
- ❏ Appropriate bedding for infant warmer

INTERVENTION

1. **Prepare the warmer.**

- Using the manual control setting, turn on the radiant warmer. *This prewarms the unit and eases the infant's transition from intrauterine to extrauterine life; it also prevents stressing of the immature infant.*

- Warm the blankets, towels, and washcloths.

2. **Assess and prepare the infant for the treatment.**

- Wipe the blood and vernix from the newborn's head and body using the prewarmed towels. *Prewarmed towels prevent loss of the infant's body heat through evaporation.*

- Wrap the infant in the preheated blankets, transfer the infant to the mother (parents), and then return him or her to the warmer.

- Remove the blankets, and apply a diaper and a head cover (if agency protocol indicates). *This allows maximal infant exposure to the heating element.* The value of a head covering in maintaining infant body heat remains debatable.

- Apply the temperature sensor to the infant's abdomen between the umbilicus and the xiphoid process. *Thin subcutaneous tissue found over the ribcage may prevent recording of an accurate temperature.*

- Cover the temperature sensor with a reflective covering (if indicated in unit manual or institutional policy). *A reflective covering decreases functional interference of the sensor by overhead lights.*

- Turn the warmer control device to the automatic setting. *This permits the infant's body temperature to control the level of heating and prevents accidental overheating or erratic warming.*

3. **Initiate the warming process.**

- Adjust the temperature setting control to the desired goal temperature. This ranges from 35.1C (97.0F) to 37.0C (98.6F). *This prevents overheating.*

- Turn the warmer on.

▶**Procedure 34–3 Applying an Infant Radiant Warmer** *continued*

- Set the temperature sensor alarm at the upper limit of the desired temperature range. *The alarm alerts the nurse if the infant's temperature exceeds upper limits of normal.*

4. **Monitor the warming process.**

- Check the infant's temperature sensor reading every 15 to 30 minutes until stable, then every 15 to 30 minutes (or as often as agency protocol dictates) until the infant's temperature reaches the desired level.

- Check the infant's axillary temperature every 15 to 30 minutes until stable, then every 2 to 4 hours (or according to agency protocol). *This verifies the accuracy of the sensor probe and the effectiveness of the treatment.*

- Monitor the sensor probe site and surrounding skin for irritation or breakdown. *Early detection of skin damage facilitates early intervention.*

5. **Terminate the warming process.**

- When the infant's temperature reaches the desired level, dress the infant in a T-shirt, diaper, and head cover. Wrap the infant in two blankets, and transfer the infant from the warmer to an open crib.

- Check the infant's axillary temperature every 2 to 4 hours (or according to agency protocol). *This allows the nurse to determine the infant's ability to maintain body temperature without assistance.*

- If the infant's temperature drops below 36.1C (97.0F), return the infant to the warmer, remove clothing, and reinitiate the warming procedure by performing the steps above.

EVALUATION FOCUS

Temperature within acceptable range; infant's ability to maintain temperature after therapy is discontinued; vital signs other than temperature within baseline data (indicates absence of environmental stress).

SAMPLE RECORDING

Date	Time	Notes
05/04/04	1032	Baby Jones born by vaginal delivery. Initial temperature 96.2F. Placed in preheated infant radiant warmer after cleaning and brief visit with parents. Temperature sensor applied to abdomen; equipment operating properly with increase noted in infant's temperature to 96.6F after 15 minutes. No signs of distress.————————————————————Pearl Gunther, RN

34–4 Managing Clients with Hyperthermia and Hypothermia Blankets

PURPOSE

- To increase or decrease the client's body temperature and prevent complications or extremes of temperatures

ASSESSMENT FOCUS

> Vital signs as baseline data; skin condition and temperature; presence of shivering; neurologic status.

EQUIPMENT

- ❏ Two pairs of nonsterile gloves
- ❏ Hyperthermia/hypothermia control module (should come with probe and blanket)
- ❏ Distilled water
- ❏ Plastic cover or thin sheet
- ❏ Lubricating jelly
- ❏ Tape
- ❏ Linen blanket (optional)

INTERVENTION

1. Prepare the client.

- Assess the client's vital signs, and explain the procedure.

- Place a blanket under the client and a pillow under the client's head. Use a sheet to insulate the client from the blanket.

- Wrap the client's hands and feet to prevent discomfort, if indicated. *This prevents chilling and promotes comfort.*

- If automatic operation is used, insert the thermistor probe and tape it in place. Rectal, axillary, or esophageal probes may be used.

- A second hyperthermia/hypothermia blanket or a bath blanket may be placed over the client. *This traps the heated or cooled air.*

2. Prepare the equipment.

- Connect the blanket pad to the modular unit, and inspect for adequate functioning.

- Inspect the pad and cords for frays or exposed wires.

- Screw (twist) the male tubing connectors of the coil blanket tubing into connectors on the modular unit.

- Check the solution level in the module, and fill with distilled water if necessary. *(The solution should be up to the fill line in order for the blanket temperature to be correct.)*

- Turn the modular unit on *to circulate the solution through the blanket.*

- Check for adequate filling of the coils throughout the blanket as the solution circulates throughout it. If you note leakage, obtain another blanket.

- Turn the client temperature control knob to the desired temperature, and determine whether the temperature gauge is functioning.

- Set the modular control knob or master switch to either the manual or automatic mode, and note the accuracy of the temperature settings.

If using the automatic mode:

- Insert the thermistor probe plug into the thermistor probe jack on modular unit.

- Check the automatic mode light to be sure it comes on.

- Set the machine to the desired temperature.

- Set the limits for the pad temperature.

If using the manual mode:

- Set the master temperature control knob to the desired temperature.

- Check the manual mode light to be sure it is operational.

- Cover the blanket with a plastic cover and a thin sheet.

- Remove and discard one glove.

3. Monitor the client closely.

- Take vital signs every 15 minutes for 1 hour, every 30 minutes for 1 hour, then hourly.

- Determine the client's neurologic status regularly as needed.

- Reposition the client every 30 minutes to 1 hour and observe the skin for indication of burns, intactness, and color. Keep the client dry and the bedclothes free of condensation. *Heat and cold can cause burning.*

- Determine any intolerance to the blanket. *Shivering may result from increased metabolic activity.*

▶ **Procedure 34–4 Managing Clients with Hyperthermia and Hypothermia Blankets** *continued*

5. **Maintain the therapy as required.**

- Check probe positioning; if a rectal probe is used, remove and clean the probe every 3 to 4 hours or when the client has a bowel movement. *When the probe is impacted with feces, the temperature reading can be distorted.*

EVALUATION FOCUS

Vital signs; skin condition; presence of shivering.

SAMPLE RECORDING

Date	Time	Notes
06/06/04	1035	Hypothermia blanket applied. T 40C, P 128, R 32, BP 90/40. Blanket set at 28C. Rectal probe inserted. Skin intact, no abrasions. Hands and feet covered with towels.————————————————————Nancy Sun, SN

LIFESPAN CONSIDERATIONS

- Monitor the older client for abrupt changes in temperature. *Decreased glandular activity and loss of body fat make older adults more vulnerable to hypothermia and hyperthermia.*

- Young clients can quickly develop an elevated body temperature. *The body's ability to control body temperature is immature.*

- Observe children with elevated temperature for seizure activity. *Accelerated temperature reduction can provoke seizure activity.*

34–5 Administering Hot Soaks and Sitz Baths

Before administering a hot soak or a sitz bath, determine (a) the type and temperature of the solution to be used; (b) the duration, frequency, and purpose of the soak, as indicated on the chart; and (c) agency protocol regarding the temperature and the length of time for soaks. Generally, a temperature of 40C to 43C (105F to 110F), as tol-erated by the client, is indicated. For a hot soak, determine whether sterile technique is required.

PURPOSES
- To hasten suppuration, soften exudates, and enhance healing
- To apply medications to a designated area
- To clean a wound in which there is sloughing tissue or an exudate
- To promote circulation and enhance healing

ASSESSMENT FOCUS

> Appearance of the affected area, such as redness, drainage (amount, color, consistency, odor), and swelling; any break in the skin; any discomfort experienced by the client; the client's mental status and ability to co-operate during the procedure; factors contraindicating heat therapy.

EQUIPMENT

(Use sterile equipment and supplies for an open wound)
- ❏ Small basin, special arm or foot bath, or sitz tub or chair
- ❏ Specified solution at the correct temperature

- ❏ Thermometer
- ❏ Disposable and sterile gloves (if the client has any open areas on the skin)
- ❏ Moisture-resistant bag
- ❏ Towels

- ❏ Bath blanket
- ❏ Required gauze squares and rolled gauze for an extremity, perineal pads and a T-binder for the perineal area

INTERVENTION

Hand or Foot Soak

1. Prepare the soak.

- Fill the container at least one-half full and test the temperature of the solution with a thermometer. *A temperature that is too high can cause burning and one that is too low will not produce the desired effect.*

- Pad the edge of the container with a towel. *Padding is necessary to prevent pressure on the body part that rests on the edge of the container.*

- Use sterile solution and a sterile thermometer if the client has an open wound.

2. Prepare and assess the client.

- Assist the client to a well-aligned, comfortable position; the position adopted will be maintained for 15 to 20 minutes. *This position helps prevent muscle strain.*

- Don disposable gloves as required, remove the dressings, and discard them in the bag. Assess the amount, color, odor, and consistency of the drainage on removed dressings.

- Inspect the appearance of the area to be soaked.

3. Commence the soak.

- Immerse the body part completely in the solution. *The entire affected area must be in contact with the solution.*

- If the soak is sterile, cover the open container with a sterile drape or the container wrapper. *Covering the open container helps prevent accidental contamination.*

- Place a large sheet or blanket over the soak. *This will help maintain the temperature of the solution.*

- Go to step 7.

Sitz Bath

4. Prepare the bath.

- Fill the sitz bath with water at above 40C (105F) (the water level in a tub should be at the umbilicus). The temperature of the water should feel comfortable to the inner aspect of the wrist.

- Pad the tub or chair with towels as required. *Padding prevents pressure on the sacrum or posterior aspects of the thighs.* When a disposable sitz bath on the toilet is used, provide a footstool. *This can prevent pressure on the back of the thighs.*

5. Prepare the client.

- Have the client void.

- Remove the gown, or fasten it above the waist.

- Don gloves if an open area or drainage is present.

▶ Procedure 34–5 Administering Hot Soaks and Sitz Baths *continued*

- Remove the T-binder and peritoneal dressings, if present, and note the amount, color, odor, and consistency of any drainage.

- Assess the appearance of the area to be soaked for redness, swelling, odor, breaks in the skin, and drainage.

- Wrap the bath blanket around the client's shoulders and over the legs as needed. *Draping the client provides warmth and prevents chilling.*

6. Begin the sitz bath.

- Assist the client into the bath and provide support for the client as needed.

- Leave a signal light within reach. Stay with the client if warranted and terminate the bath as necessary. *Some clients may become faint or dizzy and need to be able to call a nurse or have the nurse remain with them.*

7. Give the client the following instructions:

- Remain in position, and call the nurse if any discomfort is felt or an untoward reaction occurs.

8. Monitor the client.

Soak

- Assess the client and test the temperature of the solution at least once during the soak. Assess for discomfort, need for additional support, and any reactions to the soak.

- If the solution has cooled, remove the body part, empty the solution, add newly heated solution, and reimmerse the body part.

Sitz Bath

- Assess the client's comfort level, color, and pulse rate during the bath. *An accelerated pulse, dizziness, or extreme pallor may precede fainting.*

- Immediately report any unexpected or adverse responses to the nurse in charge.

- Test the temperature of the solution at least once during the bath. Adjust the temperature as needed.

9. Discontinue the soak or bath.

- At completion of a *soak*, remove the body part from the basin, and dry it thoroughly and carefully. If the soak was sterile, don sterile gloves, and dry the wound with sterile gauze pads. *Drying prevents skin maceration.*

- Assess the appearance of the affected area carefully, and reapply a dressing if required.

or

- At the completion of a *sitz bath*, assist the client out of the sitz bath, and dry the area with a towel.

- Assess the perineal area, and reapply dressings and garments as required.

10. Document all relevant information.

- Record the soak or sitz bath, including the duration, temperature, and type of solution. Include all assessments.

EVALUATION FOCUS

Redness, drainage, swelling of the affected area; any discomfort; extent of healing.

SAMPLE RECORDING

Date	Time	Notes
12/05/04	0900	43C saline soak to (L) index finger x 20 mm. 2 x 2 gauze saturated with purulent exudate. Finger measures 7 cm (down 1 cm from previous measurement) but continues to be red in color.————————Toby N. Zacharias, NS

▶ **Procedure 34–5** *continued*

LIFESPAN CONSIDERATIONS	HOME CARE CONSIDERATIONS

<table>
<tr><td>

- Provide the older client with extra warmth to prevent chilling. *Older clients have increased vulnerability to hypothermia due to decreased body fat.*

- Help the older client assume a standing position slowly, and instruct the client on how to use the safety rail when getting in and out of the tub. *Changing positions slowly prevents dizziness and helps the older client regain equilibrium.*

- For the older client, monitor the water temperature carefully, dry the skin well, and apply a moisturizer, if indicated. *The skin becomes dry and thin with age. Maceration (softening) can occur with prolonged soaking.*

</td><td>

- Assess the client's ability and willingness to perform the procedure without assistance.

- If possible, teach the client how to perform the soak or sitz bath and how to clean and store the equipment.

- If a bathtub is used, instruct the client that the tub should be cleaned and disinfected before and after the treatment. Inspect the bathroom for safety features, such as a rubber bath mat and hand rails.

- Ensure that the client has the proper equipment and knows how to obtain supplies.

</td></tr>
</table>

34–6 Administering a Cooling Sponge Bath

Before administering a cooling sponge bath, determine agency protocol. Some agencies recommend sponging the entire body. To avoid chilling, others recommend sponging only the face, arms, legs, back, and buttocks (*not the chest and abdomen*).

PURPOSE

• To reduce a client's fever by promoting body heat loss through conduction and vaporization

ASSESSMENT FOCUS

Body temperature, pulse, respirations for baseline data; other signs of fever (e.g., skin warmth, flushing, complaints of feeling hot or chilly, diaphoresis, irritability, restlessness, general malaise, or delirium).

EQUIPMENT

❑ Thermometer to measure the client's temperature
❑ Bath blanket
❑ Several washcloths and bath towels (fewer are needed if ice bags or cold packs are used)

❑ Basin for the solution
❑ Bath thermometer
❑ Solution at the correct temperature (water or equal portions of 70% alcohol and water)

❑ Ice bag or cold pack (optional)
❑ Fan (optional)

INTERVENTION

1. **Obtain all relevant baseline data.**

• If not already recorded prior to the sponge bath, measure the client's body temperature, pulse, and respirations to provide comparative baseline data.

• Assess the client for other signs of fever (see the Assessment Focus above).

2. **Prepare the client.**

• Remove the gown, and assist the client to a comfortable supine position.

• Place a bath blanket over the client.

• If ice bags or cold packs are not used, place bath towels under each axilla and shoulder. *Bath towels protect the lower bed sheet from getting wet.*

3. **Sponge the face.**

• Sponge the client's face with plain water only, and dry it.

• Apply an ice bag or cold pack to the head for comfort.

4. **Place cold applications in the axillae and groins.**

• Wet four washcloths; wring them out so that they are very damp but not dripping. *Washcloths need to be as moist as possible to be effective.*

• Place washcloths in the axillae and groins.

or

Place ice bags or cold packs in these areas. *The axillae and groins contain large superficial blood vessels, which aid the transfer of heat.*

• Leave washcloths in place for about 5 minutes, or until they feel warm. Rewet and replace them as required during the bath. *Washcloths warm up relatively quickly in such vascular areas.*

5. **Sponge the arms and legs.**

• Place a bath towel under one arm and sponge the arm *slowly* and *gently* for about 5 minutes or as tolerated by the client. *Slow,*

gentle motions are indicated because firm rubbing motions increase tissue metabolism and heat production. Cool sponges given rapidly or for a short period of time tend to increase the body's heat production mechanisms by causing shivering.

or

Place a saturated towel over the extremity, and rewet it as necessary. Give the client enough time to adjust to the initial reaction of chilliness and for the body to cool.

• Dry the arm, using a patting motion rather than a rubbing motion.

• Repeat the above steps for the other arm and the legs.

• When sponging the extremities, hold the washcloth briefly over the wrists and ankles. *The blood circulation is close to the skin surface in the wrists and ankles.*

6. **Reassess the client's vital signs after 15 minutes.**

• Compare findings with data taken before the bath. *The vital*

▶ **Procedure 34–6** *continued*

signs are checked to evaluate the effectiveness of the sponge bath. Proceed with the bath if the temperature is above 37.7C (100F); discontinue if the temperature is below 37.7C (100F), or if the pulse rate is significantly increased and remains so after 5 minutes.

7. **(Optional) Sponge the chest and abdomen.**

- Sponge these areas for 3 to 5 minutes and pat them dry.

8. **Sponge the back and buttocks.**

- Sponge the back and buttocks for 3 to 5 minutes.

- Pat these areas dry.

9. **Remove the cold applications from the axillae and groins.**

10. **Reassess vital signs.**

11. **Document assessments, including the vital signs, as well as the type of sponge bath given.**

VARIATION: Pediatric Bathing

Cooling baths for children can be given in the tub, bed, or crib.

Immersion of a child in a tepid tub bath for 20 to 30 minutes is a simple and effective method to reduce an elevated temperature.

Tub

- While the child is in the tub, firmly support the child's head and shoulders and gently squeeze water over the back and chest or gently spray water from a sprayer over the body.

- To make a tub bath more effective, lay a small infant or older child down in the water and support the head on your arm or a padded support. Small children, however, may resist any effort to place them in a horizontal position.

- For conscious children, use a floating toy or other distraction during the bath.

- Always stay with the child in a tub for safety reasons.

- Discontinue the cooling bath if there is evidence of chilling. The process of shivering generates additional heat and defeats the purpose of the bath, and chilling causes vasoconstriction so that minimal blood is carried to the skin surface.

- Dry and dress the child in light-weight clothing or only a diaper and cover the child with a light cotton blanket.

- Retake the temperature 30 minutes after removal from the tub and repeat measurement as often as indicated.

Bed or Crib Sponge

- Place the undressed child on an absorbent towel.

- Follow the steps above for a sponge bath, or use the following towel method:

    a. Apply a cool cloth or icebag to the forehead.

    b. Wrap each extremity in a towel moistened with tepid water.

    c. Place one towel under the back and another over the neck and torso.

    d. Change the towels as they warm.

    e. Continue the procedure for about 30 minutes.

EVALUATION FOCUS

Vital signs and changes in baseline assessments.

SAMPLE RECORDING

Date	Time	Notes
09/18/04	1645	T40.2, P94, R18 and shallow. c/o "burning up," face flushed, diaphoretic, and states feels "miserable and muscles aching." Dr. Kirkpatrick notified. Cooling sponge bath given.————————————Jennifer Newton, RN
	1700	T39.4, P90, R16. Face less flushed. States "feels cooler."————————————————————————Jennifer Newton, RN
	1715	T38.8, P90, R14.————————————Jennifer Newton, RN

▶**Procedure 34–6 Administering a Cooling Sponge Bath** *continued*

LIFESPAN CONSIDERATIONS	HOME CARE CONSIDERATIONS

LIFESPAN CONSIDERATIONS

- Observe older clients for chilling. Placing a warm water bottle against the feet can help prevent chills. *The skin becomes thinner and fat deposits decrease with age.*

- Observe the child with a body temperature above 103F (39.4C) for febrile seizures. Accelerated temperature reduction can also provoke seizures.

HOME CARE CONSIDERATIONS

- Make sure the room is warm and free of drafts before beginning the bath.

- Teach the caregiver how to take the client's temperature and perform the bath procedure. Instruct in signs of chilling.

- Advise the caregiver to use an electronic thermometer when taking an oral temperature. *Chills may cause the client to bite down and shatter a glass thermometer.*

- Instruct the caregiver to give antipyretic medication 15 to 20 minutes before the bath, if ordered.

34–7 Cleaning a Drain Site and Shortening a Penrose Drain

Before cleaning a drain site and shortening a Penrose drain, determine (a) agency protocol about who may shorten drains; (b) that the drain is to be shortened and the length it is to be, for example 2.5 cm (1 in); (c) whether the drain has been shortened previously (drains that have not been shortened previously are often attached to the skin by a suture, which must be removed before shortening the drain); (d) the location of the drain; and (e) the type and amount of discharge previously recorded and previous assessments of the appearance of the wound, for baseline data.

PURPOSES

Cleaning a Drain Site

- To remove any discharge from the skin, thereby reducing the danger of skin irritation
- To reduce the number of microorganisms present and therefore decrease the possibility of infection

Shortening a Drain

- To decrease the length of the drain a designated amount, thereby encouraging healing of the wound from the inside toward the outside

ASSESSMENT FOCUS

The amount of any drainage on the dressing; the color, temperature, and swelling of the skin near the dressing to provide baseline data; any discomfort associated with the wound.

EQUIPMENT

- ❏ Moistureproof bag
- ❏ Mask for the nurse and one for the client, if necessary
- ❏ Disposable gloves
- ❏ Sterile gloves
- ❏ Sterile dressing equipment, including
  - Two pairs of forceps, including at least one hemostat
  - Sterile cotton-tipped applicators

- Sterile dressing materials sufficient to cover the surgical incision and the drain site (at least two 4 × 4 gauzes are usually needed to dress the drain site, more if drainage is copious; a sterile precut gauze is needed to apply first around the drain site)

- Sterile suture scissors (if the drain has *not* been shortened previously)
- Sterile scissors
- Sterile safety pin (add this to the sterile dressing set)
- ❏ Tape, tie tapes, or other binding supplies

INTERVENTION

1. **Verify the physician's order.**

- Confirm that the drain is to be shortened by the nurse and the length it is to be, for example 2.5 cm (1 in).

2. **Prepare the client.**

- Inform the client that the drain is to be shortened and that this procedure should not be painful.

- Explain that there may be a pulling sensation for a few seconds when the drain is being drawn out before it is shortened.

- Position the client as for a dressing change.

3. **Remove dressings, and clean the incision.**

- *The incision is cleaned first because it is considered cleaner than the drain site. Moist drainage facilitates the growth of resident skin bacteria around the drain.*

4. **Clean and assess the drain site.**

- Wearing sterile gloves, clean the skin around the drain site by swabbing in half or full circles from around the drain site outward, using separate swabs for each wipe (Figure 34–14 on page 78). You may hold forceps in

▶ **Procedure 34–7 Shortening a Penrose Drain** *continued*

Figure 34–14 Cleaning the skin around a drain site.

the nondominant hand to hold the drain erect while cleaning around it. Clean as many times as necessary to remove the drainage.

- Assess the amount and character of drainage, including odor, thickness, and color.

5. **Shorten the drain.**

- If the drain has *not* been shortened before, cut and remove the suture. See Procedure 34–10. *The drain is sutured to the skin during surgery to keep it from slipping into the body cavity.*

- With a hemostat, firmly grasp the drain by its full width at the level of the skin, and pull the drain out the required length. *Grasping the full width of the drain ensures even traction.*

- Wearing sterile gloves, insert the sterile safety pin through the base of the drain as close to the skin as possible by holding the drain tightly against the skin edge and

Figure 34–15 Pinning a drain.

inserting the pin above your fingers (Figure 34–15). *The pin keeps the drain from falling back into the incision. Holding the drain securely in place at the skin level and inserting the pin above the fingers prevents the nurse from pulling the drain further out or pricking the client during this step.*

- With the sterile scissors, cut off the excess drain so that about 2.5 cm (1 in) remains above the skin (Figure 34–16). Discard the excess in the waste bag.

6. **Apply dressings to the drain site and the incision.**

- Place a precut 4 × 4 gauze snugly around the drain (Figure 34–17), or open a 4 × 4 gauze to 4 × 8, fold it lengthwise to 2 × 8, and place the 2 × 8 around the drain so that the ends overlap. *This dressing absorbs the drainage and helps prevent it from excoriating the skin. Using precut gauze or folding it as described, instead of cutting the gauze, prevents any threads from coming loose and getting into the wound, where they could cause inflammation and provide a site for infection.*

Figure 34–16 Shortening a drain.

Figure 34–17 Precut gauze in place around a drain.

- Apply the sterile dressings one at a time, using sterile gloved hands or sterile forceps. Take care that the dressings do not slide off and become contaminated. Place the bulk of the dressings over the drain area and below the drain, depending on the client's usual position. *Layers of dressings are placed for best absorption of drainage, which flows by gravity.*

- Apply the final surgipad by hand; remove gloves, and dispose of them; and secure the dressing with tape or ties.

7. **Document the procedure and nursing assessments.**

▶ **Procedure 34–7** *continued*

EVALUATION FOCUS

Amount of drainage and its color, clarity, thickness, and odor; degree of inflammation; pain at the incision or drain site.

SAMPLE RECORDING

Date	Time	Notes
12/05/04	1025	Penrose drain shortened 2.5 cm. Three 4 x 4 gauzes saturated with brownish yellow drainage. Dry dressings x 4 applied. Skin intact; no redness or irritation.————————————————————Maria L. Antonio, RN

LIFESPAN CONSIDERATIONS

• Use tape cautiously on the skin of older clients, and observe for signs of skin breakdown around the drain site and incision. *The skin becomes thin with aging.*

34–8   Establishing and Maintaining a Closed Wound Drainage System

PURPOSES
- To hasten the healing process by draining excess exudate, which interferes with the formation of granulation tissue in a wound
- To reduce the risk of infection and skin breakdown
- To maintain the patency of the wound suction

ASSESSMENT FOCUS

> The amount, color, consistency, clarity, and odor of the drainage; discomfort around the area of the drain; clinical signs of infection (e.g., elevated body temperature).

EQUIPMENT
- ❏ Disposable gloves
- ❏ Calibrated drainage receptacle

INTERVENTION

1. **Establish suction if it has not been already initiated.**

- Place the evacuator unit on a solid, flat surface and don disposable gloves.

- Open the drainage plug on top of the unit, without contaminating the unit.

- Compress the unit; while it is compressed, close the drainage plug to retain the vacuum (Figure 34–18).

- Secure the unit to the client's gown or bedding, below the level of the wound.

Figure 34–18   Compressing the Hemovac.

2. **Empty the evacuator unit.**

- When the drainage fluid reaches the line marked "Full," don disposable gloves, and open the drainage plug.

- Invert the unit, and empty it into the collecting receptacle.

- Reestablish suction as in step 1.

- Measure the amount of drainage, and note its characteristics.

3. **Document all relevant information.**

- Record the emptying of the evacuator unit and nursing assessments on the nursing progress notes.

- Record the amount and type of drainage on the intake and output record.

EVALUATION FOCUS

> Amount of drainage and its color, clarity, consistency, and odor; increased or decreased discomfort; clinical signs of infection.

SAMPLE RECORDING

Date	Time	Notes
09/09/04	1030	Hemovac emptied 20 mL dark thick red drainage. Vacuum re-established. Tubing patent and suction functioning. Drain site red, small amount of thick, white discharge. Specimen to lab for culture. No odor. No discomfort. Dry dressing applied.————————————Sarah J. Woo, RN

▶ **Procedure 34–8** *continued*

HOME CARE CONSIDERATIONS

- Schedule regular nursing visits to teach wound care and to observe the drainage site.

- Teach the client or a caregiver to empty, measure, and record the drainage at least once daily.

- Instruct the caregiver to observe the wound daily for signs of infection, such as redness, edema, tenderness, or purulent drainage. The client's temperature should be measured twice daily. *Elevated temperature can indicate infection.*

- Ensure that the client has the proper supplies and knows how to obtain new items as needed.

- Notify the physician of excess drainage, signs of infection, or occlusion of the tube.

- Determine when the physician plans to remove the drain, and help the client keep the appointment.

34–9 Applying Moist Sterile Compresses

PURPOSES

Warm Applications
- To enhance healing
- To promote comfort
- To relieve muscle spasm or pain
- To promote reabsorption in tissues or joints

Cold Applications
- To prevent or minimize bleeding
- To reduce inflammation or prevent swelling
- To anesthetize tissues and reduce pain temporarily

ASSESSMENT FOCUS

Skin integrity; size, appearance, and type of wound or injury; redness and inflammation; swelling; abrasions; character and amount of drainage; discomfort; vital signs; neurovascular integrity (circulation, sensation, and motion) of affected area.

EQUIPMENT

(Use sterile equipment and supplies for an open wound)

Compress:

❑ Container for the solution
❑ Solution at the strength and temperature specified by the physician or the agency
❑ Thermometer
❑ Petrolatum jelly
❑ Gauze squares
❑ Insulating towel
❑ Plastic underpad
❑ Hot water bottle or aquathermia pad (optional)

or

❑ Ice bag (optional)
❑ Ties or rolled gauze
❑ Nonsterile gloves
❑ Sterile gloves, forceps, and cotton applicator sticks (if compress must be sterile)

Moist pack:

❑ Flannel pieces or towel packs
❑ Hot-pack machine for heating the packs

or

❑ Basin of water with some ice chips
❑ Insulating material, such as flannel or towels
❑ Plastic
❑ Hot water bottle (optional)
or
❑ Ice bag (optional)
❑ Thermometer if a specific temperature is ordered for the pack
❑ Petrolatum jelly
❑ Sterile gloves or forceps (if sterility must be maintained)

INTERVENTION

1. Prepare the client.

- Assist the client to a comfortable position.

- Expose the area for the compress or pack.

- Provide support for the body part requiring the compress or pack.

- Don nonsterile gloves, and remove the wound dressing, if present. A dry, sterile dressing is often placed over open wounds between applications of moist heat or cold.

2. Moisten tile compress or pack.

- Place the gauze in the solution.

  or

- Heat the flannel or towel in a steamer, or chill it in the basin of water and ice.

3. Protect surrounding skin as indicated.

- With a cotton swab or an applicator stick, apply petrolatum jelly to the skin surrounding the wound, not on the wound or open areas of the skin. *Petroleum jelly protects*

the skin from possible burns, maceration, and irritating effects of some solutions.

4. Apply the moist heat.

- Wring out the gauze compress so that the solution does not drip from it. For a sterile compress, use sterile forceps or sterile gloves to wring out the gauze.

- Apply the gauze lightly and gradually to the designated area and, if tolerated by the client, mold the compress close to the body. Pack the gauze snugly against all

▶ **Procedure 34–9** *continued*

wound surfaces. *Air is a poor conductor of cold or heat, and molding excludes air.*

or

- Wring out the flannel (for a sterile pack, use sterile gloves).

- Apply the flannel to the body area, molding it closely to the body part.

5. **Immediately insulate and secure the application.**

- Cover the gauze or flannel quickly with a dry towel and a piece of plastic. *This step helps maintain the temperature of the application and thus its effectiveness.*

- Secure the compress or pack in place with gauze ties or tape.

- Optional: Apply a hot water bottle or aquathermia pad or ice bag over the plastic to maintain the heat or cold.

6. **Monitor the client.**

- Assess the client for discomfort at 5- to 10-minute intervals. If the client feels any discomfort, assess the area for erythema, numbness, maceration, or blistering.

- For applications to large areas of the body, note any change in the pulse, respirations, and blood pressure.

- In the event of unexpected reactions, terminate the treatment and report to the nurse in charge.

7. **Remove the compress or pack at the specified time.**

- Compresses and packs with external heat or cold usually retain their temperature anywhere from 15 to 30 minutes. Without external heat or cold, they need to be changed every 5 minutes.

- Apply a sterile dressing if one is required.

8. **Document relevant information.**

- Document the procedure, the time, and the type and strength of the solution.

- Record assessments, including the appearance of the wound and surrounding skin area.

EVALUATION FOCUS

Level of comfort; redness and inflammation; swelling; character, quality, and amount of discharge; appearance of wound and degree of healing; neurovascular integrity (circulation, sensation, and motion) of affected area; vital signs.

SAMPLE RECORDING

Date	Time	Notes
05/12/04	0910	Sterile normal saline compress with K-Matic 37.7 C applied to 2.5 cm open leg wound. Pink tissue surrounding wound. 1 cm diameter serosanguineous discharge on dressing. No discomfort voiced.————————————————————Olga R. Resnicoff, SN
05/12/04	0940	Compress removed. No further discharge. Wound packed with gauze and sterile dry dressing applied.————————Olga R. Resnicoff, SN

▶**Procedure 34–9 Applying Moist Sterile Compresses** *continued*

LIFESPAN CONSIDERATIONS

- Assess older clients carefully for skin breakdown or maceration (softening) after treatment. *The skin becomes thinner with aging and fat deposits are decreased.*

- Monitor the temperature of the compress carefully for older clients. *Older clients may have decreased sensations of direct heat or cold.*

- Provide extra blankets as needed for older clients. *Older clients can become chilled due to decreased fat deposits and changes in body temperature regulation.*

HOME CARE CONSIDERATIONS

- Instruct the client or caregiver on how to apply moist compresses. Provide written instructions that include when to notify the health care provider.

- Advise the client to assess the skin during and after each treatment. Measuring the temperature of the solution is especially important if the client has decreased sensation. *Tissue damage can result from direct heat applications. Intense cold may cause pain, burning, or numbness.*

- Ensure that the client has the proper equipment and knows how to obtain replacement supplies.

34–10 Removing Skin Sutures

Before removing skin sutures, verify (a) the orders for suture removal (many times only *alternate* interrupted sutures are removed one day, and the remaining sutures are removed a day or two later); (b) whether a dressing is to be applied following the suture removal; and (c) when the client may bathe or shower. Some physicians prefer no dressing; others prefer a small, light gauze dressing to prevent friction by clothing.

ASSESSMENT FOCUS

Appearance of suture line; factors contraindicating suture removal (e.g., nonuniformity of closure, inflammation, presence of drainage).

EQUIPMENT

- ❏ Moistureproof bag
- ❏ Sterile gloves
- ❏ Nonsterile gloves

- ❏ Sterile dressing equipment including:
  - • Sterile suture scissors
  - • Sterile hemostat or forceps

- • Sterile butterfly tape (optional)
- • Light sterile gauze pad
- ❏ Tape (if a dressing is to be applied)
- ❏ A prepackaged suture removal kit may be used, if available

INTERVENTION

1. Prepare the client.

- Inform the client that suture removal may produce slight discomfort, such as a pulling or stinging sensation, but should not be painful.

2. Remove dressings, and clean the incision.

- Don sterile gloves.

- Clean the suture line with an antimicrobial solution before and after suture removal. *This is generally done as a prophylactic measure to prevent infection.*

3. Remove the sutures.

Plain Interrupted Sutures

- Grasp the suture at the knot with a pair of forceps.

- Place the curved tip of the suture scissors under the suture as close to the skin as possible, either on the side opposite the knot (Figure 34–19) or directly under the knot. Cut the suture. *Sutures are cut as close to the skin as possible on one side of the visible part because the visible suture material is*

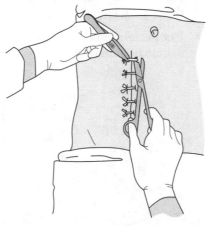

Figure 34–19 Removing a plain interrupted skin suture.

contaminated with skin bacteria and must not be pulled beneath the skin during removal. Suture material that is beneath the skin is considered free from bacteria.

- With the forceps or hemostat, pull the suture out in one piece. Inspect carefully to make sure that all suture material is removed. *Suture material left beneath the skin acts as a foreign body and causes inflammation.*

- Discard the suture onto a piece of sterile gauze or into the moistureproof bag, being careful not

to contaminate the forceps tips. Sometimes the suture sticks to the forceps and needs to be removed by wiping the tips on a sterile gauze.

- Continue to remove *alternate* sutures, such as the third, fifth, seventh, and so forth. *Alternate sutures are removed first so that remaining sutures keep the skin edges in close approximation and prevent any dehiscence from becoming large.*

- If no dehiscence occurs, remove the remaining sutures. If dehiscence does occur, do not remove the remaining sutures, and report the dehiscence to the nurse in charge.

- If a little wound dehiscence occurs, apply a sterile butterfly tape over the gap:

  a. Attach the tape to one side of the incision.

  b. Press the wound edges together.

  c. Attach the tape to the other side of the incision (Figure 34–20 on page 86). *The butterfly tape holds the wound*

▶ Procedure 34–10 Removing Skin Sutures *continued*

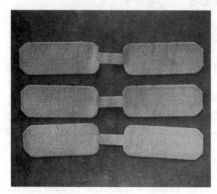

Figure 34–20 Butterfly tapes.

edges as close together as possible and promotes healing.

- If a large dehiscence occurs, cover the wound with sterile gauze, and report the problem immediately to the nurse in charge or physician.

Mattress Interrupted Sutures

- When possible, cut the visible part of the suture close to the skin at *A* and *B* in Figure 34–21, opposite the knot, and remove this small visible piece. Discard it as described above. In some sutures, the visible part opposite the knot may be so small that it can be cut only once.

- Grasp the knot *(C)* with forceps. Remove the remainder of the suture beneath the skin by pulling out in the direction of the knot.

Plain Continuous Sutures

- Cut the thread of the first suture opposite the knot at *A* in Figure 34–22. Then cut the thread of the second suture on the same side at *B*.

- Grasp the knot *(C)* with the forceps, and pull. This removes the first stitch and the piece of thread beneath the skin, which is attached to the second stitch. Discard the suture.

- Cut off the visible part of the second suture at *D*, and discard it.

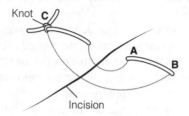

Figure 34–21 Mattress interrupted sutures.

- Grasp the suture at *E*, and pull out the underlying loop between *D* and *E*.

- Cut the visible part at *F*, and remove it.

- Repeat the above two steps at *G* through *J*, until the last knot is reached. Note that after the first stitch is removed, each thread is cut down the same side, below the original knot.

- Cut the last suture at *L*, and pull out the last suture at *K*.

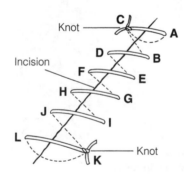

Figure 34–22 Plain continuous sutures.

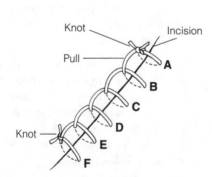

Figure 34–23 Blanket continuous sutures.

Blanket Continuous Sutures

- Cut the threads that are opposite the looped blanket edge; for example, cut at *A* through *F* in Figure 34–23.

- Pull each stitch out at the looped edge.

Mattress Continuous Sutures

- Cut the visible suture at both skin edges opposite the knot (at *A* and *B* in Figure 34–24) and the next suture opposite the knot (at *C* and *D)*. Remove and discard the visible portions as described above.

- Pull the first suture out by the knot at *E*.

- Lift the second suture between *F* and *G* to pull out the underlying suture between *G* and *C*. Cut off the visible part at *F* as close to the skin edge as possible.

- Go to the opposite side between *H* and *I*. Lift out the suture between *F* and *I*, and cut off all the visible part close to the skin at *H*.

- Lift the suture between *J* and *K* to pull out the suture between *H* and *K*, and cut the suture close to the skin at *J*.

- Repeat the above 2 steps, working from side to side of the incision, until the last suture is reached.

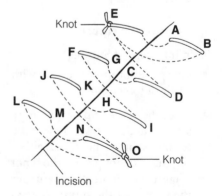

Figure 34–24 Mattress continuous sutures.

▶ **Procedure 34–10** *continued*

- Cut the visible suture opposite the knot at *L* and *M*. Pull out all remaining pieces of suture at *O*.

5. **Clean and cover the incision.**

- Clean the incision again with antimicrobial solution.

- Apply a small, light, sterile gauze dressing if any small dehiscence has occurred or if this is agency practice.

6. **Instruct the client about follow-up wound care.**

- Generally, if a wound is dry and healing well, the person can take showers in a day or two.

- Instruct the client to contact the physician if increased redness, drainage, or open areas are observed.

7. **Document the suture removal and assessment data on the appropriate records.**

EVALUATION FOCUS

Status of suture line; any wound separation or discharge.

SAMPLE RECORDING

Date	Time	Notes
12/05/04	1105	Abdominal wound sutures removed. Wound dry, edges approximated closely. No signs of inflammation or dehiscence. Gauze dressing applied.—————————————————————————————Gwen E. Owens, SN

HOME CARE CONSIDERATIONS

- Perform the procedure in a well-lighted, private area of the home.

- Instruct the client to observe the incision daily and call the health care provider if increased redness, drainage, or open areas are observed.

- Provide instructions and supplies for care of the incision, and tell the client when to shower for the first time.

- Assess the client's ability to keep the incision clean and protected at home.

35

Perioperative Nursing

35–1 Preparing the Operative Site

Before commencing the surgical skin preparation, determine the surgeon's order, relevant protocols, and recorded allergies to any solutions used in the skin preparation. Determine the agency policy for hair removal. Some agencies don't use razors to remove hair, or don't remove hair unless it's thick enough to interfere with surgery.

PURPOSE

- To reduce the risks of postoperative wound infection by removing soil and transient microbes from the skin, reducing the resident microbial count to subpathogenic levels in a short time and with the least amount of tissue irritation, inhibiting rapid rebound growth of microbes

ASSESSMENT FOCUS

Presence of growths, moles, rashes, pustules, irritations, exudate, abrasions, bruises, or broken or ischemic areas.

EQUIPMENT

- ❑ Adequate lighting for clear visibility of the hair on the skin
- ❑ Bath blanket
- ❑ Linen saver pad

Depilatory

- ❑ Cream hair remover with or without applicator
- ❑ Washcloth

- ❑ Gauze squares
- ❑ Lukewarm water

Clipping

- ❑ Electric clippers with sharp heads and unbroken teeth
- ❑ Scissors for long hair, if needed
- ❑ Antimicrobial solution and applicators, if needed

Wet Shave

- ❑ Disposable gloves
- ❑ Skin preparation set containing a disposable razor, compartmentalized basin for solutions, moisture-proof drape, soap solution, sponges, and cotton-tipped applicators
- ❑ Warm water

INTERVENTION

1. **Drape the client appropriately.**

- Expose only the area to be prepared. If using clippers or a razor, expose only small areas at a time. You will clip or shave about 15 cm (6 in) at a time.

2. **If a depilatory is to be used, test the client's reaction to it.** *Some people may experience irritation or an allergic reaction, even after prior use without an adverse effect.*

- Apply a small test dose of the depilatory to a small section of the area where hair is to be removed. Use an area at the periphery of the skin prep area or area advised by the agency policy.

- Apply the cream to the test area smoothly and thickly. Do not rub it in.

- Leave the cream on for the specified time.

- Remove the depilatory by rinsing the area thoroughly with lukewarm water and a washcloth. Do not use soap.

- Pat, rather than rub, the area dry with gauze squares.

- Wait for 24 hours, and assess the client's skin for redness or other responses.

3. **Remove hair.**

Depilatory

- If the client's skin appears normal after the skin test, apply the depilatory.

  a. Apply the depilatory as described above, and leave it in place for the *minimum* time specified by the manufacturer.

  b. Check a small area. If hair does not wipe off easily, wait a few minutes and check again, but do not leave the cream on longer than the *maximum* time recommended by the manufacturer.

  c. Remove all the depilatory as described in step 2, and pat the area dry.

Clipping

- Make sure the area is dry.

- Remove hair with clippers; do not apply pressure. *Pressure can cause abrasions, particularly over bony prominences.*

- Move the drape, and repeat the above steps until the entire area to be prepared is clipped.

- If applying antimicrobial solution, follow step 4.

▶ Procedure 35–1 Preparing the Operative Site *continued*

Wet Shave

- Don disposable gloves.

- Place the moistureproof towel under the area to be prepared.

- Lather the skin well with the soap solution. *Lathering makes the hair softer and easier to remove.*

- Stretch the skin taut, and hold the razor at about a 45° angle to the skin.

- Shave in the direction in which the hair grows. Use short strokes, and rinse the razor frequently. *Rinsing removes hairs and lather that can obstruct the blade.*

- Rinse the soap solution and loose hair from the skin with sponges.

- Move the drape, and repeat the above steps until the entire area to be prepared is shaved.

4. **Clean and disinfect the surgical area according to agency practice.**

- This may be done in the operating room.

- Clean any body crevices, such as the umbilicus, nails, and ear canals, with applicators and solutions. Dry with swabs.

- If an antimicrobial solution is used, apply to the area immediately after it is clipped. Leave it for the designated time, then dry the area with clean swabs. Agency policy will guide you on whether to use an antimicrobial solution and, if so, which to use and how long to leave it on.

5. **Inspect the skin after hair removal.**

- Closely observe the skin for reddened or broken areas.

- Report to the nurse in charge any skin lesions.

6. **Dispose of used equipment appropriately.**

- Dispose of razor blade, if used, according to agency policy to prevent injury to others.

- Discard disposable supplies.

7. **Document all relevant information.**

- Record the procedure, area prepared, and status of skin in the skin preparation area.

EVALUATION FOCUS

Presence of hairs on operative area; see also Assessment Focus.

SAMPLE RECORDING

Date	Time	Notes
12/05/04	0830	Area clipped on left lower extremity. Skin intact. Appeared tense. Stated: "I hope the scar won't show much."————————Eunice L. Lentz, NS

LIFESPAN CONSIDERATIONS

- Young children may need gentle restraint during the procedure to prevent injury. Allow the parents to help, if appropriate.

- Explain that preparing the operative site will take only a few minutes and won't be painful.

- Assess the child's understanding of the surgery and determine if further teaching is needed.

35–2 Applying Antiemboli Stockings

Before applying antiemboli stockings, determine any potential or present circulatory problems and the physician's orders involving the lower extremities.

PURPOSES
- To improve arterial and venous blood circulation to the legs and feet
- To prevent deep vein thrombosis and pulmonary embolism
- To reduce or prevent edema of the legs or feet

ASSESSMENT FOCUS

> Blood circulation to and from the feet and legs. Presence of skin lesions, drainage, or an open wound to the lower extremities. Presence of pulmonary edema.

EQUIPMENT

- ❏ Size chart
- ❏ Correct size of elastic stockings

INTERVENTION

1. **Select an appropriate time to apply the stockings.**

- Apply stockings in the morning if possible, before the client arises. *In sitting and standing positions, the veins can become distended, and edema occurs; the stockings should be applied before this happens.*

- Remove the stockings and wash the legs and feet daily. Most protocols suggest removing the stockings for a period of 30 minutes and replacing them 2–3 times a day.

- Assist the client who has been ambulating to lie down and elevate the legs for 15 to 30 minutes before applying the stockings. *This facilitates venous return and reduces swelling.*

2. **Apply the elastic stocking to the foot.**

- Assist the client to a lying position in bed.

- Dust the ankle with talcum powder, and ask the client to point the toes. *These measures ease application.*

- Turn the stocking inside out by inserting your hand into the stocking from the top and grabbing the heel pocket from the inside. The foot portion should now be inside the stocking leg.

- Remove your hand, and, with the heel pocket downward, hook your index and middle fingers of both hands into the foot section.

- Face the client, and slip the foot portion of the stocking over the client's foot, toes, and heel (Figure 35–1). As you move up the foot, stretch the stocking sideways.

Figure 35–1 Applying the inverted stocking over the client's toes.

- Support the client's ankle with one hand while using the other hand to pull the heel pocket under the heel.

- Center the heel in the pocket.

3. **Apply the remaining inverted portion of the stocking.**

- Gather the remaining portion of the stocking up to the toes, and pull only this part over the heel. With the foot already covered, the remainder of the stocking should slide easily over it.

- At the ankle, grasp the gathered portion between your index and middle fingers, and pull the stocking up the leg to the knee. You may need to support the ankle with one hand and use the other hand to stretch the stocking and distribute it evenly.

- For *thigh-* or *waist-length stockings*, ask the client to straighten the leg while stretching the rest of the stocking over the knee.

- Ask the client to flex the knee while pulling the stocking over the thigh. Stretch the stocking

▶ **Procedure 35–2 Applying Antiemboli Stockings** *continued*

from the top (front and back) to distribute it evenly over the thigh. The top should rest 2.5 to 7.5 cm (1 to 3 in) below the gluteal fold.

- For a *waist-length stocking*, ask the client to stand and continue extending the stocking up to the top of the gluteal fold.

- Apply the adjustable belt that accompanies thigh- and waist-length stockings, making sure that it does not interfere with any incision or external device (e.g., drainage tube or catheter).

- Adjust the foot section by tugging on the toe section to ensure toe comfort and smoothness of the stocking. Make sure a toe window is properly positioned.

4. **Document the application of the antiemboli stockings.**

EVALUATION FOCUS

Skin temperature and color; presence of edema; posterior tibial and dorsalis pedis pulses; pain in the calf; appearance of leg veins.

SAMPLE RECORDING

Date	Time	Notes
05/05/04	1800	Both feet warm, pink color. No edema. Tibial and pedis pulses 60/bin, equal. No pain, leg veins not visible. Applied antiemboli stockings to both legs.————————————————————————————Rosie Blakefield, SN

HOME CARE CONSIDERATIONS

- Teach the client or caregiver
  a. How to apply the stockings correctly
  b. How long the stockings are to be worn and how to care for them
  c. The importance of removing the stockings at least once a day to bathe the legs and examine the skin for irritation and breakdown

- The client will need two sets of stockings so one pair can be washed daily. The stockings should be washed in mild soap and water and allowed to air dry.

- Stockings should be replaced when they lose their elasticity.

41

Activity and Exercise

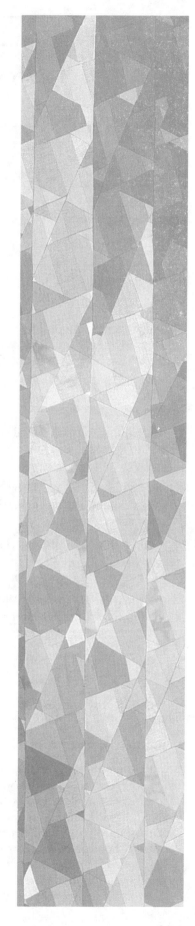

41–1   Using a Hydraulic Lift

PURPOSE
- To facilitate transfer of a dependent client to and from bed, wheelchair, tub, or toilet, without strain on the nurse

ASSESSMENT FOCUS

> Ability to comprehend instructions; degree of physical disability; weight of the client (to ensure that the lift can safely move the client); presence of orthostatic hypotension and pulse rate before transfer.

EQUIPMENT
❏ Hoyer lift with slings and canvas straps

INTERVENTION

1. Prepare the client.

- Explain the procedure, and demonstrate the lift. *Some clients are afraid of being lifted and will be reassured by a demonstration.*

2. Prepare the equipment.

- Lock the wheels of the client's bed and raise the bed to the high position.

- Put up the side rail on the opposite side of the bed, and lower the side rail near you.

- Position the lift so that it is close to the client.

- Place the chair that is to receive the client beside the bed. Allow adequate space to maneuver the lift.

- Lock the wheels, if a chair with wheels is used.

3. Position the client on the sling.

- Roll the client away from you.

- Place the canvas seat or sling under the client, with the wide lower edge under the client's thighs to the knees and the more narrow upper edge up under the client's shoulders. *This places the sling under the client's center of gravity and greatest body weight. Correct placement permits the client to be lifted evenly, with minimal shifting.*

- Raise the bed rail on your side of the bed, and go to the opposite side of the bed. Lower this side rail.

- Roll the client to the opposite side, and pull the canvas sling through.

- Roll the client to the supine position and center him on the sling.

4. Attach the sling to the swivel bar.

- Wheel the lift into position, with the footbars under the bed on the side where the chair is positioned. Set the adjustable base at the widest position to ensure stability. Lock the wheels of the lifter.

- Lower the side rail.

- Move the lift arms directly over the client and lower the horizontal bar by releasing the hydraulic valve. Lock the valve.

- Attach the lifter straps or hooks to the corresponding openings in the canvas seat. Check that the hooks are correctly placed and that matching straps or chains are of equal length. Face the hooks away from the client. *This prevents the hooks from injuring client.*

5. Lift the client gradually.

- Elevate the head of the bed to place the client in a sitting position.

- Ask the client to remove eyeglasses, and put them in a safe place. *The swivel bar may come close to the face and cause breakage of eyeglasses.*

- Nurse 1: Close the pressure valve, and gradually pump the jack handle until the client is above the bed surface. *Gradual elevation of the lift is less frightening to the client than a rapid rise.*

- Nurse 2: Assume a broad stance, and guide the client with your hands as the client is lifted. *This prepares to hold the client and provide control during the movement.*

- Check the placement of the sling before moving the client away from the bed.

6. Move the client over the chair.

- Nurse 1: With the pressure valve securely closed, slowly roll the lift until the client is over the chair. Use the steering handle to maneuver the lift.

- Nurse 2: Guide movement by hand until the client is directly over the chair (Figure 41–1). *Slow movement decreases swaying and is less frightening. Guidance also de-*

▶ **Procedure 41–1** *continued*

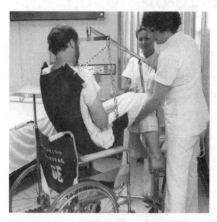

Figure 41–1 Moving the client with a hydraulic lift.

creases swaying and gives a sense of security.

7. **Lower the client into the chair.**

   • Nurse 1: Release the pressure valve very gradually. *Gradual release is less frightening than a quick descent.*

   • Nurse 2: Guide the client into the chair.

8. **Ensure client comfort and safety.**

   • Remove the hooks from the canvas seat. Leave the seat in place. *The seat is left in place in preparation for the lift back to bed.*

   • Align the client appropriately in a sitting position, and return the client's eyeglasses, if appropriate.

   • Apply a seatbelt or other restraint as needed.

   • Place the call bell within reach.

EVALUATION FOCUS

> Body alignment in sitting position; vital signs, especially pulse rate and blood pressure to determine response to the transfer; safety precautions required for clients after the transfer.

SAMPLE RECORDING

Date	Time	Notes
11/29/04	1100	Assisted to chair via hydraulic lift. Tolerated well, B/P - 128/86. AP - 82. Alert and oriented. Call bell in place.————————Kristen Morrison, SN

LIFESPAN CONSIDERATIONS

• Use special caution with older clients to prevent skin tears or bruising during the transfer. *Decreased subcutaneous fat and thinning of the skin place older clients at risk for skin breakdown.*

HOME CARE CONSIDERATIONS

• Furniture in the home may need to be rearranged to accommodate the hydraulic lift.

• The client's caregiver can operate the lift alone, but using two persons is the safest method.

• Teach the caregiver to use the device correctly and allow time to practice under supervision.

• Emphasize the importance of safety measures, such as locking the wheels while raising or lowering the client.

41–2 Providing Passive Range-of-Motion Exercises

PURPOSES
- To assess joint flexibility
- To maintain joint flexibility for effective daily functioning
- To prevent joint stiffness and contractures

ASSESSMENT FOCUS

Determine which movements are unsafe for the client because of age or pathology (e.g., adducting the hip of a client after hip surgery); degree of range-of-motion needed to perform ADLs; presence of contractures, joint swelling, redness, or pain.

INTERVENTION

1. **Prior to initiating the exercises, review any possible restrictions with the physician or physical therapist. Also refer to the agency's protocol.**

2. **Assist the client to a supine position near you, and expose the body parts requiring exercise.**

- Place the client's feet together, place the arms at the sides, and leave space around the head and the feet. *Positioning the client close to you prevents excessive reaching.*

3. **Follow a repetitive pattern and return to the starting position after each motion. Repeat each motion three times on the affected limb. To reduce discomfort, support the joint being exercised. Observe the client for nonverbal cues.**

Shoulder and Elbow Movement

Begin each exercise with the client's arm at the side. Grasp the arm beneath the elbow with one hand and beneath the wrist with the other hand, unless otherwise indicated (Figure 41–2).

4. **Flex, externally rotate, and extend the shoulder.**

- Move the arm up to the ceiling and toward the head of the bed (Figure 41–3). The elbow may

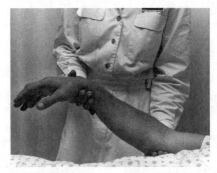
Figure 41–2 Supporting the client's arm.

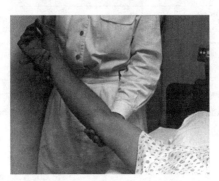
Figure 41–3 Flexing and extending the shoulder.

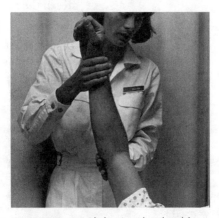
Figure 41–4 Abducting the shoulder.

need to be flexed if the headboard is in the way.

5. **Abduct and externally rotate the shoulder.**

- Move the arm away from the body (Figure 41–4) and toward the client's head until the hand is under the head (Figure 41–5).

6. **Adduct the shoulder.**

- Move the arm over the body (Figure 41–6) until the hand touches the client's other hand.

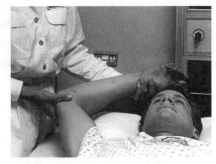
Figure 41–5 Abducting and externally rotating the shoulder.

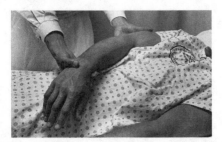
Figure 41–6 Abducting the shoulder.

▶ **Procedure 41–2** *continued*

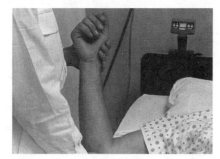

Figure 41–7   Position before rotating the shoulder.

7. Rotate the shoulder internally and externally.

- Place the arm out to the side at shoulder level (90° abduction), and bend the elbow so that the forearm is at a right angle to the mattress (Figure 41–7).

- Move the forearm down until the palm touches the mattress (Figure 41–8) and then up until the back of the hand touches the bed.

Figure 41–8   Rotating the shoulder.

8. Flex and extend the elbow.

- Bend the elbow until the fingers touch the chin, then straighten the arm (Figure 41–9).

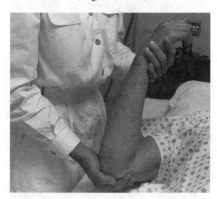

Figure 41–9   Flexing and extending the elbow.

9. Pronate and supinate the forearm.

- Grasp the client's hand as for a handshake, and turn the palm downward (Figure 41–10) and upward (Figure 41–11), ensuring that only the forearm (not the shoulder) moves.

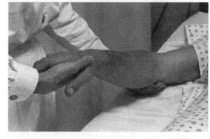

Figure 41–10   Pronating the forearm.

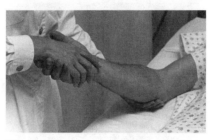

Figure 41–11   Supinating the forearm.

Wrist and Hand Movement

For wrist and hand exercises, flex the client's arm at the elbow until the forearm is at a right angle to the mattress. Support the wrist joint with one hand while your other hand manipulates the joint and the fingers (Figure 41–12).

10. Hyperextend the wrist, and flex the fingers.

- Bend the wrist backward, and at the same time flex the fingers, moving the tips of the fingers to the palm of the hand (Figure 41–13).

- Align the wrist in a straight line with the arm, and place your fingers over the client's fingers to make a fist.

11. Flex the wrist, and extend the fingers.

- Bend the wrist forward, and at the same time extend the fingers (Figure 41–14).

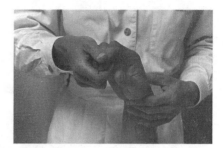

Figure 41–12   Position for wrist and hand movements.

Figure 41–13   Hyperextending the wrist and flexing the fingers.

Figure 41–14   Flexing the wrist and extending the fingers.

12. Abduct and oppose the thumb.

- Move the thumb away from the fingers and then across the hand toward the base of the little finger (Figure 41–15).

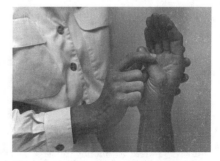

Figure 41–15   Abducting the thumb.

▶Procedure 41–2 Providing Passive Range-of-Motion Exercises *continued*

Leg and Hip Movement

To carry out leg and hip exercises, place one hand under the clients knee and the other under the ankle (Figure 41–16).

13. Flex and extend the knee and hip.

- Lift the leg and bend the knee moving the knee up toward the chest as far as possible. Bring the leg down, straighten the knee and lower the leg to the bed (Figure 41–17).

Figure 41–16 Position for knee and hip movements.

Figure 41–17 Flexing the knee and the hip.

14. Abduct and adduct the leg.

- Move the leg to the side, away from the client (Figure 41–18) and back across in front of the other leg (Figure 41–19).

Figure 41–18 Abducting the leg.

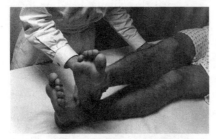

Figure 41–19 Adducting the leg.

15. Rotate the hip internally and externally.

- Roll the leg inward (Figure 41–20), then outward (Figure 41–21).

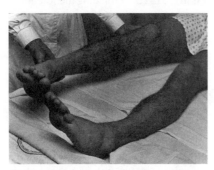

Figure 41–20 Internally rotating the hip.

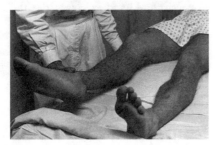

Figure 41–21 Externally rotating the hip.

Ankle and Foot Movement

For ankle and foot exercises, place your hands in the positions described, depending on the motion to be achieved.

16. Dorsiflex the foot and stretch the Achilles tendon (heel cord).

- Place one hand under the client's heel, resting your inner forearm against the bottom of the client's foot.

Figure 41–22 Dorsiflexing the foot.

- Place the other hand under the knee to support it.
- Press your forearm against the foot to move it upward toward the leg (Figure 41–22).

17. Invert and evert the foot.

- Place one hand under the client's ankle and the other over the arch of the foot.
- Turn the whole foot inward (Figure 41–23), then turn it outward (Figure 41–24).

18. Plantar flex the foot, and extend and flex the toes.

- Place one hand over the arch of the foot to push the foot away from the leg.

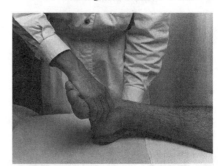

Figure 41–23 Inverting the foot.

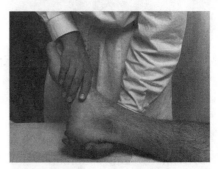

Figure 41–24 Everting the foot.

▶

► **Procedure 41–2** *continued*

- Place the fingers of the other hand under the toes, to bend the toes upward (Figure 41–25), and then over the toes, to push the toes downward (Figure 41–26).

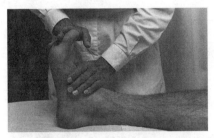

Figure 41–25 Extending the toes.

Figure 41–26 Plantar flexing the foot and flexing the toes.

Neck Movement

Remove the client's pillow.

19. Flex and extend the neck.

- Place the palm of one hand under the client's head and the palm of the other hand on the client's chin.

- Move the head forward until the chin rests on the chest, then back to the resting supine position without the head pillow (Figure 41–27).

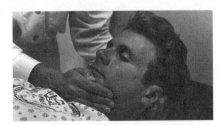

Figure 41–27 Flexing the neck.

20. Laterally flex the neck.

- Place the heels of the hands on each side of the client's cheeks.

- Move the top of the head to the right and then to the left (Figure 41–28).

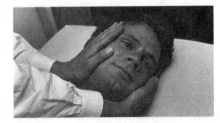

Figure 41–28 Laterally flexing the neck.

Hyperextension Movements

21. Assist the client to a prone or lateral position on the side of the bed nearest you but facing away from you.

22. Hyperextend the shoulder.

- Place one hand on the shoulder to keep it from lifting off the bed and the other under the client's elbow.

- Pull the upper arm up and backward (Figure 41–29).

23. Hyperextend the hip.

- Place one hand on the hip to stabilize it and keep it from lifting off the bed. With the other arm and hand, cradle the lower leg in the forearm, and cup the knee joint with the hand.

- Move the leg backward from the hip joint (Figure 41–30).

Figure 41–29 Hyperextending the shoulder.

Figure 41–30 Hyperextending the hip.

24. Hyperextend the neck.

- Avoid hyperextending the neck of the immobilized elderly client, because such movements can cause painful nerve damage (Hogan and Beland 1976, p. 1106).

- Remove the pillow. With the client's face down, place one hand on the forehead and the other on the back of the skull.

- Move the head backward (Figure 41–31).

Following the Exercise

25. Assess the client's pulse and endurance of the exercise.

26. Report to the nurse in charge any unexpected problems or notable changes in the client's movements (e.g., rigidity, contractures, or muscle spasms).

27. Document the exercises and your assessments.

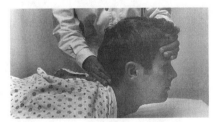

Figure 41–31 Hyperextending the neck.

▶ **Procedure 41–2 Providing Passive Range-of-Motion Exercises** *continued*

EVALUATION FOCUS

> Ability to tolerate the exercise; range of motion of the joint; any discomfort during the exercises.

SAMPLE RECORDING

Date	Time	Notes
06/14/04	1100	Passive exercises provided to R leg and foot for 5 minutes with no pain. Full ROM in hip, knee, and ankle.————————————————Sally S. Ames, SN

LIFESPAN CONSIDERATIONS

- Avoid hyperextending the joints of older clients. *Such movements can cause pain or nerve damage because joints become less flexible with age.*

- Work slowly and assess for pain when working with older clients, especially those who have arthritis. *Arthritic changes can cause contractures and enlarged, painful joints.*

- Assess for skin breakdown or reddened areas during the range-of-motion procedure. *Older clients are at risk for skin breakdown due to decreased subcutaneous fat and increased thinning of the skin.*

HOME CARE CONSIDERATIONS

Teach the client's caregiver:

- The purpose and importance of performing range-of-motion exercises at home.

- To perform the exercises at least twice daily.

- How to use correct body mechanics to prevent muscle strain while performing the exercises.

41–3 Applying a Continuous Passive Motion Device to the Knee

PURPOSES
- To prevent contractures, muscle atrophy, venous stasis, and thromboembolism
- To increase the joint range of motion
- To reduce joint swelling

ASSESSMENT FOCUS

Complaints of discomfort; appearance of joint (i.e., size and color); character and amount of drainage.

EQUIPMENT
- ❏ Continuous passive motion device
- ❏ Padding for the cradle
- ❏ Restraining straps
- ❏ Goniometer

INTERVENTION

1. Check the safety test date.

- Note the date the machine was tested for electrical safety, and ensure that it is within the guidelines established at the agency.

2. Verify the physician's orders and agency protocol.

- Determine the degrees of flexion, extension, and speed initially prescribed.

- Check agency protocol and physician's orders about increases in degrees and speed for subsequent treatments.

3. Set up the machine.

- Place the machine on the bed. Remove an egg crate mattress, if indicated. *This provides a stable surface.*

- Apply a supportive sling to the movable metal cradle.

- Attach the machine to a Balkan frame using traction equipment.

- Connect the control box to the machine.

4. Set the prescribed levels of flexion and extension and speed.

- Most postoperative clients are started on 10° to 45° of flexion and 0° to 10° of extension (Maier 1986, p. 47).

- Flexion is usually increased to 5° to 10° per shift or 20° in 24 hours if tolerated (Maier 1986, p. 47).

- Adjust the speed control to the slow to moderate range for the first postoperative day, and then increase the speed as ordered and tolerated.

- Check that the machine is functioning properly by running it through a complete cycle.

5. Position the client, and place the leg in the machine.

- Place the client in a supine position, with the head of the bed slightly elevated.

- Support the leg and, with the client's help, lift the leg and place it in the padded cradle.

- Lengthen or shorten appropriate sections of the frame to fit the machine to the client. The knee and hip should be at the hinged joints of the machine. The knee joint should correspond with the goniometer, a device for measuring range-of-motion.

- Adjust the footplate so that the foot is supported in a neutral position or slight dorsiflexion (e.g., 20°). Check agency protocol.

- Ensure that the leg is neither internally nor externally rotated.

- Apply restraining straps around the thigh and top of the foot and cradle, allowing enough space to fit several fingers under it.

6. Start the machine.

- Ensure the controls are set at the prescribed levels.

- Turn the on/off switch to the "on" position, and press the start button.

- When the machine reaches the fully flexed position, stop the machine, and verify the degree of flexion with a goniometer.

- Restart the machine, and observe a few cycles of flexion and extension to ensure proper functioning.

7. Ensure continued client safety and comfort.

- Make sure that the client is comfortable. Observe for nonverbal signs of discomfort.

- Raise the side rails to keep the machine and client contained.

▶ Procedure 41–3 Applying a Continuous Passive Motion Device to the Knee *continued*

- Stay with a confused or sedated client while the machine is on.

- Instruct a mentally alert client how to operate the on/off switch.

- Loosen the straps, and check the client's skin at least twice per shift.

- Wash the perineal area at least once per shift, and keep it dry.

- Drape a towel over the groin of a male client. *This prevents scrotal irritation by contact with the machine.*

8. Document all relevant information.

- Record the procedure, the degree of flexion, the degree of extension, the speed, and the duration of the therapy.

EVALUATION FOCUS

Response to therapy; increase in tolerance and range of motion; degree of discomfort; skin integrity of feet, elbow, sacrum, and groin.

SAMPLE RECORDING

Date	Time	Notes
07/11/04	0900	Continuous passive motion machine applied to knee as ordered for 30 minutes. Flexion control set at 80°; extension at 0°. Procedure tolerated well.————————————————————————————Michaela Nichols, RN

LIFESPAN CONSIDERATIONS

- Older clients may have limited joint flexibility.

- Older clients may need to balance periods of activity with periods of rest.

- If the older client is apprehensive, teach techniques for muscle relaxation and pain control, such as guided imagery and progressive relaxation (see Procedures 15–2 and 15–1).

HOME CARE CONSIDERATIONS

- The continuous passive motion machine can be used at home if the client or caregiver demonstrates competence.

- Teach the client or caregiver:

  a. How to set the controls and progressively increase the adjustment as the client's tolerance builds.

  b. To report excessive pain, swelling, or redness of the affected joints.

  c. To provide skin care and check for skin breakdown every 4 hours.

  d. How to clean and care for the equipment.

43

Pain Management

PROCEDURE

43–1 Managing Pain with a Transcutaneous Electric Nerve Stimulation Unit

Before applying a TENS unit, determine the presence of factors contraindicating usage (presence of a cardiac pacemaker; history of dysrhythmias, myocardial ischemia, or myocardial infarction; first-trimester pregnancy; confusion; history of peripheral vascular problems altering neurosensory perception).

PURPOSES
- To reduce chronic and acute pain (especially postoperative pain)
- To decrease opioid requirements and reduce the chances of depressed respiratory function from narcotic usage
- To facilitate client involvement in managing pain control

ASSESSMENT FOCUS

> Client's mental status and ability to follow instructions in using the TENS unit; intactness of skin and absence of signs of infection and irritation; appearance of incisional area of postoperative client; characteristics of pain (intensity, location, associated factors, precipitating factors, and alleviating factors); amount of pain medication required before and during treatment.

EQUIPMENT
- ❏ TENS Unit
- ❏ Bath basin with warm water
- ❏ Soap
- ❏ Washcloth
- ❏ Towel
- ❏ Conduction cream, gel, or water (see manufacturer's instructions)
- ❏ Hypoallergenic tape

INTERVENTION

1. **Explain the purpose and application procedure to the client and family.**

- Explain that the TENS unit may not completely eliminate pain but should reduce pain to a level that allows the client to rest more comfortably and/or carry out everyday activities.

2. **Prepare the equipment.**

- Insert the battery into the TENS unit to test its functioning.

- With the TENS unit off, plug the lead wires into the battery-operated unit at one end, leaving the electrodes at the other end.

3. **Clean the application area.**

- Wash, rinse, and dry the designated area with soap and water. *This reduces skin irritation and facilitates adhesion of the electrodes to the skin for a longer period of time.*

4. **Apply the electrodes to the client.**

- If the electrodes are not prejelled, moisten them with a small amount of water or apply conducting gel. (Consult the manufacturer's instructions). *This facilitates electrical conduction.*

- Place the electrodes on a clean, unbroken skin area. Choose the area according to the location, nature, and origin of the pain.

- Ensure that the electrodes make full surface contact with the skin. Tape all sides evenly with hypoal-lergenic tape. *This prevents an inadvertent burn.*

5. **Turn the unit on.**

- Ascertain that the amplitude control is set at level 0.

- Slowly increase the intensity of the stimulus (amplitude) until the client notes a slight increase in discomfort.

- When the client notes discomfort, slowly decrease the amplitude until the client notes a pleasant sensation. Once this has been achieved, keep the TENS unit set at this level to maintain blockage of the pain sensation. Most clients select frequencies between 60 and 100 Hertz.

6. **Monitor the client.**

▶ **Procedure 43–1** *continued*

- If the client complains of itching, pricking, or burning, explore the following options:

  a. Turn the pulse-width dial down.

  b. Check that the entire electrode surface is in contact with the skin.

  c. Increase the distance between the electrodes.

  d. Select another type of electrode suitable for the model of TENS unit in use.

  e. Discontinue the TENS, and consider the possibility of another brand of TENS.

- If the sensation of the stimulus is unpleasant, too intense, or distracting, turn down both the amplitude and the pulse-width dial.

- If the client complains of headache or nausea during application or use, turn down both the amplitude and the pulse-width dial.

Repositioning of the electrodes may also be helpful.

- If further troubleshooting is not effective, discontinue the use of the TENS unit, and notify the physician.

7. **After the treatment:**

- Turn off the controls and unplug the lead wires from the control box.

- Clean the electrodes according to the manufacturer's instructions. Clean the client's skin with soap and water.

- Replace the used battery pack with a charged battery. Begin recharging the used battery.

- If continuous therapy is used, remove the electrode patches and inspect the skin at least once daily.

8. **Provide client teaching.**

- Review with the client instructions for use, and verify that the client understands.

- Have the client demonstrate the use of the TENS unit and verbalize ways to troubleshoot if headache, nausea, or unpleasant sensations occur.

- Instruct the client not to submerge the unit in water but instead to remove and reapply it after bathing.

9. **Document all relevant information.**

- Record the date and time TENS therapy was initiated, the location of electrode placement and status of skin in that area, the character and quality of the pain, settings of TENS unit used, any side effects experienced, and the client's response.

EVALUATION FOCUS

Response of the client in terms of pain relief or side effects experienced; self-care abilities.

SAMPLE RECORDING

Date	Time	Notes
04/23/04	1000	TENS unit applied near midline abdominal incision for postoperative pain at intensity level given by client of 6–7. Lead 1 and lead 2 settings on 6.0. Verbalized minimum relief of discomfort upon initiation of treatment.——————————————————————————Mark McCormick, SN

HOME CARE CONSIDERATIONS

- TENS units are frequently ordered for home use to relieve chronic pain. Instruct the client or caregiver:

  a. How to use and care for the TENS equipment.

  b. How to troubleshoot if side effects or problems occur and who to call if the equipment malfunctions.

  c. Where and how to obtain supplies needed for the TENS unit.

  d. To remove the electrodes daily and check for skin breakdown at the electrode sites.

44

Nutrition

44–1 Assisting an Adult to Eat

PURPOSES
- To maintain the client's nutritional status
- To teach the client required eating skills
- To evaluate the client's ability to eat

ASSESSMENT FOCUS

Self-care abilities for eating and assistance required (note hand coordination, level of consciousness, and visual acuity); appetite for and tolerance of food and fluid; difficulty swallowing; anthropometric measurements for baseline data as required; any need for a special diet; any food allergies and food likes and dislikes.

EQUIPMENT

- ❏ Meal tray with the correct food and fluids
- ❏ Extra napkin or small towel
- ❏ Straw, special drinking cup, weighted glass, or other adaptive feeding aid as required

INTERVENTION

1. **Confirm the client's diet order.**

- Check the client's chart or plan of care for the diet order and to determine whether the client is fasting for laboratory tests or surgery or whether the physician has ordered "nothing by mouth" (NPO). For clients who are fasting or on NPO, ensure that the appropriate signs are placed on either the room door or the client's bed, according to agency practice.

- If there is a change in the type of food the client is to receive, notify the dietary staff.

2. **Prepare the client and overbed table.**

- Assist the client to the bathroom or onto a bedpan or commode if the client needs to urinate.

- Offer the client assistance in washing the hands prior to a meal. If the client has problems with oral hygiene, brushing the teeth or using a mouthwash can improve the taste in the mouth and hence the appetite.

- Clear the overbed table so that there is space for the tray. If the client must remain in a lying position in bed, arrange the overbed table close to the bedside so that the client can see the food.

3. **Position the client and yourself appropriately.**

- Assist the client to a comfortable position for eating. Most people sit during a meal; if it is permitted, assist the client to sit in bed (Figure 44–1) or in a chair.

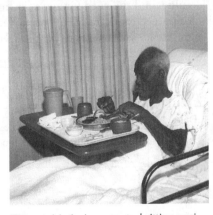

Figure 44–1 A supported sitting position contributes to a client's comfort while eating.

or

If the client is unable to sit, assist the client to a lateral position. *People will swallow more easily in these positions than in a back-lying position.*

- If the client requires assistance with feeding, assume a sitting position, if possible, beside the client. *This conveys a more relaxed presence and encourages the client to eat an adequate meal.*

4. **Assist the client as required.**

- Check each tray for the client's name, the type of diet, and completeness. If the diet does not seem to be correct, check it against the client's chart. Confirm the client's name by checking the wristband before leaving the tray. Do *not* leave an incorrect diet for a client to eat.

- Encourage the client to eat independently, assisting as needed. Do not take over the feeding process. *Participation by the client enhances feelings of independence.*

- Remove the food covers, butter the bread, pour the drink, and cut the meat, if needed.

▶Procedure 44–1 Assisting an Adult to Eat *continued*

- For a blind person, identify the placement of the food as you would describe the time on a clock. For instance, say, "The potatoes are at 8 o'clock; the chicken at 12 o'clock; and the green bean salad at 4 o'clock." (Figure 44–2).

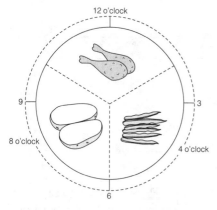

Figure 44–2 The clock system used to describe the location of food on the plate for a blind client.

- If the client needs assistance with feeding:

  a. Ask in which order the client desires to eat the food.

  b. Use normal utensils whenever possible. *Using ordinary utensils enhances self-esteem.*

  c. If the client cannot see, tell which food you are giving.

  d. Warn the client if the food is hot or cold.

  e. Allow ample time for the client to chew and swallow the food before offering more.

  f. Provide fluids as requested, or, if the client is unable to tell you, offer fluids after every three or four mouthfuls of solid food.

  g. Use a straw or special drinking cup for fluids that would spill from normal containers.

  h. Make the time a pleasant one, choosing topics of conversation that are of interest to the client, if the person wants to talk.

5. **After the meal, ensure client comfort.**

- Assist the client to clean the mouth and hands.

- Reposition the client.

- Replace the food covers, and remove the food tray from the bedside.

6. **Document all relevant information.**

- Note how much and what the client has eaten and the amount of fluid taken. Record fluid intake and calorie count as required.

- If the client is on a special diet or is having problems eating, record the amount of food eaten and any pain, fatigue, or nausea experienced.

- If the client is not eating, notify the nurse in charge so that the diet can be changed or other nursing measures can be taken (e.g., rescheduling the meals, providing smaller, more frequent meals, or obtaining special self-feeding aids).

EVALUATION FOCUS

Appetite; tolerance of food and fluids taken; amount of fluid intake, if being measured; calorie count, if required; any chewing or swallowing difficulties and the need for any adjustments in food consistency (e.g., minced or pureed foods, need for special feeding aids); comparison of anthropometric measurements to baseline data, as required.

SAMPLE RECORDING

Date	Time	Notes
05/13/04	0800	Refused all solid food. Ingested 120 mL milk. Nauseated. Dull crampy pain persists in epigastric region.———Wendy B. Low, SN

▶ **Procedure 44–1** *continued*

LIFESPAN CONSIDERATIONS	HOME CARE CONSIDERATIONS

LIFESPAN CONSIDERATIONS

- For older clients, offer fluids frequently to prevent dry mouth. Initially avoid dry foods such as crackers and sticky foods such as bananas. *Saliva production decreases with age.*

- Allow the older client time to eat and offer to re-warm the food if needed. *Hand tremors and arthritic joint changes may slow the eating process for older clients.*

- Observe for dysphagia (difficulty swallowing) and adapt the older client's diet accordingly. *Esophageal nerve degeneration, which often occurs with aging, can affect the ability to swallow.*

- Older clients may need extra seasoning on food. *Aging decreases the ability to taste, especially sweet and salty foods.*

HOME CARE CONSIDERATIONS

- Assess the home for adequate facilities to prepare and store food, such as a working refrigerator and stove.

- Assess the client's and caregiver's ability to obtain food and prepare meals.

- Evaluate problems that can interfere with eating, such as ill-fitting dentures, sore gums, constipation, diarrhea, or a special diet.

- Instruct the caregiver about the importance of regular, nutritious meals and allowing the client to remain independent when possible.

- Provide written guidelines for the client's diet and any special feeding techniques.

44–2 Bottle-Feeding an Infant

PURPOSES
- To provide the nutrients required for normal growth and life
- To provide feelings of love and security to the infant for sound psychologic development

ASSESSMENT FOCUS

The infant's general nutritional status; weight gain or loss; development of suck reflex; eagerness to take fluids; family history of allergy. The mother's education level or ability to understand feeding instructions; previous experience with infant feeding.

EQUIPMENT

- ❑ Sterile bottle
- ❑ Sterile nipple
- ❑ Sterile formula
- ❑ Bib or clean cloth

INTERVENTION

1. **Obtain essential information before the feeding:**

- The type of formula recommended by the physician

- The amount per feeding, e.g., 4 to 5 oz

- The type of bottle and nipple used

- The frequency of feeding, e.g., every 4 hours, and the specific times of day

- How the formula is prepared, i.e., at what dilution

- What other fluids, e.g., water or apple juice, are given at scheduled times per day and the amounts

2. **Prepare the bottle, nipple, and formula.**

- If the formula is refrigerated, warm it to room temperature. The formula should feel lukewarm to the inner wrist when a few drops are shaken onto it. *Babies digest formula at room temperature more quickly than cold formula and are less likely to develop abdominal cramps.*

- Test the size of the nipple holes by turning the bottle upside down. If a drop of milk appears at the tip of the nipple, the holes are the correct size. If no milk appears or if milk flows out freely, the nipple needs to be changed. *Nipple holes should be large enough for the baby to get formula with normal sucking, but not allow milk to flow freely. Large holes can cause choking and regurgitation. Nipple holes that are too small require too much energy to suck, and too much air is sucked with them.*

3. **Ensure infant comfort.**

- Change the infant's diaper, if needed. Handle the infant calmly, gently, and unhurriedly. *A clean, dry diaper is conducive to pleasurable feeding. Calm, gentle handling soothes the infant.*

- Arrange a quiet, comfortable environment in which to feed the infant. *A calm environment is conducive to successful feeding.*

- Carry the infant, using the football hold, to the feeding chair (see Figure 44–3). *The football hold supports the infant's head and back yet frees one of the nurse's hands to carry the bib and formula.*

- Sit comfortably in the chair, and relax. *Discomfort and tension can be transmitted to the infant and can interfere with feeding and digestion.*

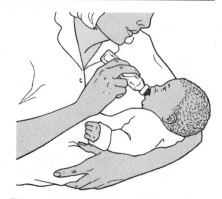

Figure 44–3 Position of infant and bottle when bottle-feeding an infant.

- Tuck the bib or clean cloth under the infant's chin.

4. **Position the infant appropriately.**

- Cradle the baby in your arms, with the head slightly elevated. Support the head and neck in the bend of your elbow while the buttocks rest on your lap. *Elevating the head facilitates swallowing. Infants need to be held while being fed to feel warm and loved.*

- If the baby cannot be removed from an isolette or crib because of therapy (e.g., an oxygenated croupette or traction), provide as much hand contact as possible, and stay with the infant during the feeding.

▶ **Procedure 44–2** *continued*

- Never leave an infant with a propped bottle. *The infant can suck in excessive air or ingest the formula too quickly. Both circumstances induce regurgitation and possible aspiration of fluid into the lungs, which can cause pneumonia in the baby.*

5. **Insert the nipple, and feed the infant.**

- Insert the nipple gently along the infant's tongue and hold the bottle at about a 45° angle so that the nipple is filled with formula and not air (Figure 44–3). *Excessive swallowed air causes gas, abdominal distention, discomfort, and possible regurgitation.*

6. **Remove the bottle periodically and burp (bubble) the baby.**

- Small infants may need to be burped after every ounce or at least at the middle and end of the feeding. With some collapsible feeding bottles, infants suck in very little air and may need to be burped only at the end of the feeding. The infant who was crying before the feeding may have swallowed air and may need to be burped before the feeding begins or after taking just enough formula to calm down. *Periodic burping helps the infant expel the swallowed air and therefore consume the maximum amount of formula.*

- Place the baby either
   a. Over your shoulder (Figure 44–4).
   b. In a supported sitting position on your lap (Figure 44–5). *This position is often preferred because the infant's responses can be observed continuously.*
   c. In a prone position over your lap (Figure 44–6).

- Place the bib where it will protect your clothing. *Newborns frequently regurgitate small amounts of*

Figure 44–4   Burping an infant over the shoulder.

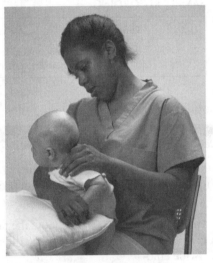

Figure 44–5   Burping an infant in a supported sitting position.

feedings. This normal occurrence may be due initially to excessive mucus and gastric irritation from foreign substances in the stomach from birth. Later, regurgitation may occur when the infant feeds too rapidly and swallows air, or when the infant is overfed and the cardiac sphincter allows the excess to be regurgitated.

- Rub or pat the infant's back gently. *Patting encourages relaxation of the cardiac sphincter of the stomach and the expulsion of air.*

7. **Continue with the feeding until the formula is finished and/or the baby is satisfied.**

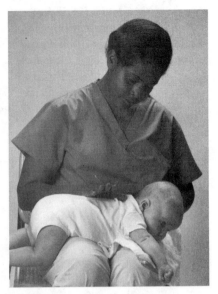

Figure 44–6   Burping an infant in a prone position.

- An infant feeding generally takes about 30 minutes. *Prolonged feeding times tend to foster lazy eating habits.*

- For newborns who need encouragement to continue sucking during initial feedings, provide gentle tactile stimulation to the feet and hands. *Stimulation helps maintain sucking for a sufficient time to complete a feeding.*

- Once feedings are established, encourage the infant to set the pace.

- Avoid overfeeding or feeding every time the infant cries. *Overfeeding results in infant obesity. A fat baby is not necessarily healthy.*

8. **Ensure infant safety and comfort after the feeding.**

- Return the infant to the crib or isolette.

- Check whether the diaper needs changing, and change it if necessary. *Smaller infants commonly move their bowels while feeding because of the gastrocolic reflex.*

- Position the infant on the side with the head to one side. *In this*

▶ Procedure 44–2 Bottle-Feeding an Infant *continued*

position, the infant is less likely to aspirate any fluid that may be regurgitated. For infants in whom regurgitation is a problem, a right side-lying position tends to facilitate the expulsion of air without regurgitation, since the cardiac sphincter is on the left side of the stomach.

- Ensure that the crib sides are elevated before leaving the infant.

- Assess the infant for signs of allergic reaction, particularly with initial formula usage or when formula type is changed.

9. **Document all relevant information.**

- Record the type and the amount of the feeding taken and all assessments.

EVALUATION FOCUS

Responses of the infant (e.g., amount and frequency of regurgitation, whether the infant seems satisfied after the feeding and rests quietly, any allergy), weight gain or loss; color and characteristics of the feces or urine.

SAMPLE RECORDING

Date	Time	Notes
06/06/04	0700	5 oz Similac taken well. Regurgitated small amount formula × 1. Resting quietly on right side.————————Sally R. Duprez, SN

HOME CARE CONSIDERATIONS

- Evaluate the home environment and the parents' ability to prepare formula and follow feeding instructions. *The safe home must have hot water, a refrigerator, and be relatively insect- and rodent-free.*

- Observing a parent feeding the infant can help determine the parents' learning needs. Provide emotional support and take time to answer questions. *New parents often feel overwhelmed when feeding problems occur.*

- Stress the importance of adequate nutrition for the infant and provide written nutritional guidelines. *Proper nutrition in early years is critical to development.*

- Support the family unit and encourage siblings to help feed the infant, if appropriate. *Family-focused care recognizes the importance of other children living in the home.*

44–3 Feeding Solid Foods to an Infant

PURPOSES
- To provide nutrients and calories to meet the infant's needs
- To promote muscular development of the mouth and tongue

ASSESSMENT FOCUS

Developmental status (e.g., extrusion reflex); appetite; food likes and dislikes; food allergies.

EQUIPMENT
- ❏ Small feeding spoon and un-breakable dishes
- ❏ Proper food (e.g., pureed or diced) at room temperature
- ❏ Bib
- ❏ Infant seat or high chair, if required

INTERVENTION

1. **Prepare the infant and yourself for the meal.**

- Change the diaper if damp or soiled.

- Wash hands.

- Approach the infant in a pleasant, relaxed manner, and provide a calm environment. *An infant old enough to eat solids will be well aware of this, because interest in the surroundings is increasing.*

- Put the bib on the infant, and place the infant on your lap or in the infant seat or highchair.

- Seat yourself comfortably, and relax. *Feeding times need to be un-hurried and relaxed to promote good eating habits and good digestion.*

2. **Promote acceptance and digestion of the food.**

- Control the infant's hands with your free hand by giving something to hold or by gently holding the arms (Figure 44–7). *Holding the arms prevents young infants from smearing their food.*

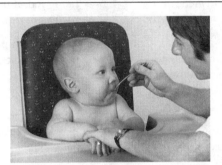

Figure 44–7 Controlling an infant's hands when feeding the infant in a highchair.

- Offer plain foods before sweet ones (e.g., cereal and vegetables before fruits). *Infants may reject plain foods after eating the sweeter tasting ones.*

- Place small spoonfuls of food well back on the infant's tongue. *Putting food well back in the mouth overcomes the extrusion reflex, if it is present.*

- Scrape up any food that is pushed back out of the mouth, and refeed it.

- Continue to feed at a pace appropriate for the infant until the infant is satisfied. Hungry infants tend to eat quickly and show frustration if the food is given too slowly.

- Talk to the infant throughout the meal. *Friendly talk at meal-times is conducive to digestion and socialization.*

3. **Provide follow-up care as needed.**

- Wash and dry the infant's face and hands.

- Feed a young infant the recommended formula.

- Change the diaper, if required.

- Place the infant in a safe position in the crib. (See Procedure 44–2, step 8). Encourage the child to nap or rest. Ensure that the crib sides are elevated before leaving the infant.

4. **Document all relevant information.**

- Record assessments, the type and amount of feeding taken, and the infant's responses.

▶**Procedure 44–3 Feeding Solid Foods to an Infant** *continued*

EVALUATION FOCUS

Type and amount of food ingested; weight gain or loss; specific food likes and dislikes.

SAMPLE RECORDING

Date	Time	Notes
05/29/04	1000	Tolerated 30mL of rice cereal mixed with formula well.————————————————————————————————Corey Newton, SN

HOME CARE CONSIDERATIONS

- Evaluate the home environment for hygiene and safety. *The safe home must have hot water, a refrigerator, and be relatively free of insects and rodents.*

- Assess the parents' ability to provide adequate food for the infant and refer the family to social services as needed. *There may be inadequate food in the home due to lack of transportation, neglect, or lack of funds.*

- Teach the parents how to introduce solid foods and take time to answer questions. Observe the infant being fed, if possible. *Parents may feel overwhelmed by changes in feeding.*

- Stress the importance of adequate nutrition and regular feeding times for the infant. *Proper nutrition in early years is critical to development.*

- Support the family unit by encouraging siblings to help with feeding, if appropriate. *Family-focused care recognizes the importance of other children living in the home.*

45

Fecal Elimination

PROCEDURES

45–1 Obtaining and Testing a Specimen of Feces

Before obtaining a specimen, determine the reason for collecting the stool specimen and the correct method of obtaining and handling it (e.g., how much stool to obtain, whether a preservative needs to be added to the stool, and whether it needs to be sent immediately to the laboratory). It may be necessary to confirm this information by checking with the agency laboratory. In many situations, only a single specimen is required; in others, timed specimens are necessary, and every stool passed is collected within a designated time period.

PURPOSE

- To determine the presence of occult blood, parasites, bacteria, viruses, or other abnormal constituents in the stool

ASSESSMENT FOCUS

Client's need for assistance to defecate or use a bedpan; any abdominal discomfort before, during, or after defecation; status of perianal skin for any irritation, especially if the client defecates frequently and has liquid stools; any interventions related to the specimen collection, such as dietary or medication orders; presence of hemorrhoids that may bleed (particularly important for clients who are constipated, because constipated stool can aggravate existing hemorrhoids; any bleeding can affect test results); any interventions (e.g., medication) ordered to follow a defecation.

EQUIPMENT

Collecting a Specimen of Feces

- ❏ Clean or sterile bedpan or bedside commode (for an infant, the stool is scraped from the diaper)
- ❏ Disposable gloves
- ❏ Cardboard or plastic specimen container (labeled) with a lid or, for stool culture, a sterile swab in a test tube, as policy dictates

- ❏ Two tongue blades
- ❏ Paper towel
- ❏ Completed laboratory requisition
- ❏ Air freshener

Testing for Occult Blood in the Feces

- ❏ Clean bedpan or bedside commode

- ❏ Disposable gloves
- ❏ Two tongue blades
- ❏ Paper towel
- ❏ Test product

INTERVENTION

1. **Give clients the following information and instructions.**

- The purpose of the stool specimen and how the client can assist in collecting it.

- Defecate in a clean or sterile bedpan or bedside commode.

- Do not contaminate the specimen with urine or menstrual discharge. Void before the specimen collection.

- Do not place toilet tissue in the bedpan after defecation, because contents of the paper can affect the laboratory analysis.

- Notify the nurse as soon as possible after defecation, particularly for specimens that need to be sent to the laboratory immediately after collection.

2. **Assist clients who need help.**

- Assist the client to use a bedside commode or a bedpan placed on a bedside chair or under the toilet seat in the bathroom.

- After the client has defecated, cover the bedpan or commode. *Covering the bedpan reduces odor and embarrassment to the client.*

- Put on gloves to prevent hand contamination, and clean the client as required. Inspect the skin around the anus for any irritation, especially if the client defecates frequently and has liquid stools.

▶ **Procedure 45–1** *continued*

3. **Transfer the required amount of stool to the stool specimen container.**

- Use one or two tongue blades to transfer some or all of the stool to the specimen container, taking care not to contaminate the outside of the container. The amount of stool to be sent depends on the purpose for which the specimen is collected. Usually 2.5 cm (1 in) of formed stool or 15 to 30 ml of liquid stool is adequate. For some timed specimens, however, the entire stool passed may need to be sent. Visible pus, mucus, or blood should be included in the sample.

  or

  For a culture, dip a sterile swab into the specimen, preferably where purulent fecal matter is present in the feces. Place the swab in a sterile test tube using sterile technique.

  or

  For an occult blood test, see step 5 below.

- Wrap the used tongue blades in a paper towel before disposing of them in a plastic-lined waste container. *These measures help prevent the spread of microorganisms by contact with other articles.*

- Place the lid on the container as soon as the specimen is in the container. *Putting the lid on immediately prevents the spread of microorganisms.*

4. **Ensure client comfort.**

- Empty and clean the bedpan or commode, and return it to its place.

- Remove and discard the gloves.

- Provide an air freshener for any odors unless contraindicated by the client; e.g., a spray may increase dyspnea.

5. **Label and send the specimen to the laboratory.**

- Ensure that the specimen label and the laboratory requisition have the correct information on them and are securely attached on the specimen container. *Inappropriate identification of the specimen can lead to errors of diagnosis or therapy for the client.*

- Arrange for the specimen to be taken to the laboratory. Specimens to be cultured or tested for parasites need to be sent immediately. If this is not possible, follow the directions on the specimen container. In some instances refrigeration is indicated because bacteriologic changes take place in stool specimens left at room temperature.

  or

Test the stool for occult blood.

- Select a test product.

- Put on gloves.

- Follow the manufacturer's directions. For example:

  a. For a Guaiac test, smear a thin layer of feces on a paper towel or filter paper with a tongue blade, and drop reagents onto the smear as directed.

  b. For a Hematest, smear a thin layer of feces on filter paper, place a tablet in the middle of the specimen, and add two drops of water as directed.

  c. For a Hemoccult slide, smear a thin layer of feces over the circle inside the envelope, and drop reagent solution onto the smear.

- Note the reaction. For all tests, a blue color indicates a positive result, i.e., the presence of occult blood.

6. **Document all relevant information.**

- Record the collection of the specimen on the client's chart and on the nursing care plan. Include in the recording the date and time of the collection and all nursing assessments. See Evaluation Focus.

- For an occult blood test, record the type of test product used and the reaction.

▶**Procedure 45–1 Obtaining and Testing a Specimen of Feces** *continued*

EVALUATION FOCUS

Color, odor, consistency, and amount of feces; presence of abnormal constituents (e.g., blood or mucus); results of test for occult blood if obtained; discomfort during or after defecation; status of perianal skin; any bleeding from the anus after defecation.

SAMPLE RECORDING

Date	Time	Notes
08/12/04	0830	Stool specimen obtained for parasites and sent to laboratory. Stool is light brown, soft and without form. No evidence of blood or mucus. Perianal skin intact.————————————Stacey McNamara, RN *or* Guaiac test performed for occult blood. Results positive.————————————————————————Stacey McNamara, RN

LIFESPAN CONSIDERATIONS

- A child who is toilet trained should be able to provide a fecal specimen, but may prefer being assisted by a parent.

- Teach the parent how to collect the specimen and provide disposable wipes, a specimen container (if needed), and gloves.

- When explaining the procedure to the child, use words appropriate for the child's age rather than medical terms. Ask the parent what words the family normally uses to describe a bowel movement.

HOME CARE CONSIDERATIONS

- Unless the nurse happens to be present when a bowel movement occurs, the client or a caregiver will need to collect the fecal specimen.

- Teach the client or caregiver how to perform the procedure, and provide the necessary equipment. Emphasize the need for body fluid precautions when handling the stool.

- Ask the client or caregiver to call when the specimen is obtained. If a laboratory test is needed, the nurse can pick up the specimen or a family member may take it to the laboratory.

- Place the specimen inside a plastic biohazard bag. Carry the bag in a sealed container marked "biohazard" and take it to the laboratory promptly. Do not expose the specimen to extreme temperatures in the car.

- Ensure that all containers are properly labeled and the laboratory knows where the results should be reported.

45–2 Removing a Fecal Impaction Digitally

Digital removal involves breaking up the fecal mass digitally and removing it in portions. Because the bowel mucosa can be injured during this procedure, some agencies restrict and specify the personnel permitted to conduct digital disimpactions. Rectal stimulation is also contraindicated for some people because it may cause an excessive vagal response resulting in cardiac arrhythmia. After a disimpaction, the nurse can use various interventions to remove remaining feces, such as a cleansing enema or the insertion of a suppository.

PURPOSES
- To relieve pain and discomfort caused by blockage of impacted feces
- To reestablish normal defecation

ASSESSMENT FOCUS

Pattern of defecation; presence of an impaction confirmed by digital examination; presence of nausea, headache, abdominal pain, malaise, or abdominal distention.

EQUIPMENT

- ❑ Bath blanket
- ❑ Bedpan and cover
- ❑ Toilet tissue
- ❑ Disposable gloves
- ❑ Lubricant
- ❑ Soap, water, and towel
- ❑ Disposable linen-saver pads

INTERVENTION

1. **Prepare the client.**

- Explain to the client what you plan to do and why. This procedure is distressing, tiring, and uncomfortable, so the person may desire the presence of another nurse or support person.

- Assist the client to a right or left lateral or Sims' position with the back toward you. *When the person lies on the right side, the sigmoid colon is uppermost, thus, gravity can aid removal of the feces. Positioning the client on the left side allows easier access to the sigmoid colon.*

- Cover the client with the bath blanket.

2. **Prepare the equipment.**

- Place the linen-saver pad under the client's hips, and arrange the top bedclothing so that it falls obliquely over the hips, exposing only the buttocks.

- Place the bedpan and toilet tissue nearby on the bed or a bedside chair.

- Put on the gloves.

- Lubricate the gloved index finger. *Lubricant reduces resistance by the anal sphincter as the finger is inserted.*

3. **Remove the impaction.**

- Gently insert the index finger into the rectum, moving toward the umbilicus.

- Gently massage around the stool. *Gentle action prevents damage to the rectal mucosa. A circular motion around the rectum dislodges the stool, stimulates peristalsis, and relaxes the anal sphincter.*

- Work the finger into the hardened mass of stool to break it up. If you cannot break up the impaction with one finger, insert two fingers and try to break up the impaction scissor style.

- Work the stool down to the anus, remove it in small pieces, and place them in the bedpan.

- Carefully continue to remove as much fecal material as possible; at the same time, assess the client for signs of pallor, feelings of faintness, shortness of breath, and perspiration. Terminate the procedure if these occur. *Manual stimulation could result in excessive vagal nerve stimulation and subsequent cardiac arrhythmia.*

- Assist the client to a position on a clean bedpan, commode, or toilet. *Digital stimulation of the rectum may induce the urge to defecate.*

4. **Assist the client with hygienic measures as needed.**

- Wash the rectal area with soap and water and dry gently.

- Remove and discard the gloves.

5. **If appropriate, teach the client measures to promote normal elimination. Alterations in diet and fluid intake and the use of stool softeners may be necessary.**

6. **Document the procedure and all assessments.**

▶**Procedure 45–2 Removing a Fecal Impaction Digitally** *continued*

EVALUATION FOCUS

Color, consistency, odor, and amount of feces; presence of abnormal constituents; passage of flatus; client comfort; vital signs; abdominal distention.

SAMPLE RECORDING

Data	Time	Notes
09/28/04	1000	Rectal examination for fecal impaction. Moderate amount dark brown feces removed digitally. Vital signs stable. Unable to defecate following procedure.————————————Bruce L. Ching, NS

LIFESPAN CONSIDERATIONS

- Constipation is a frequent problem for older clients. *Aging causes decreased anal muscle tone and sensations.*

- Teach the older client how to prevent fecal impaction by altering diet and fluid intake, increasing exercise, and using stool softeners. *Older clients may not receive adequate fluid or bulk from their diet. Some clients restrict fluids to avoid frequent urination.*

HOME CARE CONSIDERATIONS

- Obtain an order from the physician and check the client's medical history before removing a fecal impaction.

- Perform the procedure in a private area of the home with facilities nearby to dispose of soiled material.

- Ask the client or caregiver to keep a record of bowel movements and notify the health care provider if more than two days pass without a bowel movement.

45–3 Irrigating a Colostomy

Before commencing a colostomy irrigation, determine (a) whether the stoma needs to be dilated; (b) which is the distal stoma and which is the proximal stoma, if the colostomy is not an end colostomy; and (c) why the irrigation is being performed and which stoma is to be irrigated (usually the proximal stoma is irrigated, to stimulate evacuation of the bowel; however, it may be necessary to irrigate the distal stoma in preparation for diagnostic procedures, such as roentgenography).

PURPOSE

- To distend the bowel and stimulate peristalsis and evacuation of feces

ASSESSMENT FOCUS

Bowel sounds; presence of abdominal distention; type of colostomy and functioning stoma; client readiness to select and use the equipment; client's mobility status to determine where the irrigation will be done.

EQUIPMENT

- ❏ Disposable bedpad and a bedpan, if the client is to remain in bed
- ❏ Bath blanket
- ❏ Irrigation equipment:
  A bag to hold the solution
  Tubing attached to the bag
  Tubing clamp or flow regulator
  #28 rubber colon catheter, calibrated in either centimeters or inches, with a stoma cone or seal
  Disposable stoma-irrigation drainage sleeve with belt to direct the fecal contents into the toilet or bedpan
- ❏ IV pole
- ❏ Moisture-resistant bag
- ❏ Clean gloves to protect the nurse's hands from contamination, and one glove to dilate the stoma if ordered by the physician
- ❏ Lubricant
- ❏ Clean colostomy appliance or dressings
- ❏ Wash cloth and towel

INTERVENTION

1. Prepare the client.

- Assist the client who must remain in bed to a side-lying position. Place a disposable bedpad on the bed in front of the client, and place the bedpan on top of the disposable pad, beneath the stoma.

- Assist an ambulatory client to sit on the toilet or on a commode in the bathroom. Ensure that the client's gown or pajamas are moved out of the way to prevent soiling, and cover the client appropriately with the bath blanket to prevent undue exposure.

- Throughout the procedure, provide explanations, and encourage the client to participate.

2. Prepare the equipment.

- Fill the solution bag with 500 mL of warm (body temperature) tap water, or other solution as ordered.

- Hang the solution bag on an IV pole so that the bottom of the container is at the level of the client's shoulder, or 30 to 45 cm (12 to 18 in) above the stoma. *This height provides a pressure gradient that allows fluid to flow into the colon.*

- Attach the colon catheter securely to the tubing.

- Open the regulator clamp, and run fluid through the tubing to expel all air from it. Close the clamp until ready for the irrigation. *Air should not be introduced into the bowel because it distends the bowel and can cause cramps.*

3. Remove the colostomy bag and then position the irrigation drainage sleeve.

- Remove the soiled colostomy bag, and place it in the moisture-resistant bag. *Placing the colostomy bag in this container prevents the transmission of microorganisms and helps reduce odor.*

- Center the irrigation drainage sleeve over the stoma, and attach it snugly. *This prevents seepage of the fluid onto the skin.*

- Direct the lower, open end of the drainage sleeve into the bedpan or between the client's legs into the toilet.

4. If ordered by the physician, dilate the stoma.

- Put on gloves.

- Lubricate the tip of the little finger.

- Gently insert the finger into the stoma, using a massaging motion

▶ Procedure 45–3 Irrigating a Colostomy *continued*

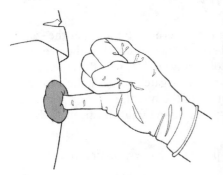

Figure 45–1 Dilating a colostomy stoma.

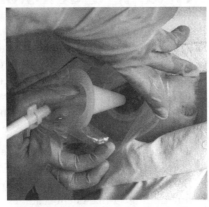

Figure 45–2 The client is participating in the colostomy irrigation by directing the cone.

(Figure 45–1). *A massaging motion relaxes the intestinal muscles.*

- Repeat the previous two steps, using progressively larger fingers, until maximum dilation is achieved. *Stoma dilation is performed to stretch and relax the stomal sphincter and to assess the direction of the proximal colon prior to an irrigation.*

5. **Insert the stoma cone or colon catheter.**

- Lubricate the tip of the stoma cone or colon catheter. *Lubricating the tip of the cone or catheter eases insertion and prevents injury to the stoma.*

- Using a rotating motion, insert the catheter or stoma cone through the opening in the top of the irrigation drainage sleeve and gently through the stoma (Figure 45–2). *A rotating motion on insertion helps to open the stoma.*

- Insert a catheter only 7 cm (3 in); insert a stoma cone just until it fits snugly. Many practitioners prefer using a cone to avoid the risk of perforating the bowel.

- If you have difficulty inserting the catheter or cone, do not apply

force. *Forcing the cone or catheter may traumatize or perforate the bowel.*

6. **Irrigate the colon.**

- Open the tubing clamp, and allow the fluid to flow into the bowel. If cramping occurs, stop the flow until the cramps subside and then resume the flow. *Fluid that is too cold or administered too quickly may cause cramps.*

- If the fluid flows out as fast as you put it in, press the stoma cone or seal more firmly against the stoma to occlude it. If a stoma cone or seal is not available, press around the stoma with your fingers to close the stoma against the catheter.

- After all the fluid is instilled, remove the catheter or cone and allow the colon to empty. Although not always indicated, you may ask the client to gently massage the abdomen and sit quietly for 10 to 15 minutes until initial emptying has occurred. *Massaging the abdomen encourages initial emptying.*

In some agencies the stoma cone is left in place for 10 to 15 minutes before it is removed.

7. **Seal the drainage sleeve and allow complete emptying of the colon.**

- Clean the base of the irrigation drainage sleeve, and seal the bottom with a drainage clamp, following the manufacturer's instructions.

- Encourage an ambulatory client to move around for about 30 minutes. *Complete emptying of the colon often takes up to half an hour. Moving around promotes peristalsis.*

8. **Empty and remove the irrigation sleeve.**

9. **Ensure client comfort.**

- Clean the area around the stoma, and dry it thoroughly.

- Put a colostomy appliance on the client as needed. See Procedure 45–2 in *Fundamentals of Nursing.*

10. **Document and report relevant information.**

- Document all assessments and interventions. Include the time of the irrigation, the type and amount of fluid instilled, the returns, any problems experienced, and the client's response.

- Promptly report to the nurse in charge any problems, such as no fluid or stool returns, difficulties inserting the tube, peristomal skin redness or irritation, and stomal discoloration.

▶ **Procedure 45–3** *continued*

EVALUATION FOCUS

Amount and consistency of fluid returns; status of stoma and peristomal skin; any difficulties encountered inserting the tube or dilating the stoma; client's response and participation.

SAMPLE RECORDING

Date	Time	Notes
12/05/04	0900	Colostomy irrigated with 750 mL warm tap water. Water and large amount soft brown stool expelled. Tube inserted without difficulty. Peristomal skin intact. Stoma is pink. Asked questions about irrigation, looked at stoma for first time. Observed stoma care and pouch application.————————————————————Chung-Hao Jen, NS

LIFESPAN CONSIDERATIONS

- Older clients may need assistance with the procedure due to arthritic joint changes, hand tremors, or poor eyesight. *Offer to assist only as needed, so the client can remain independent.*

- Younger clients who work outside the home may have special concerns about odor and appearance. Provide information about ostomy care and community support groups. A visit from a person who has a colostomy can be helpful.

HOME CARE CONSIDERATIONS

- Perform the procedure in a warm, private area of the home.

- Assess the client's attitude toward the colostomy and willingness to learn colostomy care. Encourage the expression of feelings. *Many clients are repulsed by the colostomy at first and are reluctant to even look at the site.*

- Teach a caregiver how to assist the client or how to perform the irrigation if the client is unable to do so.

- Ensure that the client knows where to obtain ostomy supplies.

46

Urinary Elimination

46–1 Collecting a Routine Urine Specimen from an Adult or a Child Who Has Urinary Control

PURPOSE
- To screen the client's urine for abnormal constituents

ASSESSMENT FOCUS

Client's ability to provide the specimen; medications that may discolor urine or affect the test results.

EQUIPMENT

- ❏ Nonsterile gloves as needed
- ❏ Clean bedpan, urinal, or commode for clients who are unable to void directly into the specimen container
- ❏ Wide-mouthed specimen container
- ❏ Completed laboratory requisition
- ❏ Completed specimen identification label

INTERVENTION

1. **Give ambulatory clients the following information and instructions.**

- Explain the purpose of the urine specimen and how the client can assist.

- Explain that all specimens must be free of fecal contamination, so voiding needs to occur at a different time from defecation.

- Instruct female clients to discard the toilet tissue in the toilet or in a waste bag rather than in the bedpan, because tissue in the specimen makes laboratory analysis more difficult.

- Give the client the specimen container, and direct the client to the bathroom to void 120 ml (4 oz) into it.

2. **Assist clients who are seriously ill, physically incapacitated, or disoriented.**

- Provide required assistance in the bathroom, or help the client to use a bedpan or urinal in bed.

- Wear gloves when assisting the client to void into a bedpan or urinal and transferring the urine from the bedpan, urinal, or commode to the specimen container.

- Empty the bedpan or urinal.

- Remove gloves if worn, and wash your hands.

3. **Ensure that the specimen is sealed and the container clean.**

- Put the lid tightly on the container. *This prevents spillage of the urine and contamination of other objects.*

- If the outside of the container has been contaminated by urine, clean it with soap and water. *This prevents the spread of microorganisms.*

4. **Label and transport the specimen to the laboratory.**

- Ensure that the specimen label and the laboratory requisition have the correct information on them. Attach them securely to the specimen container. *Inappropriate identifiction of the specimen can lead to errors of diagnosis or therapy for the client.*

- Arrange for the specimen to be taken immediately to the laboratory or placed in a refrigerator. *Urine deteriorates relatively rapidly from bacterial contamination when left at room temperture; specimens should be analyzed immediately after collection.*

5. **Document all relevant information.**

- Document the collection of the specimen on the client's chart. Include the date and time of collection and the appearance and odor of the urine.

▶**Procedure 46–1 Collecting a Routine Urine Specimen from an Adult or a Child** *continued*

EVALUATION FOCUS

> Color, odor, and character of the urine.

SAMPLE RECORDING

Date	Time	Notes
02/27/04	0600	Random urine specimen collected for admission urinalysis. Urine clear, straw colored, and without odor. Specimen sent to lab.— ————————————————————————Joyce Daynard, SN

LIFESPAN CONSIDERATIONS

- Explain the procedure in simple terms to a child and ask the child to void in a potty chair or a bedpan placed inside the toilet.

- Give a child a clean specimen container to play with.

- Allow a parent to assist with a child, if possible. *The child may feel more comfortable with a parent.*

HOME CARE CONSIDERATIONS

- Explain why the test is needed and ask the client to obtain the specimen in the bathroom. Help a bedfast client use the bedpan.

- Place the urine specimen in a plastic biohazard bag and transport inside a closed container marked "biohazard." Use a cooler with ice to transport the sample, if needed.

- Take the sample to the laboratory as soon as possible. Don't expose the sample to extreme temperatures inside the car.

- Ensure that the laboratory knows where to report the findings.

46–2 Collecting a Timed Urine Specimen

For timed urine specimens, appropriate specimen containers with or without preservative in accordance with the specific test are generally obtained from the laboratory and placed in the client's bathroom or in the utility room. Alert signs are placed in the client's unit to remind staff of the test in progress. Specimen identification labels need to indicate the date and time of each voiding in addition to the usual identification information. They may also be numbered sequentially (e.g., 1st specimen, 2nd specimen, 3rd specimen).

PURPOSES
- To assess the ability of the kidney to concentrate and dilute urine
- To determine disorders of glucose metabolism, such as diabetes mellitus
- To determine levels of specific constituents, such as albumin, amylase, creatinine, urobilinogen, certain hormones (e.g., estriol or corticosteroids) in the urine

ASSESSMENT FOCUS

Client's ability to understand instructions and to provide urine samples independently; any fluid or dietary requirements associated with the test; any medication restrictions or requirements for the test.

EQUIPMENT
- ❏ Appropriate specimen containers with or without preservative in accordance with the specific test
- ❏ Completed specimen identification labels
- ❏ Completed laboratory requisition
- ❏ Bedpan or urinal
- ❏ Alert card on or near the bed indicating the specific times for urine collection
- ❏ Antiseptic
- ❏ Nonsterile gloves, as needed
- ❏ Ice-filled container if a refrigerator isn't available

INTERVENTION
1. **Give the client the following information and instructions.**

- The purpose of the test and how the client can assist.

- When the specimen collection will begin and end. For example, a 24-hour urine test commonly begins at 0700 hours and ends at the same hour the next day.

- That all urine must be saved and placed in the specimen containers once the test starts.

- That the urine must be free of fecal contamination and toilet tissue.

- That each specimen must be given to the nursing staff immediately so that it can be placed in the appropriate specimen bottle.

2. **Start the collection period.**

- Ask the client to void in the toilet or bedpan or urinal. Discard this urine (check agency procedure), and document the time the test starts with this discarded specimen. Collect all subsequent urine specimens, including the one at the end of the period.

- Ask the client to ingest the required amount of liquid for certain tests or to restrict fluid intake. Follow the test directions.

- Instruct the client to void all subsequent urine into the bedpan or urinal and to notify the nursing staff when each specimen is provided. Some tests require voiding at specified times.

- Number the specimen containers sequentially, e.g., 1st specimen, 2nd specimen, 3rd specimen, if separate specimens are required.

- Place alert signs in the client's unit to remind staff of the test in progress.

3. **Collect all of the required specimens.**

- Place each specimen into the appropriately labeled container. For some tests, each specimen is not kept separately but is poured into a large bottle.

- If the outside of the specimen container is contaminated with urine, clean it with soap and water. *Cleaning prevents the transfer of microorganisms to others.*

- Ensure that each specimen is refrigerated throughout the timed collection period. In some agencies, a cooler with ice is kept in the client's bathroom to store the urine specimens. *Refrigeration or other form of cooling prevents bacterial decomposition of the urine.*

- Measure the amount of each urine specimen as required.

▶ Procedure 46–2 Collecting a Timed Urine Specimen *continued*

- Ask the client to provide the last specimen 5 to 10 minutes before the end of the collection period.

- Inform the client that the test is completed.

- Remove the alert signs and the specimen equipment from the client's unit and bathroom.

4. Document all relevant information.

- Record the starting time of the test and completion of the specimen collection on the client's chart. Include the date and specific time. In addition, if indicated for the specific test, note the time each urine specimen was collected, the volume of each specimen, the appearance of the urine, and other relevant data such as fluid intake or restrictions.

EVALUATION FOCUS

Each urine specimen for color, odor, and clarity; results of laboratory analysis when available.

SAMPLE RECORDING

Date	Time	Notes
03/21/04	0700	24-hour urine collection for quantitative albumin started after client voided. Client informed of need to save all urine and inform nursing staff after each voiding. Specimen collection bottle labeled and placed on ice in bathroom.————————Annette Campinola, R.N.
03/22/04	0700	24-hour urine collection for albumin completed. Specimen sent to lab. Urine cloudy.————————————Thomas Timothy, R.N.

LIFESPAN CONSIDERATIONS

- Older clients may void frequently, especially if taking a diuretic medication.

- A toilet-trained child will need careful instructions that use terms the child can understand. Allow the parents to help, if possible.

- Both children and older clients may need frequent reminders to take extra fluids (if ordered) or follow other guidelines for the test.

HOME CARE CONSIDERATIONS

- Explain why the test is needed, and teach the client how to obtain the specimens. Provide written instructions and specimen containers.

- Assess the client's ability and willingness to collect the specimens as ordered. If poor eyesight or hand tremors are a problem, suggest using a funnel to pour the urine into the container.

- The home should have a refrigerator or other method for cooling the urine samples.

- Tell the client to keep the specimen container in a plastic or paper bag in the refrigerator, separate from other contents. Or the client may use a cooler with ice.

- Wash the outside of the specimen container before taking it from the home. For transport, place the specimens in a plastic biohazard bag inside a closed container, such as a cooler marked "biohazard."

- Take the specimen to the laboratory promptly, avoiding extreme temperatures in the car.

- Ensure that the laboratory knows where to send the test results.

46–3 Collecting a Urine Specimen from an Infant

PURPOSE

- To screen the infant's urine for abnormal constituents

ASSESSMENT FOCUS

Skin status of infant's perineal area

EQUIPMENT

- ❏ Plastic disposable urine collection bag
- ❏ Sterile cotton balls
- ❏ Soap and a basin of water
- ❏ Antiseptic solution
- ❏ Sterile water
- ❏ Diaper
- ❏ Specimen container
- ❏ Disinfectant
- ❏ Completed specimen label
- ❏ Completed laboratory form
- ❏ Nonsterile gloves, as needed

INTERVENTION

1. **Prepare the parents and the infant.**

- If parents are present, explain why a urine specimen is being taken and the method of obtaining it.

- Before and throughout the procedure, handle the infant gently, and talk in soothing tones.

- Remove the infant's diaper and clean the perineal-genital area with soap and water and then with an antiseptic. *Cleaning is necessary to remove powder, baby oil, lotions, secretions, and fecal matter from the genitals. It also reduces the number of microorganisms on the skin and subsequent contamination of the voided urine.*

  a. For girls, separate the labia and wash, rinse, and dry the perineal area from the front to the back (clitoris to anus) on each side of the urinary meatus, and then over the meatus (Figure 46–1). Repeat this procedure, using the antiseptic solution to clean, the sterile water to rinse, and some dry cotton balls to dry.

  b. For boys, clean and disinfect both the penis and the scrotum in the manner described

Figure 46–1 Cleaning the perineal area of a female infant.

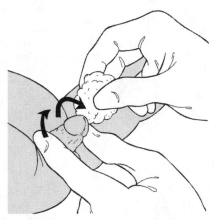

Figure 46–2 Cleaning the tip of the penis.

above. Wash the penis in a circular motion from the tip toward the scrotum, and wash the scrotum last (Figure 46–2). Retract the foreskin of an uncircumcised boy. *Freeing the skin of all moisture and secretions facilitates proper adhesion of the urine collection bag and prevents leakage of urine.*

2. **Apply the specimen bag.**

- Remove the protective paper from the bottom half of the adhesive backing of the collection bag (Figure 46–3).

- Spread the infant's legs apart as much as possible. *Spreading the legs separates and flattens the folds of the skin.*

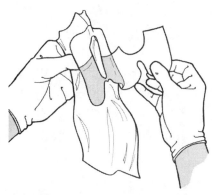

Figure 46–3 Removing the bottom half of the adhesive backing.

▶ Procedure 46–3 Collecting a Urine Specimen from an Infant *continued*

- Place the opening of the collection bag over the urethra or the penis and scrotum. The base of the opening needs to cover the vagina or to fit well up under the scrotum (Figure 46–4).

- Press the adhesive portion firmly against the infant's skin, starting at the perineum (the area between the anus and the genitals) and working outward. *This*

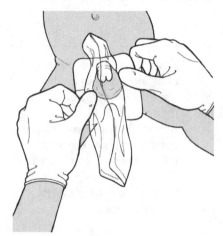

Figure 46–4 Placing the opening of the collection bag over the penis and scrotum.

method prevents wrinkles, which could cause leakge of urine.

- Remove the protective paper from the top half of the adhesive backing, and press it firmly in place, working from the top center outward.

- Apply a loose-fitting diaper. *A diaper helps keep the urine bag in place.*

- Elevate the head of the crib mattress to semi-Fowler's position. *Semi-Fowler's position aids the flow of urine by gravity into the collection portion of the urine bag.*

3. **Remove the bag, and transfer the specimen.**

- After the child has voided a desired amount, gently remove the bag from the skin.

- Empty the urine from the bag through the opening at its base into the specimen container.

- Discard the urine bag.

- If the outside of the specimen container has been contaminated, clean it with a disinfectant. *Clean-*

ing the outside of the container prevents the spread of microorganisms.

4. **Ensure client comfort.**

- Apply the infant's diaper.

- Leave the infant in a comfortable and safe position held by a parent or in a crib.

5. **Transport the specimen.**

- Ensure that the specimen label and the laboratory requisition have the correct information on them. Attach them securely to the specimen. *Incorrect identification of the specimen can lead to subsequent errors of diagnosis or therapy for the infant.*

- Arrange for the specimen to be sent to the laboratory immediately or refrigerate it.

6. **Document all relevant information.**

- Record collection of the urine specimen and your assessments.

EVALUATION FOCUS

Color, odor, and character of the urine.

SAMPLE RECORDING

Date	Time	Notes
02/27/04	0600	Random urine specimen collected for admission urinalysis. Urine clear, straw colored, and without odor. Specimen sent to lab.——————————————————————————Joyce Daynard, SN

▶ **Procedure 46–3** *continued*

HOME CARE CONSIDERATIONS

- Take all the necessary equipment to the home, including a spare urine collection bag and an extra specimen container. *Extra supplies will be needed if the bag becomes dislodged or the specimen container is contaminated.*

- Explain to the parents why the test was ordered and how the urine specimen will be obtained.

- Apply the urine bag at the beginning of the visit, giving the infant more time to void while you are in the home.

- Transport the specimen container in a plastic biohazard bag placed inside a closed container marked "biohazard."

- Use a cooler with ice to keep the specimen cool, and transport it to the laboratory as quickly as possible.

- Ensure that the laboratory knows where to send the test results.

Changing a Urinary Diversion Ostomy Appliance

Various types of vinyl urinary stoma appliances are available. The disposable one-piece pouch may be attached either to a nonallergenic adhesive-backed faceplate, which may or may not be precut, or to a semipermeable skin barrier, which is permeable to vapor and oxygen but impermeable to liquid. The latter attachment maintains skin integrity more effectively. Reusable pouches have opaque faceplates, which may or may not

be attached to the pouch. Some have belt attachments, and one type has an adaptable insert that can be adjusted to stoma size. The enterostomal therapy nurse selects the pouch that best suits the client by considering the type of ostomy, the stoma location and shape, and the peristomal skin surface, as well as the client's body size and contour, physical and mental abilities, skin allergies, financial status, and lifestyle.

Generally, a urinary diversion appliance adheres to the skin for 2 to 5 days. It is usually changed twice a week. The nurse's responsibilities include stoma and peristomal care.

46–4　Changing a Urinary Diversion Ostomy Appliance

PURPOSES
- To assess and care for the peristomal skin
- To collect urinary drainage for the assessment of the amount and type of output

ASSESSMENT FOCUS

> Stoma size and shape; color of stoma; presence of swelling; condition of peristomal skin; type and size of appliance currently in use; client and family learning needs; client emotional status and responses; level of comfort; behavior and attitude toward ostomy; skills learned.

EQUIPMENT

If a commercially prepared stoma care kit is not available, the following supplies need to be assembled:

- ❑ Disposable gloves
- ❑ Ostomy pouch with adhesive-backed faceplate
- ❑ Ostomy pouch belt (optional)
- ❑ Graduated pitcher or receptacle for the urine
- ❑ Cleaning materials including basin filled with warm water, soap (optional), cotton balls, and towel

- ❑ Tampon
- ❑ Scissors
- ❑ Gauze pads
- ❑ Skin barrier (Skin Prep liquid or wipes or similar product, e.g., Stomahesive or ready-made wafer-type or disc-type barrier) for the peristomal skin
- ❑ Stoma measuring guide
- ❑ Pen or pencil

- ❑ Adhesive solvent in the form of presaturated sponges or liquid (optional)
- ❑ Adhesive cement (optional) for reusable pouches if double-faced adhesive disc is not used
- ❑ Electric razor or scissors
- ❑ Waterproof bag for the soiled appliance

INTERVENTION

1. **Determine the need for appliance change.**

- Assess the appliance in use for leakage of urine. *Urine can irritate the peristomal skin.*

- Ask the client about any discomfort at or around the stoma. *Com-*

plaints of burning may indicate urine leakage and skin breakdown beneath the faceplate.

- Drain the pouch into a graduated cylinder when it is one-third to one-half full and prior to removing the pouch.

- With any evidence of leakage or discomfort at or around the stoma, change the appliance.

2. **Communicate acceptance and support of the client throughout the procedure.** *This procedure may evoke negative emotional and psychologic responses.*

▶ **Procedure 46–4** *continued*

3. **Select an appropriate time.**

- The best time is early in the morning prior to taking fluids. *Urine output is lower at this time.* Avoid mealtimes or visiting hours. *The ostomy may embarrass the client or affect appetite.*

- Avoid times immediately after the administration of diuretics which will increase urine output. *It is best to change the pouch when urine output is at its lowest flow rate.*

4. **Prepare the client and support persons.**

- Explain the procedure to the client and support persons. Changing an ostomy appliance should not result in discomfort, but it may be distressful to the client. *Providing information to support persons will assist them in providing support.*

- Change the appliance competently and quickly and provide privacy, preferably in the bathroom, where clients can deal with the ostomy as they would at home.

- Assist the client into a comfortable sitting or lying position in bed or, preferably, a sitting or standing position in the bathroom. *Lying or standing positions may facilitate pouch application by avoiding skin wrinkles.*

- Don gloves, and unfasten the belt if one is being worn.

5. **Shave the peristomal skin of well-established ostomies as needed.**

- Use an electric razor or scissors on a regular basis to remove excessive hair. *Hair follicles can become irritated or infected by repeated pulling out hairs during removal of the appliance and skin barrier.*

6. **Remove the emptied ostomy appliance.**

- Assess the volume and character of output.

- Peel the bag off slowly while holding the client's skin taut. *Holding the skin taut minimizes client discomfort and prevents abrasion of the skin.*

- If the appliance is disposable, discard it in a moisture-proof bag.

7. **Clean and dry the peristomal skin and stoma.**

- Use a tampon or rolled piece of cotton-free gauze to wick urine from the stoma until the appliance is reapplied. *The capillary action of the gauze will keep urine away from the skin.*

- Using cotton balls, carefully wash the peristomal skin with warm water and mild soap if needed. Thoroughly rinse the soap from the skin. *Washing the area will remove any urine on the skin. Soap left on the skin can prevent proper adherence of the appliance and may be irritating.*

- Pat dry the skin with a towel or cotton balls. Excessive rubbing may abrade the skin.

8. **Assess the stoma and peristomal skin.**

- Inspect the color, size, and shape of the stoma. Note any frank bleeding.

- Inspect the peristomal skin for any redness, ulcerations, or irritation. *Transient redness after the removal of adhesive is normal.*

Applying the Skin Barrier (Peristomal Seal)

9. **If using Skin Prep liquid or wipes or other similar product:**

- Cover the stoma with a gauze pad to avoid getting the Skin Prep on the stoma.

- Either wipe the Skin Prep evenly around the peristomal skin or use an applicator to apply a thin layer of the liquid plastic coating to the area. Allow the Skin Prep to dry.

10. **If using a wafer- or disc-type barrier, read the manufacturer's directions as well as the steps below.** (Note that the karaya ring seal, although effective in protecting the skin, is less effective with urinary ostomies than with bowel ostomies because urine tends to melt the karaya.)

- Use the stoma measuring guide to measure the size of the stoma.

- Trace a circle on the backing of the skin barrier the same size as the stomal opening.

- Make a template of the stoma pattern. *A template aids other nurses and the client with future appliance changes.*

- Cut out the traced stoma pattern to make an opening in the skin barrier.

- Remove the backing on one side of the skin barrier to expose the sticky adhesive.

- Attach the skin barrier to the faceplate of the ostomy appliance when it is prepared. *Assembling the skin barrier and the appliance before application enhances the speed of application, an important consideration for constantly draining urostomies.*

11. **Prepare the clean appliance.**

To prepare a disposable pouch with adhesive square:

- If the appliance does not have the precut opening, trace a circle no more than 2–3 mm (1 in.) larger than the stoma size on the appliance's adhesive square. *The opening is made slightly larger than the*

▶ **Procedure 46–4 Changing a Urinary Diversion Ostomy Appliance** *continued*

stoma to prevent rubbing, cutting, or trauma to the stoma.

- Cut out the traced circle in the adhesive. Take care not to cut any portion of the pouch.

- Peel off the backing from the adhesive seal, and attach the seal to a disc-type skin barrier or, if a liquid product was used, to the client's peristomal skin.

To prepare a reusable pouch with faceplate attached:

- Depending on the type of appliance, apply either adhesive cement or a double-faced adhesive disc to the faceplate. Follow the manufacturer's directions.

To prepare a reusable pouch with detachable faceplate:

- Remove the protective paper strip from one side of the double-faced adhesive disc.

- Apply the sticky side of the disc to the back of the faceplate.

- Remove the remaining protective paper strip from the other side of the adhesive disc.

- Attach the faceplate to a disc-type skin barrier or, if a liquid product was used, to the client's peristomal skin.

12. Applying the clean appliance
For a disposable pouch:

- Remove the gauze pad or tampon over the stoma before applying the pouch.

- Gently press the adhesive backing onto the skin and smooth out any wrinkles, working from the stoma outward. *Wrinkles allow seepage of urine, which can irritate the skin and soil clothing.*

- Remove the air from the pouch. *Removing the air helps the pouch lie flat against the abdomen.*

- Attach the spout of the pouch to a urinary drainage system or cap the spout. Temporary disposable pouches are often attached to drainage systems.

For a reusable pouch with faceplate attached:

- Insert a coiled paper guidestrip into the faceplate opening. The strip should protrude slightly from the opening and expand to fit it. *The guidestrip helps in centering the appliance over the stoma and prevents pressure or irritation to the stoma by the appliance.*

- Using the guidestrip, center the faceplate over the stoma.

- Firmly press the adhesive seal to the peristomal skin. The guidestrip will fall into the pouch; commercially prepared guidestrips will dissolve in the pouch.

- Place a deodorant in the bag (optional).

- Close the spout of the pouch with the designated cap.

- Optional: Attach the pouch belt and fasten it around the client's waist. Wash a soiled belt with warm water and mild soap, rinse, and dry if needed.

For a reusable pouch with detachable faceplate:

- Press and hold the faceplate against the client's skin for a few minutes to enhance the seal.

- Press the adhesive around the circumference of the adhesive disc.

- Tape the faceplate to the client's abdomen using four or eight 7.5-cm (3-in.) strips of tape. Place the strips around the faceplate in a "picture-framing" manner, one strip down each side, one across the top, and one across the bottom. The additional four strips can be placed diagonally over the other tapes to enhance the seal.

- Stretch the opening on the back of the pouch, and position it over the base of the faceplate. Ease it over the faceplate flange.

- Place the lock ring between the pouch and the faceplate flange to secure the pouch against the faceplate.

- Close the spout of the pouch with the appropriate cap.

- Optional: Attach the pouch belt and fasten it around the client's waist.

13. Document relevant information.

- Document the date and time of appliance change.

- Record the color and size of stoma; amount, color, and character of urine output, condition of peristomal skin; client response; type and size of the appliance.

- Document client's behavior and attitudes toward ostomy and skills learned.

14. Adjust the client's teaching plan and nursing care plan as needed. Include on the teaching plan the equipment and procedure used. *Learning to care for the ostomy is facilitated if procedures implemented by nurses are consistent.* The client will also need to learn self-care and ways to reduce odor. Use of deodorant tablets in the appliance, soaking a reusable pouch in dilute vinegar solution, a diet that makes the urine more acid, and drinking plenty of fluids all help to control odor. *A high fluid intake dilutes the urine, making it less odorous. Ascorbic acid and cranberry juice increase the acidity of urine, which in turn inhibits bacterial action and odor. Information about ostomy clubs and other community services should also be included.*

▶ **Procedure 46–4** *continued*

EVALUATION FOCUS

Stoma size and shape; color of stoma; presence of swelling; condition of peristomal skin; type and size of appliance currently in use; client and family learning needs; client emotional status and responses; level of comfort; behavior and attitudes toward ostomy; skills learned.

SAMPLE RECORDING

Date	Time	Notes
01/8/04	800	Ureterostomy appliance changed. 200 cc clear yellow urine. Stoma pink, 6 cm. Peristomal skin intact. Denies discomfort. 1-inch two piece drainage system applied. Helped to clean peristomal skin and measure appliance.————————————Kerry Andrews, SN

LIFESPAN CONSIDERATIONS

- Younger clients who work outside the home may have special concerns about odor. Provide information about odor control and community support groups.

- Older clients may need assistance with the ostomy care due to arthritic joint changes, hand tremors, or poor eyesight. *Offer to assist as needed, but encourage the client to be independent.*

HOME CARE CONSIDERATIONS

- Assess the client's learning needs and attitude toward the ostomy. Determine if a caregiver in the home is willing to help.

- Demonstrate and teach ostomy care in a private area of the home. Give the client adequate time to practice using the equipment and ask questions.

- Teach the client how to clean and store the ostomy equipment.

- Ensure that the client knows where and how to obtain ostomy supplies.

- Teach the client to recognize signs of urinary tract infection, including strong odor, cloudy urine, and fever.

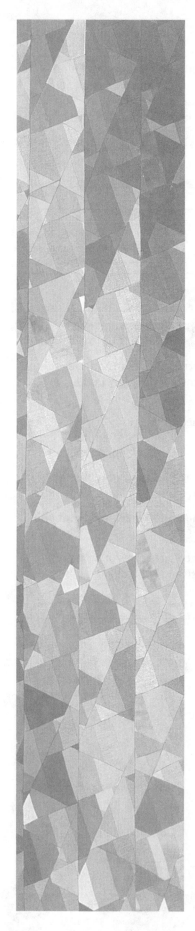

47

Oxygenation

PROCEDURES

47–1   Collecting a Sputum Specimen

Before collecting a sputum specimen, identify the purpose for which it is to be obtained. This often determines the number of specimens to obtain and the time of day to obtain them.

PURPOSES
- To identify a specific microorganism and its drug sensitivities or the presence of cancerous cells
- To assess the effectiveness of therapy

ASSESSMENT FOCUS

Client's ability to cough and expectorate secretions; type of assistance required to produce the specimen (e.g., the need to splint an abdominal incision, the need to be placed in postural drainage position beforehand, or the need to perform deep-breathing exercises beforehand); skin color and rate, depth, and pattern of respirations as baseline data.

EQUIPMENT

- ❏ Sterile specimen container with a cover
- ❏ Disposable gloves (if assisting the client)
- ❏ Disinfectant and swabs, or liquid soap and water
- ❏ Paper towels
- ❏ Completed label
- ❏ Completed laboratory requisition
- ❏ Mouthwash

INTERVENTION

1. **Give the client the following information and instructions:**

- The purpose of the test, the difference between sputum and saliva, and how to provide the sputum specimen.

- Not to touch the inside of the sputum container.

- To expectorate the sputum directly into the sputum container.

- To keep the outside of the container free of sputum, if possible.

- How to hold a pillow firmly against an abdominal incision if the client finds it painful to cough.

- The amount of sputum required. Usually 1 to 2 tsp (5 to 10 mL) of sputum is sufficient for analysis.

2. **Provide necessary assistance to collect the specimen.**

- Assist the client to a standing or a sitting position (e.g., high- or semi-Fowler's position, or on the edge of a bed or in a chair). *These positions allow maximum lung ventilation and expansion.*

- Ask the client to hold the sputum cup on the outside, or, for a client who is not able to do so, don gloves and hold the cup (Figure 47–1).

- Ask the client to breathe deeply and then cough up secretions. *A deep inhalation provides sufficient air to force secretions out of the airways and into the pharynx.*

- Hold the sputum cup so that the

Figure 47–1   Sputum specimen container.

client can expectorate into it, making sure that the sputum does not come in contact with the outside of the container. *Containing the sputum within the cup restricts the spread of microorganisms to others.*

- Assist the client to repeat coughing until a sufficient amount of sputum has been collected.

- Cover the container with the lid immediately after the sputum is in the container. *Covering the container prevents the inadvertent spread of microorganisms to others.*

- If spillage occurs on the outside of the container, clean the outer surface with a disinfectant. Some agencies recommend washing the outside of all containers with liquid soap and water and then drying with a paper towel.

- Remove and discard the gloves.

3. **Ensure client comfort.**

- Assist the client to rinse the mouth with a mouthwash as needed.

▶ Procedure 47–1 Collecting a Sputum Specimen *continued*

- Assist the client to a position of comfort that allows maximum lung expansion as required.

4. **Label and transport the specimen to the laboratory.**

- Ensure that the specimen label and the laboratory requisition carry the correct information. Attach them securely to the specimen. *Inaccurate identification and/or information on the specimen container can lead to errors of diagnosis or therapy.*

- Arrange for the specimen to be sent to the laboratory immediately. *Bacterial cultures must be started immediately, before any contaminating organisms can grow, multiply, and produce false results.*

5. **Document all relevant information.**

- Document the collection of the sputum specimen on the client's chart. Include the amount, color, consistency, and odor of the sputum, any measures needed to obtain the specimen (e.g., postural drainage), the general amount of sputum produced, and any discomfort experienced by the client.

EVALUATION FOCUS

Amount, color, and consistency (thick, tenacious, watery) of sputum; presence of hemoptysis; respiration rate and any abnormalities or difficulty breathing after the specimen collection; color of the client's skin and mucous membranes, especially any cyanosis, which can indicate impaired blood oxygenation.

SAMPLE RECORDING

Date	Time	Notes
06/21/04	0600	Sputum specimen sent to laboratory. Produced approximately 2 tbsp of green-yellow thick sputum. States has "sharp, knifelike pain" in right anterior lower chest when coughing.——Sheila O. Wry, NS

LIFESPAN CONSIDERATIONS

- The older client may need encouragement to cough. *A decreased cough reflex occurs with aging.*

- Allow time for the client to rest and recover between coughs. *Older clients may become short of breath after coughing because lung compliance, expiratory volume, and chest expansion decrease with aging.*

- Offer frequent mouth care to the elderly client. *Aging causes mucous membrane to become dry.*

HOME CARE CONSIDERATIONS

- Use a private area of the home to obtain the specimen and place supplies on a clean towel or pad.

- Place the specimen in a plastic biohazard bag and store in a container marked "biohazard."

- Transport the specimen in a cooler with ice and take it to the laboratory as quickly as possible. Avoid exposing specimens to extreme temperatures in the car.

- Ensure that the laboratory knows where the results should be reported. Call the physician immediately with abnormal or critical results.

47–2 Obtaining Nose and Throat Specimens

Before collecting a nose or throat specimen, determine (a) whether the client is suspected of having a contagious disease, such as diphtheria, which requires special precautions; and (b) whether a specimen is required from the nasal cavity as well as from the pharynx and/or the tonsils.

PURPOSE

• To identify the presence of specific organisms and their drug sensitivities.

ASSESSMENT FOCUS

Appearance of nasal mucosa and throat (note in particular areas of inflammation and purulent drainage); complaints of soreness or tenderness; clinical signs of infection (e.g., fever, chills, fatigue).

EQUIPMENT

❏ Gloves
❏ Two sterile swabs in sterile culture tubes
❏ Penlight
❏ Tongue blade (optional)

❏ Otoscope with a nasal speculum (optional)
❏ Container for the used nasal speculum

❏ Completed labels for each specimen container
❏ Completed laboratory requisition

INTERVENTION

1. **Prepare the client and the equipment.**

• Assist the client to a sitting position. *This is the most comfortable position for many people and the one in which the pharynx is most readily visible.*

• Don gloves in case the client's mucosa is touched.

• Open the culture tube and place it on the sterile wrapper. *This prevents microorganisms from entering the tube.*

• Remove one sterile applicator, and hold it carefully by the stick end, keeping the remainder sterile. *The swab end is kept from touching any objects that could contaminate it.*

2. **Collect the specimen.**

For a Throat Specimen

• Ask the client to open the mouth, extend the tongue, and say "ah." *When the tongue is extended, the pharynx is exposed. Saying "ah" relaxes the throat muscles and helps minimize contraction of the constric-*tion muscle of the pharynx (the gag reflex).

• Use the penlight to illuminate the posterior pharynx while depressing the tongue with a tongue blade. Depress the tongue firmly without touching the throat (Figure 47–2). *Touching the throat stimulates the gag reflex.*

• Insert a swab into the mouth without touching any part of the mouth or tongue. *The swab should not pick up microorganisms in the mouth.*

• Quickly run the swab along the tonsils, making sure to contact any areas on the pharynx that are particularly erythematous (reddened) or that contain exudate. *By moving the swab quickly, you can avoid initiating the gag reflex or causing discomfort. Erythematous areas and areas with exudate will likely have the most microorganisms.*

• Remove the swab without touching the mouth or lips. *This prevents the swab from transmitting microorganisms to the mouth.*

• Insert the swab into the sterile tube containing transport medium without allowing it to touch the outside of the container. Make sure the swab is placed in the correctly labeled tube. *Touching the outside of the tube could transmit microorganisms to it and then to others.*

• Crush the ampule of culture medium at the bottom of the tube and push the swab into the medium.

• Place the top securely on the tube, taking care not to touch the inside of the cap. *Touching the inside of the cap could transmit additional microorganisms into the tube.*

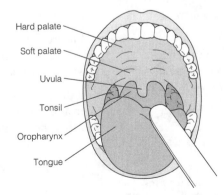

Hard palate
Soft palate
Uvula
Tonsil
Oropharynx
Tongue

Figure 47–2 Diagram of the mouth.

▶ Procedure 47–2 Obtaining Nose and Throat Specimens *continued*

- Repeat the above steps with the second swab.

- Discard the tongue blade in the waste container.

- Discard gloves.

For a Nasal Specimen

- If using a nasal speculum, gently insert the lighted speculum up one nostril.

- Insert the sterile wire swab carefully through the speculum, without touching the edges. *This*

prevents the swab from picking up microorganisms from the speculum. When working without a speculum, pass the swab along the septum and the floor of the nose.

- After passing the swab about 3 to 4 inches into the nasopharynx, rotate the swab.

- Remove the swab without touching the speculum, and place it in a sterile tube.

- Repeat the above steps for the other nostril.

3. Label and transport the specimens to the laboratory.

- See Procedure 47–1, step 4.

4. Document all relevant information.

- Record the collection of the nose and/or throat specimens on the client's chart. Include the assessments of the nasal mucosa and pharynx, and any discomfort the client experienced.

EVALUATION FOCUS

Appearance of nasal mucosa and throat; color of any drainage; any complaints of the client.

SAMPLE RECORDING

Date	Time	Notes
06/22/04	0800	Throat specimen for culture and sensitivity sent to lab. Throat is inflamed with patches of yellow discharge on tonsillar pillars. Unable to swallow fluids without soreness.————————Glenda Irvine, RN

LIFESPAN CONSIDERATIONS

Younger Clients

- The young child will need to be restrained gently while the specimens are collected. Allow the parents to assist, and explain that the procedure will be over quickly and isn't painful.

- Do not use a tongue depressor if signs of epiglottitis are present (drooling and a croaking sound with inspiration). *The tongue depressor can cause a laryngospasm, which may obstruct the airway.*

- Observe the young client for signs of an ear infection (e.g., rubbing the ears). *A child's short respiratory tract allows bacteria to migrate easily to the ears.*

- Avoid occluding an infant's nose. *Infants normally breathe only through the nose.*

Older Clients

- Older clients are vulnerable to upper respiratory infections due to decreased ciliary activity, dry mucous membranes, and decreased coughing ability.

HOME CARE CONSIDERATIONS

- Use a private area of the home to obtain the specimens, and place supplies on a clean towel or pad.

- Pack the culture tubes in a plastic biohazard bag and store in a container marked "biohazard."

- Transport the specimens in a cooler with ice and take them to the laboratory as quickly as possible. Avoid exposing specimens to extreme temperatures in the car.

- Ensure that the laboratory knows where the results should be reported. Call the physician immediately with abnormal or critical results.

- If the client is debilitated by a respiratory infection, ensure that a caregiver is available in the home. Instruct the caregiver to provide rest and extra fluids.

47–3 Assisting a Client to Use a Sustained Maximal Inspiration (SMI) Device

Before assisting a client to use an SMI device, determine the prescribed inspiratory volume level.

PURPOSES

- To improve pulmonary ventilation
- To counteract the effects of anesthesia and/or hypoventilation
- To loosen respiratory secretions
- To facilitate respiratory gaseous exchange
- To expand collapsed alveoli

ASSESSMENT FOCUS

Vital signs; breathing pattern (rhythm, ease or effort of breathing, volume); chest movements (retractions, flail chest); character of secretions and cough; breath sounds; presence of pallor or cyanosis; presence of clinical signs of hypoxia (e.g., restlessness, increased heart rate, anxiety, rapid or deep respirations); location of a surgical incision that could impede lung expansion.

EQUIPMENT

- ❏ Flow-oriented or volume-oriented SMI
- ❏ Mouthpiece or breathing tube
- ❏ Label for mouthpiece
- ❏ Nose clip (optional)

INTERVENTION

1. Prepare the client.

- Explain the procedure.

- Assist the client to an upright sitting position in bed or in a chair. If the person is unable to assume a sitting position for a flow spirometer, have the person assume any position. *A sitting position facilitates maximum ventilation of the lungs.*

For a Flow-Oriented SMI

2. Set the spirometer.

- If the spirometer has an inspiratory volume-level pointer, set the pointer at the prescribed level. The physician's or respiratory therapist's order should indicate the level.

3. Instruct the client to use the spirometer as follows:

- Hold the spirometer in the upright position. *A tilted spirometer requires less effort to raise the balls or discs.*

- Exhale normally.

- Seal the lips tightly around the mouthpiece; take in a slow deep breath to elevate the balls: and then hold the breath for 2 seconds initially, increasing to 6 seconds (optimum), to keep the balls elevated if possible. Instruct the client to avoid brisk low-volume breaths that snap the balls to the top of the chamber. The client may use a noseclip if the person has difficulty breathing only through the mouth. *A slow, deep breath ensures maximal ventilation. Greater lung expansion is achieved with a very slow inspiration than with a brisk shallow breath, even though a slow inspiration may not elevate or keep the balls elevated while the client holds the breath (Luce,* Tyler, and Pierson 1984). *Sustained elevation of the balls ensures adequate alveolar ventilation.*

- Remove the mouthpiece, and exhale normally.

- Cough productively, if possible and not contraindicated, after using the spirometer. *Deep ventilation may loosen secretions, and coughing can facilitate their removal.*

- Relax, and take several normal breaths before using the spirometer again.

- Repeat the procedure several times and then one or two times hourly. *Practice increases inspiratory volume, maintains alveolar ventilation, and prevents atelectasis.*

For a Volume-Oriented SMI

4. Set the spirometer.

- Set the spirometer to the predetermined volume. Check the

▶ Procedure 47–3 Assisting a Client to Use an SMI Device *continued*

physician's or respiratory therapist's order.

- Since some SMIs are battery-operated, ensure that the spirometer is functioning. Place the device on the client's bedside table.

5. **Instruct the client to use the spirometer as follows:**

- Exhale normally.

- Seal the lips tightly around the mouthpiece, and take in a slow, deep breath until the piston is elevated to the predetermined level. The piston level may be visible to the client, or lights or the word "Hold" may be illuminated to identify the volume obtained.

- Hold the breath for 6 seconds to ensure maximal alveolar ventilation.

- Remove the mouthpiece, and exhale normally.

- Cough productively, if possible and not contraindicated, after using the spirometer. *Deep ventilation may loosen secretions, and coughing can facilitate their removal.*

- Relax, and take several normal breaths before using the spirometer again.

- Repeat this procedure several times and then one or two times hourly. *Practice increases inspiratory volume, maintains alveolar ventilation, and prevents atelectasis.*

For All Devices

6. **Clean the equipment.**

- Clean the mouthpiece with water, and shake it dry. Label the mouthpiece and a disposable SMI with the client's name. A disposable SMI may be left at the bedside for the client to use as prescribed. *Only the mouthpiece of a*

volume SMI is stored with the client because volume SMIs are used by many clients. Change the disposable mouthpieces every 24 hours.

7. **Document all relevant information.**

- Record the procedure, including type of spirometer, number of breaths taken, volume or flow levels achieved, and results of auscultation.

- For a flow SMI, calculate the volume achieved by multiplying the setting by the length of time the client kept the balls elevated. For example, if the setting was 500 mL and the balls were kept suspended for 2 seconds, the volume is 500×2, or 1000 mL.

- For a volume SMI, take the volume directly from the spirometer (e.g., 1500 mL).

EVALUATION FOCUS

> Sounds heard on auscultation of the lungs to compare with those heard before procedure.

SAMPLE RECORDING

Date	Time	Notes
07/06/04	1100	Instructed in use of Triflo II spirometer. 5 breaths taken at volume of 1,000 mL (500 mL × 2 sec). Bilateral breath sounds normal on auscultation before and after spirometry.————Nicholas Coscos, SN

LIFESPAN CONSIDERATIONS

- The SMI device can be a game for young clients. Demonstrate the procedure beforehand, and show the child how to take slow, deep breaths.

- Nasal clips may be needed if the younger client doesn't understand how to prevent breathing through the nose.

HOME CARE CONSIDERATIONS

- Show the client how to use and clean the SMI device.

- Make certain the client understands how often to use the SMI and how to document the volume achieved.

- Evaluate the client's ability and willingness to follow instructions and comply with treatment.

47–4 Administering Percussion, Vibration, and Postural Drainage (PVD) to Adults

Before administering PVD to an adult client, determine (a) the lung segments affected; (b) the ordered sequence of percussion, vibration, and postural drainage and the length of time specified; (c) whether the bronchodilator or moisturizing nebulization therapy is ordered prior to the postural drainage (secretions are easier to raise after the bronchi are dilated and secretions are thinned); and (d) preexisting or potential respiratory conditions.

PURPOSES
- To assist the removal of accumulated secretions
- To prevent the accumulation of secretions in clients at risk, e.g., the unconscious and those receiving mechanical ventilation

ASSESSMENT FOCUS

> Lung sounds by auscultation; whether the cough is productive or nonproductive; color, amount, and character of expectoration; rate, depth, and pattern of respirations; vital signs.

EQUIPMENT
- Bed that can be placed in Trendelenburg's position
- Pillows
- Gown or pajamas
- Towel
- Sputum container
- Tissues
- Mouthwash
- Specimen label and requisition, if a specimen of sputum is required
- Suction, as needed

INTERVENTION

1. **Prepare the client.**

- Provide visual and auditory privacy. *Coughing and expectorating secretions can embarrass the client and disturb others.*

- Explain which positions the client will need to assume, and explain about percussion and vibration techniques.

2. **Assist the client to the appropriate position for the postural drainage.**

- Use pillows to support the client comfortably in the required positions.

3. **Percuss the affected area.**

- Ensure that the area to be percussed is covered by a gown or towel. *Percussing the skin directly can cause discomfort.*

- Ask the client to breathe slowly and deeply. *Slow deep breathing promotes relaxation.*

- Cup your hands (i.e., hold your fingers and thumb together, and flex them slightly to form a cup, as you would to scoop up water). *Cupped hands trap the air against the chest. The trapped air sets up vibrations through the chest wall to the secretions, helping to loosen them.*

- Relax your wrists, and flex your elbows. *Relaxed wrists and flexed elbows help obtain a rapid, hollow, popping action.*

- With both hands cupped, alternately flex and extend the wrists rapidly to slap the chest (Figure 47–3). *The hands must remain cupped so that the air cushions the impact and injury to the client can be avoided.*

- Percuss each affected lung segment for 1 to 2 minutes. The per-

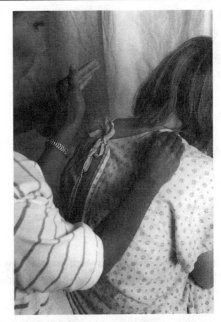

Figure 47–3 Percussing the upper posterior chest.

cussing action should produce a hollow, popping sound when done correctly.

▶ **Procedure 47–4 Administering PVD to Adults** *continued*

4. Vibrate the affected area.

- Place your flattened hands, one over the other (or side by side) against the affected chest area (Figure 47–4).

- Ask the client to inhale deeply through the mouth and exhale slowly through pursed lips or the nose.

- During the exhalation, straighten your elbows, and lean slightly against the client's chest while tensing your arm and shoulder muscles in isometric contractions. *Isometric contractions will transmit fine vibrations through the client's chest wall.*

- Vibrate during five exhalations over one affected lung segment.

- Encourage the client to cough and expectorate secretions into

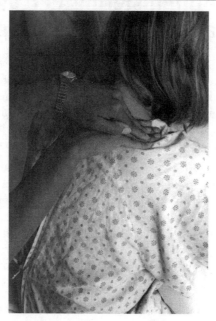

Figure 47–4   Vibrating the upper posterior chest.

the sputum container. Offer the client tissues and mouthwash as required. *Secretions may leave a foul taste in the mouth.*

- Auscultate the client's lungs, and compare the findings to the baseline data.

5. Label and transport the specimen, if obtained.

- Ensure that the specimen label and requisition carry the correct information.

- Arrange for the specimen to be sent to the laboratory immediately, or refrigerated.

6. Document the percussion, vibration, and postural drainage and assessments.

EVALUATION FOCUS

Amount, appearance, and character of secretions; tolerance of therapy (note signs of intolerance such as pallor, diaphoresis, dyspnea, or fatigue); change in breath sounds and rate, depth, and pattern of respirations.

SAMPLE RECORDING

Date	Time	Notes
06/06/04	0600	PVD for right anterior basal segment performed for 5 mm. Large amount thick grey sputum produced. Specimen sent to lab. No pain or dyspnea. Inspiratory crackles unchanged.————————————————————————Robert Loo, RN

LIFESPAN CONSIDERATIONS

- Modify the positions as needed for older clients. *Persons with arthritis or decreased joint flexibility may have difficulty assuming and holding the positions.*

- Allow rest periods for older clients, especially if shortness of breath is noted.

- Provide extra blankets for warmth. *Older clients have decreased ability to maintain the body temperature.*

HOME CARE CONSIDERATIONS

- Perform the procedure in a private area of the home, if possible. Allow the client to choose the location.

- Use rolled up towels or blankets if extra pillows are not available.

- If frequent treatments are ordered, teach a caregiver how to perform the procedure.

PVD for Infants and Children

Percussion, vibration, and postural drainage for infants and children is similar to that for the adult. It is usually performed three to four times daily and is more effective following bronchodilation and/or nebulization therapy. The length and duration of therapy depend on the child's condition and tolerance. To minimize the chance of vomiting, PVD is performed before meals (or 1 to 1½ hours after meals) and at bedtime. In a hospital setting, an older child can be positioned over the elevated knee rest of the hospital bed. Smaller children and infants can be positioned with pillows or over the nurse's lap.

Various methods may be employed to stimulate deep breathing, such as blowing feathers, blowing up balloons, using whistle toys, or using blow bottles designed to move colored liquid from one container to another.

Because many children have difficulty coughing when in a dependent position, they should be allowed to sit up while they cough. The nurse can also reinforce the child's efforts by encircling the chest with the hands and compressing the sides of the lower chest during the cough.

For an infant whose chest is too small for conventional hand percussion, a small face mask or bulb syringe cut in half can be used. Cut the syringe, leaving the nozzle with one half, and tape the cut edge to cushion it. Hold the bulb by the nozzle for percussion (Figure 47–5 on page 146). To make a vibrator for an infant, remove the brush from a portable electric toothbrush and tape padding over the vibrating end.

Procedure 47–5 explains how to provide PVD to infants and children.

47–5 Administering Percussion, Vibration, and Postural Drainage (PVD) to Infants and Children

Before administering PVD to an infant or child, determine (a) the lung segments affected; (b) the ordered sequence of percussion, vibration, and postural drainage and the length of time specified; (c) whether the bronchodilator or moisturizing nebulization therapy is ordered prior to the postural drainage (secretions are easier to raise after the bronchi are dilated and secretions are thinned); and (d) preexisting or potential respiratory conditions.

PURPOSES
- To assist the removal of accumulated secretions
- To prevent the accumulation of secretions

ASSESSMENT FOCUS

> Lung sounds; whether the cough is productive or nonproductive; color, amount, and character of expectorations; rate, depth, and pattern of respirations; vital signs.

EQUIPMENT

- ❏ Pillows
- ❏ Gown or shirt and diapers
- ❏ Towel
- ❏ Face mask or other percussion device for small infant

- ❏ Sputum container (optional)
- ❏ Tissues
- ❏ Mouthwash, if the child is old enough to use it

- ❏ Suction apparatus as required
- ❏ Specimen label and requisition, if a specimen of sputum is required

▶Procedure 47–5 Administering PVD to Infants and Children *continued*

INTERVENTION

1. Prepare the infant or child.

- Provide an explanation that is suitable to the child's age.

- Assist the child to the appropriate position for postural drainage.

- Use pillows to support the client comfortably in the required positions.

2. Perform PVD as ordered.

- Percuss the affected area, using a percussion device if appropriate (Figure 47–5) or three fingertips flexed and held together.

- Vibrate the affected area as appropriate, using a vibrator

Figure 47–5 A bulb syringe modified for chest percussion.

appropriate to the child's age. See Procedure 47–4, step 4.

- Instruct the child to sit up, and encourage deep breathing and coughing to remove loosened secretions.

or

Suction airway.

- Repeat percussion, vibration, deep breathing, and coughing for each lobe requiring drainage.

3. Document the PVD and all assessments.

- See Sample Recording in Procedure 47–4.

EVALUATION FOCUS

Changed breath sounds; cough; amount, color, and character of expectorated secretions; rate, depth, and pattern of respirations; dyspnea; tolerance of treatment.

HOME CARE CONSIDERATIONS

- If frequent treatments are ordered, teach a parent or caregiver to perform PVD at home. Ask for a return demonstration of the procedure.

- Emphasize the importance of performing PVD before meals to prevent vomiting.

- Instruct the caregiver in the signs of respiratory infection, such as thick, purulent secretions, fever, and increased coughing.

- Consider performing the procedure away from the child's bedroom, so the room does not become associated with treatments.

Infant Bulb Suctioning

A bulb syringe is frequently used to suction the oral and nasal cavities of infants and children, particularly when secretions are not severe enough to require deeper suctioning. This technique may be used for a newborn who has amniotic fluid in the air passages or an infant with increased mucus that is causing labored breathing. The technique requires medical aseptic practice rather than surgical asepsis, since only the mouth or nose is entered, not the pharynx. The bulb syringe should be sterile initially, but it can be rinsed and used for subsequent suctions without resterilizing. The same syringe can be used for the nose and mouth. See Procedure 47–6.

47–6 Bulb Suctioning an Infant

PURPOSES
- To establish and maintain a patent airway
- To prevent or relieve labored respirations

ASSESSMENT FOCUS

Rate and depth of respirations; presence or absence of breath sounds and chest movements: color and pulse rate; color, consistency, and amount of secretions.

EQUIPMENT

- ❏ Large towel or blanket
- ❏ Clean towel or bib
- ❏ Bulb syringe
- ❏ Kidney basin or other receptacle
- ❏ Disposable gloves as needed

INTERVENTION

1. **Position the infant appropriately for the procedure.**

- Bundle the infant in a large towel or blanket to restrain the arms, or cradle the child in your arm, tucking the infant's near arm behind your back and holding the other arm securely with your hand (Figure 47–6).

- Put the bib or towel under the infant's chin.

2. **Suction the oral and nasal cavities.**

- Compress the bulb of the syringe with your thumb before inserting the syringe (Figure 47–7). *Compressing the bulb while the tip is in the mouth or nose can force secretions deeper into the respiratory tract.*

- Keeping the bulb compressed, insert the tip of the syringe into the infant's nose or mouth.

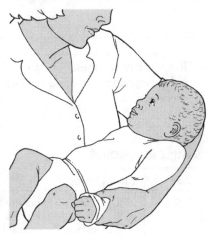

Figure 47–6 Restraining the arms of an infant for bulb suctioning. The infant's right arm is tucked behind the nurse's back.

- Release the bulb compression gradually, and slowly move it outward to aspirate the secretions.

- Remove the syringe, hold the tip over the waste receptacle, and compress the bulb again.

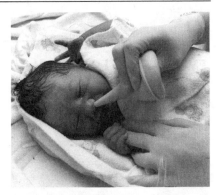

Figure 47–7 Maintaining compression of the bulb of the syringe during insertion into the nose. *Source:* S. B. Olds, M. L. London, and P. W. Ladewig, *Maternal-newborn nursing: A family-centered approach,* 4th ed. (Redwood City, Calif.: Addison-Wesley Nursing, 1992), p. 899.

Compressing the bulb expels the contents into the waste receptacle.

- Repeat the above until the infant's nares and mouth are clear of secretions and the breathing sounds are clear.

▶ Procedure 47–6 Bulb Suctioning an Infant *continued*

3. Ensure infant comfort and safety.

- Cuddle and soothe the infant as necessary; and place the infant in a side-lying position after suctioning. *In a back-lying position, the infant is more likely to aspirate secretions.*

4. Ensure availability of the equipment for the next suction.

- Rinse the syringe and the waste receptacle.

- Place the syringe in a clean folded towel at the cribside for use as needed.

5. Document all relevant information.

- Report to the nurse in charge any problems or untoward responses of the infant.

- Record the procedure and relevant observations in the appropriate records.

VARIATION: The DeLee Suction Device (Mucus Trap)

The DeLee mucus trap is a negative-pressure mouth suction device used for infants (Figure 47–8). To use the device, carefully insert the catheter to 12 cm (3 to 5 in) into the infant's nose or mouth without applying suction, and connect the other end to low suction. Apply suction as the tube is removed. Continue to reinsert the tube and provide suction as long as fluid is aspirated. Avoid excessive suctioning. *This can cause vagal stimulation and subsequent bradycardia.*

The DeLee device is commonly used in the delivery room to clear the neonate's nose, mouth, and pharynx of mucus and amniotic fluid and to initiate breathing. Suctioning of the mouth is often needed as soon as the neonate's head presents. The mouth is suctioned before the nose. *Nasal stimulation can precipitate the sneezing reflex and cause the infant to inhale and aspirate any secretions in the mouth.*

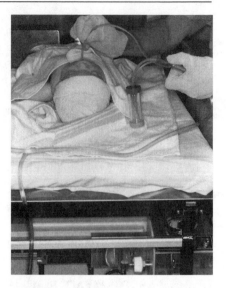

Figure 47–8 Suctioning a neonate using the DeLee suction device. *Source:* S. B. Olds, M. L. London, and P. W. Ladewig, *Maternal-newborn nursing: A family-centered approach,* 4th ed. (Redwood City, Calif.: Addison-Wesley Nursing, 1992), p. 678.

Suctioning is often repeated after the neonate's first cry.

EVALUATION FOCUS

Response to suctioning in terms of respiratory rate, rhythm, and depth; pulse rate and rhythm; skin color; and appearance of secretions suctioned.

SAMPLE RECORDING

Date	Time	Notes
11/02/04	0730	Admitted to nursery from delivery room. Color pink, P 142, R 30. Clear mucous drainage removed from mouth and nose with bulb syringe. Placed in side-lying position.————Kay Kergstra, RN

HOME CARE CONSIDERATIONS

- Teach the parents or caregiver how to use the bulb syringe at home.

- Emphasize the importance of placing the infant in a side-lying position to prevent aspiration.

- Teach the parents that keeping the nasal passages clear is important because infants normally breathe only through the nose.

Humidity Tent and Incubator

A variety of humidity/oxygen tents are available for children beyond early infancy until they are old enough to cooperate and use a nasal cannula. Each unit generally comes with the manufacturer's instructions for use. However, all have common elements. The tent consists of a rectangular, clear, plastic canopy with outlets that connect to an oxygen or compressed air source and to a humidifier that moisturizes the air or oxygen (Figure 47–9). Because the enclosed tent becomes very warm, some type of cooling mechanism such as an ice chamber or a refrigeration unit is provided to maintain the desired temperature. Administering oxygen by humidity tent is discussed in Procedure 47–7.

Figure 47–9   A humidity tent.

47–7 Administering Oxygen by Humidity Tent

Before administering oxygen by humidity tent, determine (a) whether the damper valve is to be kept open, kept partially open, or intermittently closed and opened; and (b) whether aerosol medications are to be administered. Check the physician's orders.

PURPOSES
- To facilitate breathing by humidifying respiratory membranes and loosening secretions
- To increase blood oxygenation levels if oxygen is required
- To cool the body and reduce body temperature to normal range

ASSESSMENT FOCUS

See Procedure 47–2 in *Fundamentals of Nursing*.

EQUIPMENT
- ❑ Gown or cotton blanket
- ❑ Humidity tent
- ❑ Ice
- ❑ Sterile distilled water
- ❑ Oxygen source or compressed air
- ❑ Additional gowns and bath blankets
- ❑ Small pillow or rolled towel

INTERVENTION
1. **Verify the physician's orders.**

2. **Prepare the child.**

- Provide an explanation appropriate to the age of the child, and offer emotional support.

- Cover the child with a gown or a cotton blanket. Some agencies provide gowns with hoods, or a small towel may be wrapped around the head. *The child needs protection from chilling and from the dampness and condensation in the tent.*

3. **Prepare the humidity tent.**

- Close the zippers on each side of the tent.

- Fanfold the front part of the canopy into the bedclothes or into an overlying drawsheet, and ensure that all sides of the canopy are tucked well under the mattress (Figure 47–9, earlier).

- If cool mist is ordered, fill the trough with ice to the depth indicated by a line on the trough.

▶**Procedure 47–7 Administering Oxygen by Humidity Tent** *continued*

- Ensure that the drainage tube for the trough is in place.

- Fill the water reservoir with sterile distilled water. *The water moisturizes the air or the oxygen.*

- Connect the tent to the wall oxygen or compressed air.

- Flood the tent with oxygen by setting the flow meter at 15 liters per minute for about 5 minutes. Then, adjust the flow meter according to orders (e.g., 10 to 15 liters per minute). *Flooding the tent quickly increases the oxygen to the desired level.*

- Open the damper valve for about 5 minutes to increase humidity. The valve controls mist output and may be left open or partially open.

4. **Place the child in the tent, and assess the child's respiratory status.**

- Assess vital signs, skin color, breathing, and chest movements.

5. **Provide required care for the child.**

- Change the bedding and clothing as they become damp.

- Encourage parents to stay with the child. Allow the parents to take the child outside the tent to provide comfort if the child becomes fussy. *Crying increases oxygen consumption.*

- Monitor the child frequently for condition changes. *The mist inside the tent can make observation difficult.*

- The child can have toys inside the humidity tent, but stuffed toys should be discouraged because they absorb moisture.

- An infant can be placed in an infant seat within the humidity tent. *A more upright position helps mobilize secretions.*

6. **Monitor the functioning of the humidity tent.**

- Monitor air or oxygen flows frequently to maintain required concentrations, and ensure that all connections are airtight.

- Minimize opening of the tent to avoid lowering the prescribed oxygen concentration. Plan care accordingly.

- Monitor the concentration of oxygen inside the tent according to agency protocol.

- Maintain the temperature of the tent at 20C to 21C (68F to 70F).

7. **Document relevant data.**

- Record the initiation of therapy, all assessments, and the data from oxygen analyzer.

EVALUATION FOCUS

Vital signs; cough; skin color; lung sounds; signs of hypoxia, hypercarbia; blood gas levels.

SAMPLE RECORDING

Date	Time	Notes
05/5/04	0600	Placed in humidity tent. T 98.6, P 108, R 32, Slightly cyanotic. 02 set at 8 L/min., mist continuous.————————Nina Sims, SN
	0630	P 96, R 24, no cyanosis, Resting————————Nina Sims, SN

HOME CARE CONSIDERATIONS

- Evaluate the parents' ability and willingness to use the humidity tent correctly.

- Assess the home environment. The home must have electricity and running water and should be relatively free of rodents and insects.

- Teach the parents how to set up, use, and clean the humidity tent.

- Explain the need to prohibit smoking if the child is receiving oxygen. Battery-operated toys can spark or trigger an electric shock and cause a fire.

47–8 Inserting and Maintaining a Pharyngeal Airway

PURPOSES
- To prevent obstruction of the airway by the tongue of an unconscious client (oropharyngeal tube)
- To maintain a patent air passage for clients who have or may become obstructed

ASSESSMENT FOCUS

> Level of consciousness and presence or absence of gag reflex; clinical signs indicating need for airway (e.g., upper airway "gurgling," labored respiration, increased respiratory and pulse rates).

EQUIPMENT

- Disposable gloves
- Tongue blade (for oropharyngeal tube)
- Water-soluble lubricant or cool water
- Sterile oropharyngeal airway of the appropriate size (length should extend from the teeth to the end of the jawline)

or

- Nasopharyngeal airway of the appropriate size (diameter should be slightly narrower than the client's naris)
- Soft tissues or washcloth
- Topical anesthetic, if ordered (for nasopharyngeal tube)
- Tape
- Suction equipment

INTERVENTION

1. Insert the airway.

Oropharyngeal Airway

- Explain the procedure, even if the client is not alert. Check for and remove dentures.

- Place the client in a supine position with the neck hyperextended or with a pillow placed under the shoulders. *This position prevents the tongue from falling back to block the pharynx.* Note: This position may be contraindicated for clients with head, neck, or back injuries.

- Don disposable gloves, open the client's mouth, and place a tongue depressor on the anterior half of the tongue. *This flattens the tongue and facilitates airway insertion.*

- Lubricate the airway with a water-soluble lubricant or with cool water.

- Turn the airway upside down, with the curved end upward or sideways, and advance it along the roof of the mouth.

- When the airway passes the uvula (or is at the posterior half of the tongue), rotate the airway until the curve of the airway follows the natural curve of the tongue.

- Remove excess lubricant from the client's lips with a soft tissue or washcloth.

Nasopharyngeal Airway

- Determine the size of airway needed by measuring the diameter of the client's nostril and the distance from the tip of the nose to the ear lobe. Use an airway with slightly smaller diameter than the nostril and slightly longer length than measured.

- Assess the patency of each naris. Ask the client, if conscious, to breathe through one naris while occluding the other.

- Ask the client, if conscious, to blow the nose to clear it of excess secretions.

- Lubricate the entire tube with a topical anesthetic (if ordered). *This prevents irritation of the nasopharyngeal mucosa and undue discomfort.*

- Hold the airway by the wide end, and insert the narrow end into the naris, applying gentle inward and downward pressure when advancing the airway. Follow the natural course of the nasal passage.

- Advance the airway until the external horn fits against the outer naris.

- If resistance is felt, try the other naris.

- Remove excess lubricant from the nares, as required.

2. Tape the airway in position, if required. *Stabilizing the airway maintains the airway's position and prevents injury to the oropharyngeal or nasopharyngeal mucosa. Smith and Johnson (1990) recommend the following method:*

- Prepare two long strips of tape–one 35 cm (14 in), and the other 60 cm (24 in). This should be performed before donning the gloves.

▶ Procedure 47–8 Inserting and Maintaining a Pharyngeal Airway *continued*

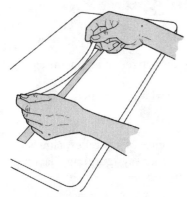

Figure 47–10 Attaching the shorter tape over the center of the longer tape.

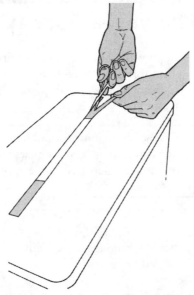

Figure 47–11 Splitting one end of the longer tape.

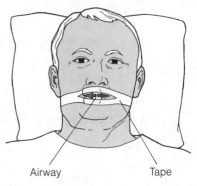

Airway   Tape

Figure 47–12 An oral airway taped in place.

- Lay the longer strip down, sticky side up.

- Place the shorter strip, sticky side down, over the center (Figure 47–10).

- Split each end of the longer tape (Figure 47–11).

- Place the nonsticky tape under the client's neck.

- For an *oral airway*, press half of the split tape across the upper airway flange and the other across the lower flange (Figure 47–12).

  or

- For a *nasal airway*, press half of the split tape across the upper lip and the other half around the tube without occluding the nares. Repeat for the other side.

- In some agencies, airways are not taped in place. *Taping can delay removal of the airway in an emergency situation.*

3. Ensure the client's comfort and safety.

Oropharyngeal Tube

- Maintain the client in a lateral or semiprone position so that any blood, vomitus, and mucus will drain out of the mouth and not be aspirated.

- Suction secretions as required.

- Provide mouth care at least every 4 hours, and check mucous membranes for ulceration.

- Remove the airway once the client has regained consciousness and has the swallow, gag, and cough reflexes.

Nasopharyngeal Tube

- Remove the tube, clean it in warm, soapy water, and insert it in the other nostril at least every 8 hours, or as ordered by the physician, to prevent irritation of the mucosa.

- Provide nasal hygiene every 4 hours or more often if needed.

4. Document all relevant information.

- Record the time the airway was inserted, type of airway inserted, client response to insertion, and character of any secretions suctioned.

▶ **Procedure 47–8** *continued*

EVALUATION FOCUS

Client response to insertion (e.g., comparison of respiratory rate and depth and pulse rate to baseline data); integrity of oral or nasal mucous membrane and lips; character of secretions suctioned.

SAMPLE RECORDING

Date	Time	Notes
04/6/04	0930	Responding to painful stimuli only. Gurgling during aspiration. R 14, P 88. Oral airway inserted. Clear secretions suctioned from mouth. Turned to L lateral position. Mouth care given. Skin on lips and oral mucous membrane intact.————————Mary Beth Holly, RN

LIFESPAN CONSIDERATIONS

- Older clients may need more frequent mouth care to keep the mucous membranes moist. *Oral secretions decrease with aging.*

- Use extra care not to bump the teeth when inserting or removing an airway for an older client. *Teeth become more brittle with aging due to enamel loss and retraction of gums.*

- When checking for a gag reflex, keep in mind that the gag reflex decreases with aging.

47–9 Plugging a Tracheostomy Tube

PURPOSE
- To establish ventilation through the natural airway

ASSESSMENT FOCUS

Vital signs and respiratory effort before plugging the tube; excessive secretions in the respiratory tract (may contraindicate plugging of the tube).

EQUIPMENT

- ❏ Suction apparatus
- ❏ Sterile suction catheters
- ❏ Sterile 10-mL syringe
- ❏ Sterile gloves
- ❏ Sterile tracheostomy plug

INTERVENTION

1. Position the client.

- Assist the client to a semi-Fowler's position if not contraindicated. *This position enhances lung expansion and may decrease fears about not being able to breathe.*

2. Suction the airways.

- Suction the client's nasopharynx and oropharynx if there are any secretions present.

- Change suction catheters and suction the tracheostomy. If there are excessive secretions, report this finding to the nurse in charge or physician to determine whether to proceed with the procedure.

3. Deflate the tracheal cuff if ordered.

- Suction the tracheostomy tube again if secretions are present.

4. Insert the tracheostomy plug.

- Using sterile gloves, fit the tracheostomy plug into either the inner or the outer cannula, depending on whether the tracheostomy tube has a double or single cannula.

- Monitor the client closely for 10 minutes for signs of respiratory distress, such as noisy and/or rapid respirations and use of accessory muscles for breathing. At the first signs of distress, remove the tracheostomy plug, and suction the tracheostomy if necessary.

- Clean the inner cannula, if it was removed, so that it is ready to be reinserted.

- Observe the client frequently while the tube is plugged.

5. Remove the plug at the designated time.

- After removing the plug, suction the tracheostomy if indicated, and replace the inner cannula if removed.

- Reinflate the cuff if ordered.

6. Document all relevant information.

- Document the amount, color, and consistency of the secretions, the times the plug was inserted and removed, and your assessments.

EVALUATION FOCUS

Respiratory status while the tube is plugged (e.g., breath sounds, respiratory rate, and the use of accessory muscles for breathing).

SAMPLE RECORDING

Date	Time	Notes
07/11/04	1500	P82 regular, R 14 and effortless. Tracheostomy tube plugged after suctioning nasopharynx and tracheostomy tube. Cuff deflated–2.5 mL air withdrawn.
	1515	Breathing effortless while plug in place, pulse rate and respiratory rate unchanged. Plug removed.————————Briona R. King, SN

▶ **Procedure 47–9** *continued*

LIFESPAN CONSIDERATIONS	HOME CARE CONSIDERATIONS
• Observe the older client carefully for signs of respiratory distress, and stress the importance of slow, deep breathing. *Decreased lung compliance is part of the aging process.*	• Suction equipment should be available in the home when performing this procedure.
• Teach the older client how to cough and breathe deeply to keep the airway clear. *Decreased ability to cough occurs with aging.*	• Use a clean, private area of the home for the procedure, and place equipment on a clean towel or drape.
	• Stay with the client while the tracheostomy is plugged, and observe for signs of respiratory distress.
	• Don't perform the procedure at home if the client is short of breath or extremely anxious. Have a plan of action in case problems occur, and notify the physician immediately.

47–10 Assisting with the Insertion of a Chest Tube

Prior to assisting with the insertion of a chest tube, verify that an informed consent has been obtained and that the client has been prepared for the procedure.

PURPOSES
- To remove air, fluid, and/or blood from the pleural space
- To allow full re-expansion of the lungs and relieve respiratory distress caused by pulmonary compression
- May be used to permit the administration of sclerosing agents in the treatment of malignant effusions

ASSESSMENT FOCUS

Respiratory rate, rhythm, and quality; vital signs, bilateral breath sounds; chest expansion and respiratory excursion; chest movements; presence/absence of retractions; dressing site; presence/absence of drainage and subcutaneous emphysema; level of comfort; client's emotional status.

EQUIPMENT

- ❏ Sterile chest tube tray, which includes:
  Drapes
  10-mL syringe
  Sponges
  1-in #22 gauge needle
  5/8-in #25 gauge needle
  Scalpel
  #11 blade
  Forceps
- ❏ Two rubber-tipped clamps for each tube inserted

- ❏ Several 4 × 4 gauze squares
- ❏ Split drain gauzes
- ❏ Chest tube with a trocar
- ❏ Suture materials (e.g., 2-0 silk with a needle)
- ❏ Pleural drainage system with sterile drainage tubing and connectors
- ❏ Y-connector, if two tubes will be inserted

- ❏ Sterile gloves for the physician and the nurse
- ❏ Vial of local anesthetic (e.g., 1% lidocaine) if required
- ❏ Alcohol sponges to clean the top of the vial
- ❏ Antiseptic (e.g., povidone-iodine)
- ❏ Tape (nonallergenic is preferable)
- ❏ Sterile petrolatum gauze (optional)

INTERVENTION

1. Prepare the client.

- Explain the procedure to the client and family.

- Explain placement and rationale for chest tube(s) to the client and family.

- Position the client as directed by the physician, with the area to receive the tube facing upward. Determine from the physician whether to have the bed in the supine position or semi-Fowler's position. *A supine position is generally preferred for tube insertion into the second or third intercostal space, a*

semi-Fowler's position for the sixth to eighth intercostal spaces.

2. Prepare the equipment.

- Open the chest tube tray and the sterile gloves on the overbed table.

- Assist the physician to clean the insertion site with povidone-iodine solution, as needed.

- After cleansing rubber stopper of local anesthetic with an alcohol swab, invert vial and hold it for physician to aspirate the medication.

- Once the tube is inserted, assist with clamping or connecting the tube to the thoracic drainage system.

- Be sure to maintain sterile technique.

3. Provide emotional support and monitor the client as required.

4. Provide an airtight dressing.

After tube insertion:

- Don sterile gloves. Wrap a piece of sterile petrolatum gauze

▶ **Procedure 47–10** *continued*

around the chest tube. Place drain gauzes around the insertion site (one from the top and one from the bottom). Place several 4 × 4 gauze squares over these. *The gauze makes an airtight seal at the insertion site.*

- Remove your gloves and tape the dressings, covering them completely.

5. **Secure the chest tube appropriately.**

- Tape the chest tube to the client's skin away from the insertion site. *Taping prevents accidental dislocation of the tube.*

- Tape the connections of the chest tube to the drainage tube and to the drainage system. *Taping prevents inadvertent separation.*

- Coil the drainage tubing, and secure it to the bed linen, ensuring enough slack for the person to turn and move. *This prevents kinking of the tubing and impairment of the drainage system.*

6. **When all drainage connections are completed, ask the client to**

- Take a deep breath and hold it for a few seconds.

- Slowly exhale. *These actions facilitate drainage from the pleural space and lung re-expansion.*

7. **Prepare the client for a portable chest x-ray to check placement of the tube and lung re-expansion.**

8. **Ensure client safety.**

- Place rubber-tipped chest tube clamps at the bedside. *These are used to clamp the chest tube and prevent pneumothorax if the tube becomes disconnected from the drainage system or the system breaks or cracks.*

- Assess the client regularly for signs of pneumothorax and subcutaneous emphysema. *Subcutaneous emphysema can result from a poor seal at the chest tube insertion site. It is manifested by a "crackling" sound that is heard when the area around the insertion site is palpated. This doesn't present an immediate danger to the client, but should be reported, documented, and monitored.*

- Assess the client's vital signs every 15 minutes for the first hour following tube insertion and then as ordered, e.g., every hour for 2 hours, then every 4 hours or as often as the client's condition indicates.

- Auscultate the lungs at least every 4 hours for breath sounds and the adequacy of ventilation in the affected lung.

- Check for intermittent bubbling in the water of the water-seal bottle or chamber. *Intermittent bubbling normally occurs when the system removes air from the pleural space, especially when the client takes a deep breath or coughs. Absence of bubbling usually indicates that the pleural space has healed and is sealed, but it may also indicate obstructed tubing. Continuous bubbling or a sudden change from the established pattern can indicate a break in the system, such as an air leak, and should be reported immediately.*

- Check for gentle bubbling in the suction-control chamber or bottle. *Gentle bubbling indicates proper suction pressure.*

- Inspect the drainage in the collection container at least every 30 minutes during the first 2 hours after chest tube insertion and then every 2 hours. Report bright red bleeding or drainage over 100 cc per hour to the physician.

9. **Document relevant information.**

- Document the date and time of chest tube insertion and the name of the physician.

- Include the insertion site, drainage system used, presence of bubbling, characteristics of the drainage, vital signs, breath sounds by auscultation, and any other assessment findings.

▶ Procedure 47–10 Assisting with the Insertion of a Chest Tube *continued*

EVALUATION FOCUS

Respiratory rate, rhythm, and quality; vital signs; breath sounds; dressing and character, quality, and amount of any drainage; patency of drainage system and character, quality and amount of drainage; presence/absence of subcutaneous emphysema.

SAMPLE RECORDING

Date	Time	Notes
12/6/04	2200	Sudden sharp pain in L chest, diaphoretic, pale, and dyspneic.——————————Karen P. Smith, RN
12/6/04	2300	BP 100/70, TPR 98.6, 105, 24. Diminished breath sounds in L lung and absence of chest movement. Two chest tubes inserted by Dr. Jung in L 2nd and 8th CS. Connected by Y-connector and attached to Pleur-evac. Drainage system patent. Fluid level in water-seal chamber fluctuating with respiration. Drainage 25 cc clear amber.————————————Karen P. Smith, RN
12/6/04	2305	BP 110/70, TPR 98.6, 100, 20. Breath sounds present in L lung.——————————Karen P. Smith, RN

LIFESPAN CONSIDERATIONS

- Provide pillows and support to help the older client maintain the correct position. *Arthritis and joint stiffness can make position changes difficult.*

- Use care when applying tape to the skin of older clients. *Skin becomes thinner and less elastic with aging.*

- Teach the older client to cough and breathe deeply to help clear secretions and promote lung expansion. *Shallow breathing and decreased ability to cough can occur with aging.*

47–11 Monitoring a Client with Chest Drainage

PURPOSES
- To maintain patency of the chest drainage system and facilitate lung reexpansion
- To prevent complications associated with chest drainage (e.g., infection)

ASSESSMENT FOCUS

See Intervention, step 1.

EQUIPMENT

To Remedy Tube Problems
- ❏ Sterile gloves
- ❏ Two rubber-tipped Kelly clamps
- ❏ Sterile petrolatum gauze
- ❏ Sterile drainage system
- ❏ Antiseptic swabs
- ❏ Sterile 4 × 4 gauzes
- ❏ Air-occlusive tape

To Milk Tubing
- ❏ Lubricating gel, soap, hand lotion, or alcohol sponge

To Obtain a Specimen
- ❏ Povidone-iodine swab
- ❏ Sterile #18 or #20 gauge needle

- ❏ 3- or 5-mL syringe
- ❏ Needle protector
- ❏ Label for the specimen container
- ❏ Laboratory requisition
- ❏ Sterile specimen container

INTERVENTION

1. Assess the client.

- Assess vital signs every 4 hours, or more often, as indicated.

- Determine ease of respirations, breath sounds, respiratory rate and depth, and chest movements.

- Monitor the client for signs of pneumothorax.

- Inspect the dressing for excessive and abnormal drainage, such as bleeding or foul-smelling discharge. Palpate around the dressing site, and listen for a crackling sound indicative of subcutaneous emphysema. *Subcutaneous emphysema can result from a poor seal at the chest tube insertion site. It is manifested by a "crackling" sound that is heard when the area around the insertion site is palpated.*

- Assess level of discomfort. *Analgesics often need to be administered before the client moves or does deep-breathing and coughing exercises.*

2. Implement all necessary safety precautions.

- Keep two 15- to 18-cm (6- to 7-in) rubber-tipped Kelly clamps within reach at the bedside, to clamp the chest tube in an emergency (e.g., if leakage occurs in the tubing).

- Keep one sterile petrolatum gauze within reach at the bedside to use with an air-occlusive material if the chest tube becomes dislodged.

- Keep an extra drainage system unit available in the client's room. To change the drainage system:

    a. Clamp the chest tube close to the insertion site with two rubber-tipped clamps placed in opposite directions (Figure 47–13).

    b. Reestablish a water-sealed drainage system and remove the clamps.

- Keep the drainage system below chest level and upright at all times, unless the chest tubes are clamped. *Keeping the unit below chest level prevents backflow of fluid from the drainage chamber into the*

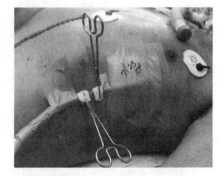

Figure 47–13 Clamping a chest tube.

pleural space. Keeping the unit upright maintains the glass tube below the water level, forming the water seal.

3. Maintain the patency of the drainage system.

- Check that all connections are secured with tape to ensure that the system is airtight.

- Inspect the drainage tubing for kinks or loops dangling below the entry level of the drainage system.

- Coil the drainage tubing and secure it to the bed linen, ensuring

▶ Procedure 47–11 Monitoring a Client with Chest Drainage *continued*

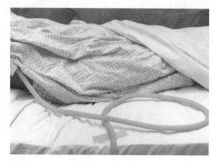

Figure 47–14 Coiled drainage tubing secured to the bed linen.

enough slack for the client to turn and move (Figure 47–14). *This prevents kinking of the tubing and impairment of the drainage system.*

- Inspect the air vent in the system periodically to make sure it is not occluded. A vent must be present to allow air to escape. *Obstruction of the air vent causes an increased pressure in the system that could result in pneumothorax.*

- Milk or strip the chest tubing **as ordered and only in accordance with agency protocol.** *Too vigorous milking can create excessive negative pressure that can harm the pleural membranes and/or surrounding tissues.* Always verify the physician's orders before milking the tube; milking of only short segments of the tube maybe specified (e.g., 10 to 20 cm, or 4 to 8 in). To milk a chest tube, follow these steps:

  a. Lubricate about 10 to 20 cm (4 to 8 in) of the drainage tubing with lubricating gel, soap, or hand lotion, or hold an alcohol sponge between your fingers and the tube. *Lubrication reduces friction and facilitates the milking process.*

  b. With one hand, securely stabilize and pinch the tube at the insertion site.

  c. Compress the tube with the thumb and forefinger of your other hand and milk it by sliding them down the tube,

moving away from the insertion site. *Milking the tubing dislodges obstructions such as blood clots. Milking from the insertion site downward prevents movement of the obstructive material into the pleural space.*

  d. If the entire tube is to be milked, reposition your hands farther along the tubing, and repeat steps **a** through **c** in progressive overlapping steps, until you reach the end of the tubing.

4. **Assess any fluid level fluctuations and bubbling in the drainage system.**

- In gravity drainage systems, check for fluctuation (tidaling) of the fluid level in the water-seal glass tube of a bottle system or the water-seal chamber of a commercial system as the client breathes. Normally, fluctuations of 5 to 10 cm (2 to 4 in) occur until the lung has reexpanded. In suction drainage systems, the fluid line remains constant. *Fluctuations reflect the pressure changes in the pleural space during inhalation and exhalation. The fluid level rises when the client inhales and falls when the client exhales. The absence of fluctuations may indicate tubing obstruction from a kink, dependent loop, blood clot, or outside pressure (e.g., because the client is lying on the tubing), or may indicate that full lung reexpansion has occurred.*

- To check for fluctuation in suction systems, temporarily turn off the suction. Then observe the fluctuation.

- Check for intermittent bubbling in the water of the water-seal bottle or chamber. *Intermittent bubbling normally occurs when the system removes air from the pleural space, especially when the client takes a deep breath or coughs. Absence of bubbling indicates that the pleural*

space has healed and is sealed. Continuous bubbling or a sudden change from an established pattern can indicate a break in the system, such as an air leak, and should be reported immediately.

- Check for gentle bubbling in the suction-control bottle or chamber. *Gentle bubbling indicates proper suction pressure.*

5. **Assess the drainage.**

- Inspect the drainage in the collection container at least every 30 minutes during the first 2 hours after chest tube insertion and every 2 hours thereafter.

- Every 8 hours, mark the time, date, and drainage level on a piece of adhesive tape affixed to the container or mark it directly on a disposable container (Figure 47–15).

- Note any sudden change in the amount or color of the drainage.

- If drainage exceeds 100 mL per hour or if a color change indicates hemorrhage, notify the physician immediately.

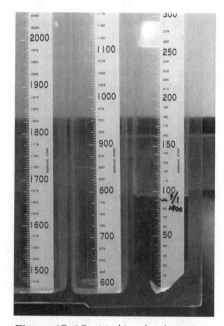

Figure 47–15 Marking the date, time, and drainage level.

▶ **Procedure 47–11** *continued*

6. **Watch for dislodgement of the tubes, and remedy the problem promptly.**

- If the chest tube becomes disconnected from the drainage system

  a. Have the client exhale fully.

  b. Clamp the chest tube close to the insertion site with two rubber-tipped clamps placed in opposite directions. *Clamping the tube prevents external air from entering the pleural space. Two clamps ensure complete closure of the tube.*

  c. Quickly clean the ends of the tubing with an antiseptic, reconnect them, and tape them securely.

  d. Unclamp the tube as soon as possible. *Having the client exhale and clamping the tube for no longer than necessary prevents an air or fluid buildup in the pleural space, which can cause further lung collapse.*

  e. Assess the client closely for respiratory distress (dyspnea, pallor, diaphoresis, blood-tinged sputum, or chest pain).

  f. Check vital signs every 10 minutes or as the client's condition indicates.

- If the chest tube becomes dislodged from the insertion site

  a. Remove the dressing, and immediately apply pressure with the petrolatum gauze, your hand, or a towel.

  b. Cover the site with a petrolatum gauze dressing and sterile 4 × 4 squares.

  c. Tape the dressings with air-occlusive tape.

  d. Notify the physician immediately.

  e. Assess the client for respiratory distress every 10 to 15

minutes or as client condition indicates.

- If the drainage system is accidentally tipped over

  a. Immediately return it to the upright position.

  b. Ask the client to take several deep breaths. *Deep breaths help force air out of the pleural cavity that might have entered when the water seal was not intact.*

  c. Notify the nurse in charge and assess the client for respiratory distress.

7. **If continuous bubbling persists in the water-seal collection chamber, indicating an air leak, determine its source.** *Continuous bubbling in the water-seal collection chamber normally occurs for only a few minutes after a chest tube is attached to drainage, because fluid and air initially rush out from the intrapleural space under high pressure.*

- To detect an air leak, follow the next steps sequentially (Quinn 1986 and Palau 1986):

  a. Check the tubing connection sites. Tighten and retape any connection that seems loose. *The tubing connection sites are the most likely places for leaks to occur. Bubbling will stop if these are the sources of the leak.*

  b. If bubbling continues, clamp the chest tube near the insertion site, and see whether the bubbling stops while the client takes several deep breaths. *Clamping the chest tube near the insertion site will help determine whether the leak is proximal or distal to the clamp. Chest tube clamping must be done only for a few seconds at a time. Clamping for long periods can aggravate an existing*

pneumothorax or lead to a recurrent pneumothorax.

  c. If bubbling stops, proceed with the next step. The source of the air leak is above the clamp, i.e., between the clamp and the client. It may be either at the insertion site or inside the client.

  d. If bubbling continues, the source of the air leak is below the clamp, i.e., in the drainage system below the clamp. See next step below.

- To determine whether the air leak is at the insertion site or inside the client:

  a. Unclamp the tube and palpate gently around the insertion site. If the bubbling stops, the leak is at the insertion site. To remedy this situation, apply a petrolatum gauze and a 4 × 4 gauze around the insertion site, and secure these dressings with adhesive tape.

  b. If the leak is not at the insertion site, it is inside the client and may indicate a dislodged tube or a new pneumothorax, a new disruption of the pleural space. In this instance, leave the tube unclamped, notify the physician, and monitor the client for signs of respiratory distress.

- To locate an air leak below the chest tube clamp

  a. Move the clamp a few inches farther down and keep moving it downward a few inches at a time. Each time the clamp is moved, check the water-seal collection chamber for bubbling. The bubbling will stop as soon as the clamp is placed between the air leak and the water-seal drainage.

▶ Procedure 47–11 Monitoring a Client with Chest Drainage *continued*

b. Seal the leak when you locate it by applying tape to that portion of the drainage tube.

c. If bubbling continues after the entire length of the tube is clamped, the air leak is in the drainage device. To remedy this situation, replace the drainage system according to agency protocol.

8. Take a specimen of the chest drainage as required.

- Specimens of chest drainage may be taken from a disposable chest drainage system because these systems are equipped with self-sealing ports. If a specimen is required

a. Use a povidone-iodine swab to wipe the self-sealing diaphragm on the back of the drainage collection chamber. Allow it to dry.

b. Attach a sterile #18 or #20 gauge needle to a 3- or 5-mL syringe, and insert the needle into the diaphragm (Figure 47–16).

c. Aspirate the specimen (discard the needle in the appropriate container), transfer the fluid to a sterile specimen container, label the container, and send it to the laboratory with the appropriate requisition form.

9. Ensure essential client care.

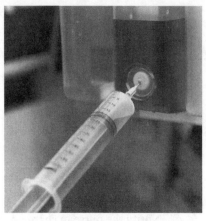

Figure 47–16 Obtaining a specimen through a self-sealing port.

- Encourage deep-breathing and coughing exercises every 2 hours if indicated (this may be contraindicated in clients with a lobectomy). Have the client sit upright to perform the exercises, and splint the tube insertion site with a pillow or with a hand to minimize discomfort. Provide pain medication, as ordered, before the exercise. *Deep breathing and coughing help remove accumulations from the pleural space, facilitate drainage, and help the lung to reexpand.*

- While the client takes deep breaths, palpate the chest for thoracic expansion. Place your hands together at the base of the sternum so that your thumbs meet. As the client inhales, your thumbs should separate at least 2.5 to 5 cm (1 to 2 in). Note whether chest expansion is symmetric.

- Reposition the client every 2 hours. When the client is lying on the affected side, place rolled towels beside the tubing. *Frequent position changes promote drainage, prevent complications, and provide comfort. Rolled towels prevent occlusion of the chest tube by the client's weight.*

- Assist the client with range-of-motion exercises of the affected shoulder three times per day to maintain joint mobility.

- When transporting and ambulating the client:

a. Attach rubber-tipped forceps to the client's gown for emergency use.

b. Keep the water-seal unit below chest level and upright.

c. Disconnect the drainage system from the suction apparatus before moving the client, and make sure the air vent is open.

10. Document all relevant information.

- Record patency of chest tubes; type, amount, and color of drainage; presence of fluctuations, appearance of insertion site; laboratory specimens taken; respiratory assessments; client's vital signs and level of comfort; and all other nursing care provided to the client.

► **Procedure 47–11** *continued*

EVALUATION FOCUS

Amount and appearance of drainage; rate, depth, and pattern of respirations; breath sounds, pulse, blood pressure, and body temperature; complaints of discomfort; status of chest tube insertion site; amount and appearance of insertion site drainage.

SAMPLE RECORDING

Date	Time	Notes
08/6/04	0800	Respirations 12 and effortless. Breath sounds auscultated in all lung lobes. Chest expansion is symmetric. T 37.6, P 78, BP 126/78. 25 mL of serosanguineous chest drainage in last hour. Fluid level in water-seal chamber fluctuating with respiration. Dressing dry and intact. Chest tubes intact.————————————Holly Wilson, RN

LIFESPAN CONSIDERATIONS

- Coughing and deep breathing exercises are especially important for older clients. *Shallow breathing and decreased ability to cough occur with aging.*

- Encourage the client to ask for pain medication as needed. *Older clients may be reluctant to take pain medication due to fears of addiction.*

- Use care when applying tape to the skin of older clients, and check bony prominences for skin breakdown. *Skin becomes thinner and less elastic with aging.*

47–12 Assisting with the Removal of a Chest Tube

PURPOSE

- To remove a chest tube when the lung is re-expanded

ASSESSMENT FOCUS

Respiratory rate, rhythm, and quality; vital signs, bilateral breath sounds; chest expansion and respiratory excursion; chest movements; presence/absence of retractions; dressing site; presence/absence of drainage and subcutaneous emphysema; level of comfort; client's emotional status.

EQUIPMENT

- ❏ Nonsterile gloves to remove the dressing
- ❏ Sterile gloves to remove the tube
- ❏ Sterile suture removal set, with forceps and suture scissors

- ❏ Sterile petrolatum gauze
- ❏ Several 4 × 4 gauze squares
- ❏ Air-occlusive tape, 2 or 3 in wide (nonallergenic is preferred)
- ❏ Absorbent linen-saver pad

- ❏ Moistureproof bag
- ❏ Sterile swabs or applicators in sterile containers to obtain a specimen (optional)

INTERVENTION

1. Prepare the client.

- Administer an analgesic, if ordered, 30 minutes before the tube is removed.

- Ensure that the chest tube is securely clamped. *Clamping prevents air from entering the pleural space.*

- Assist the client to a semi-Fowler's position or to a lateral position on the unaffected side.

- Put the absorbent pad under the client beneath the chest tube. *The pad protects the bed linen from drainage and provides a place for the chest tube after removal.*

- Instruct the client how to perform the Valsalva maneuver (exhale fully and bear down) when the physician removes the chest tube.

2. Prepare sterile field and sterile air-tight gauze.

- Open the sterile packages, and prepare a sterile field.

- Wearing sterile gloves, place the sterile petrolatum gauze on a 4 × 4 gauze square. *This will quickly provide an airtight dressing over the insertion site after the tube is removed.*

3. Remove the soiled dressing.

- Wearing gloves, be careful not to dislodge the tube when removing underlying gauzes.

- Discard soiled dressings in the moisture-resistant bag.

4. Assist with removal of the tube.

- While the physician takes out the sutures and removes the tube, assist the client to perform Valsalva's maneuver, and provide emotional support.

- Immediately apply the petrolatum gauze dressing over the insertion site and cover it with air-occlusive tape. *This makes the dressing as airtight as possible.*

5. Provide emotional support and monitor the client's response to removal of the chest tube.

6. Assess the client.

- Monitor the vital signs, and assess the quality of the respirations as the client's condition indicates (e.g., every 15 minutes for the first hour following tube removal and then less often or as condition indicates).

- Auscultate the client's lungs every hour for the first 4 hours to assess breath sounds and the adequacy of ventilation in the affected lung.

- Assess the client regularly for signs of pneumothorax, subcutaneous emphysema, and infection.

7. Document relevant information.

- Document the date and time of chest tube insertion or removal and the name of the physician.

- Include the amount, color, and consistency of drainage, and vital signs.

8. Prepare the client for a chest x-ray, which is usually done 1 to 2 hours after removal of chest tube to assess lung expansion.

▶ **Procedure 47–12** *continued*

EVALUATION FOCUS

Respiratory rate, rhythm, and quality; vital signs; breath sounds; dressing and character, quality, and amount of any drainage; presence/absence of subcutaneous emphysema.

SAMPLE RECORDING

Date	Time	Notes
12/12/04	1000	Chest tubes removed by Dr. Jung. 100 mL clear pink drainage. Occlusive dressing applied. Respirations are nonlabored. Denies discomfort. Bedside chest x-ray completed. BP 120/70, TPR 98.6, 76, 16.————————————————Susan March, RN

LIFESPAN CONSIDERATIONS

• Encourage older adults to perform frequent coughing and deep breathing exercises. *Shallow breathing and decreased ability to cough occur with aging.*

• Observe the older client carefully for signs of respiratory distress. *Decreased lung compliance is part of the aging process.*

Clearing an Obstructed Airway

There are several possible causes of airway obstruction and, as a result, several different ways of clearing an obstructed airway. Causes include

- Aspirated food, mucus plug, or foreign bodies, such as partial dentures or small toys. Food is the most common cause of choking, particularly meat that has been ineffectively chewed.
- Unconsciousness or seizures, which cause the tongue to fall back and block the airway.
- Severe trauma to the nose, mouth, or neck that produces blood clots that obstruct the airway, especially in unconscious victims.
- Acute edema of the trachea, from smoke inhalation, facial and neck burns, or anaphylaxis. In these instances, a tracheostomy is often indicated.

Foreign bodies may cause either partial or complete airway obstruction. When an airway is partially obstructed, the victim may have either good air exchange or poor air exchange. If sufficient air is obtained, even though there is frequent wheezing between coughs, do *not* interfere with the victim's attempts to expel the foreign object. Stay with the individual and call the emergency medical service (EMS). Partial obstructions with inadequate air exchange are dealt with in the same manner as complete obstructions.

The victim with complete airway obstruction is unable to speak, breathe, or cough and may clutch at the neck. *Subdiaphragmatic abdominal thrusts* (also known as the Heimlich maneuver) are recommended to relieve the obstruction for persons over 1 year of age. By elevating the diaphragm, this maneuver forces air from the lungs to create an artificial cough to expel the obstruction. It may be necessary to perform this maneuver numerous times to clear the airway. Abdominal thrusts can be performed when the victim is conscious and standing or sitting. For infants under 1 year of age, a combination of back blows and chest thrusts is recommended. Chest thrusts are used with clients who are pregnant or markedly obese.

Any individual who receives intervention to treat an obstructed airway should seek immediate follow-up medical evaluation, even if the person remains conscious and the airway is cleared with abdominal thrusts.

47-13   Clearing an Obstructed Airway

PURPOSE
- To clear an obstructed airway in order to permit adequate ventilation

ASSESSMENT FOCUS

> Patency of airway (inability to speak, breathe, or cough); hand(s) at throat (universal sign of choking); rate, rhythm, and quality of respirations, quality of cough; skin color; level of consciousness.

EQUIPMENT

❑ Mouth shield, if indicated
❑ Nonsterile gloves, if indicated

INTERVENTION

Abdominal Thrusts to a Standing or Sitting Victim

To perform abdominal thrusts to a conscious victim who is standing or sitting:

1. **Identify yourself as a trained rescuer.**

- Stand behind the victim, and wrap your arms around the victim's waist.

- Direct a bystander to contact EMS.

2. **Give abdominal thrusts.**

- Make a fist with one hand, tuck the thumb inside the first, and

place the flexed thumb just above the victim's navel and below the xiphoid process. (*A protruding thumb could inflict injury.*)

- With the other hand, grasp the fist (see Figure 47–17), and press it into the victim's abdomen with a firm, quick upward thrust (see Figure 47–18). Avoid tightening

▶ **Procedure 47–13** *continued*

Figure 47–17 The hand and fist position used to deliver abdominal thrusts to a conscious victim.

Figure 47–18 The position to provide abdominal thrusts to a conscious victim.

the arms around the rib cage, and thrust in the direction of the chin. Deliver quick upward thrusts.

- Deliver successive thrusts as separate and complete movements until the victim's airway clears or the victim becomes unconscious.

- If the victim becomes unconscious, lower the person carefully to the floor, supporting the head and neck to prevent injury.

Abdominal Thrusts to an Unconscious Victim Lying on the Ground

To implement abdominal thrusts to an unconscious victim who is lying on the ground:

1. Direct a bystander to contact EMS.

2. Open the airway.

- Tilt the victim's head back, lift the chin, and pinch the nose shut. Put on mouth shield, if available.

- Give two slow breaths.

- If unable to ventilate, re-tilt the head and repeat breaths.

3. Give abdominal thrusts.

- Straddle one or both of the victim's legs.

- Place the heel of one hand slightly above the victim's navel and well below the xiphoid process.

- Place the other hand directly on top of the first. Your shoulders should be over the victim's abdomen and your elbows should be straight.

- Point the fingers of both hands toward the victim's head and give five quick inward and upward abdominal thrusts. See Figure 47–19. Perform the thrusts to the middle of the abdomen, not to the left or right.

4. Check for foreign objects.

- Using your fingers and thumb, lift the victim's lower jaw and tongue. Slide one finger down in-

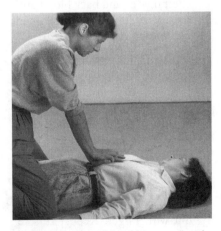

Figure 47–19 The position to provide abdominal thrusts to an unconscious victim.

side the victim's cheek and attempt to hook the object out, being careful not to push it down. In children, try hooking out the object only if you can see it.

5. Repeat abdominal thrusts, airway maneuvers, and foreign object checks until the airway clears or the victim breathes.

Chest Thrusts to a Conscious Standing or Sitting Victim

Chest thrusts are to be administered only to women in advanced stages of pregnancy and markedly obese persons who cannot receive abdominal thrusts. To administer chest thrusts:

1. Identify yourself as a trained rescuer.

- Stand behind the victim with your arms under the victim's armpits and encircling the victim's chest.

- Direct a bystander to contact EMS.

- Place the thumb side of the fist on the middle of the breast bone, not on the xiphoid process.

2. Deliver thrusts.

- Grab the fist with the other hand and deliver a quick backward thrust.

- Repeat thrusts until the obstruction is relieved or the victim becomes unconscious.

Chest Thrusts to an Unconscious Victim Lying Flat

Chest thrusts to unconscious victims lying on the ground are administered only to women in advanced stages of pregnancy or markedly obese persons. To administer this maneuver:

1. Open the airway.

- Tilt the victim's head back, lift the chin, and pinch the nose

▶ **Procedure 47–13 Clearing an Obstructed Airway** *continued*

shut. Put on mouth shield, if available.

- Give two slow breaths.

- If unable to ventilate, re-tilt the head and repeat breaths.

2. **Deliver thrusts.**

- Position the victim supine and kneel close to the side of the victim's trunk.

- Position the hands as for cardiac compression with the heel of the hand on the lower half of the sternum. (See Procedure 47–15, step 4.)

3. **Check for foreign objects.**

- Using your fingers and thumb, lift the victim's lower jaw and tongue. Slide one finger down inside the victim's cheek and attempt to hook the object out, being careful not to push it down.

4. **Repeat chest thrusts, airway maneuvers, and foreign object checks until the airway clears or the person breathes.**

Back Blows and Chest Thrusts for Infants

To administer a combination of back blows and chest thrusts to infants:

1. **Deliver back blows.**

- Straddle the infant over your forearm with his or her head lower than the trunk.

- Support the infant's head by firmly holding the jaw in the hand.

- Rest your forearm on your thigh.

- With the heel of the free hand, deliver five sharp blows to the back over the spine between the shoulder blades. (See Figure 47–20.)

2. **Deliver chest thrusts.**

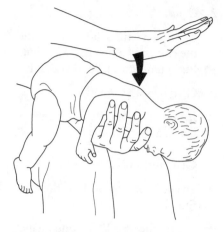

Figure 47–20 The correct position to administer back blows to an infant.

- Turn the infant as a unit to the supine position:

    a. Place the free hand on the infant's back.

    b. While continuing to support the jaw, neck, and chest with the other hand, turn and place the infant on the thigh with the baby's head lower than the trunk.

- Using two fingers, administer five chest thrusts over the sternum in the same location as external chest compression for cardiac massage, one finger width below the nipple line. See Procedure 47–15.

- For a conscious infant, continue chest thrusts and back blows until the airway is cleared or the infant becomes unconscious.

- If the infant is unconscious, assess the airway and give two breaths. If unable to ventilate, retilt the infant's head and try to give two breaths. If the air does not go in, then give back blows and chest thrusts (see above). Following the chest thrusts, lift the jaw and tongue and check for foreign object. If an object is noted, sweep it out with finger. Repeat this sequence of foreign object checks, breaths, back blows, and chest

thrusts until the airway clears or the infant begins to breathe.

Finger Sweep

If foreign material is visible in the mouth it must be expediently removed. The finger sweep maneuver should be used only on unconscious persons and with extreme caution in infants and children since the foreign material can be pushed back into the airway, causing increased obstruction. To remove visible foreign material from the mouth:

1. **Prepare victim.**

- Don nonsterile gloves.

- Open the person's mouth by grasping the tongue and lower jaw between the thumb and fingers, and lifting the jaw upward (see Figure 47–21). This pulls the tongue away from the back of the throat.

2. **Perform finger sweep.**

- To remove solid material insert the index finger of your free hand along the inside of the person's cheek and deep into the throat. With your finger hooked, use a sweeping motion to try to dislodge and lift out the foreign object. If these measures fail, try more abdominal thrusts in adults

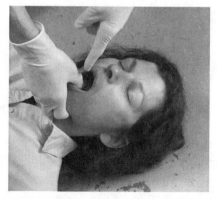

Figure 47–21 The finger sweep maneuver.

▶ **Procedure 47–13** *continued*

and children. In infants, give back blows and chest thrusts.

- After removing the foreign object, clear out liquid material, such as mucus, blood, or emesis, with a scooping motion, using two fingers wrapped with a gauze pad, tissue, or piece of cloth.

3. **Assess air exchange.**

- After the digital maneuver, assess air exchange. If it is ineffective, proceed with Procedures 47–14 and 47–15, as indicated.

4. **Document relevant information.**

- Document the date and time of the procedure, including the precipitating events and the client's response to the intervention.

- Describe the type of the procedure, the duration of breathlessness, and the type and size of any foreign object.

- Note vital signs, any complications, and type of follow-up care.

EVALUATION FOCUS

Patency of airway; rate, rhythm, and quality of respirations; level of consciousness; bilateral breath sounds; complications (injuries).

SAMPLE RECORDING

Date	Time	Notes
06/17/04	1800	Found choking in bed during evening meal, conscious with both hands on neck. Five abdominal thrusts given with quick return of 1″ by 1″ piece of meat. Alert, able to speak following thrusts. R 20, even and unlabored. Breath sounds clear to auscultation. Dr. Hood in to examine.————————————Matthew B. Corwin, RN

LIFESPAN CONSIDERATIONS

- Young children are most likely to choke on objects such as small toys. *Children don't understand the danger of placing objects in the mouth.*

- Older clients can be injured by incorrect placement of the rescuer's hands. *The sternum becomes more brittle with aging.*

- Older clients have a decreased gag reflex.

HOME CARE CONSIDERATIONS

- If a client has difficulty swallowing, teach the caregiver how to clear an obstructed airway.

- After removal of an airway obstruction at home, the client should receive a medical evaluation. *The client may have aspirated foreign material, which can cause airway edema and infection.*

- Teach parents how to clear an obstructed airway and emphasize the importance of keeping small objects away from a young child. *Children often put objects in their mouths while teething.*

47–14 Administering Oral Resuscitation

PURPOSES
- To provide ventilation during a respiratory or cardiac arrest
- To provide oxygen to the brain, heart, and vital organs during a respiratory or cardiac arrest

ASSESSMENT FOCUS

Patency of airway; rate, rhythm, quality of respirations; level of consciousness; skin color; presence/absence of carotid pulse.

EQUIPMENT

❏ Pocket face mask with one-way valve or mouth shields, or hand-compressible breathing bag with mask with one-way valve (see Figure 47–22).

❏ Disposable gloves

INTERVENTION

1. **Clear mouth and throat of obstructive material, and position the client appropriately.**

- Clear mouth and throat using finger sweeps.

- If the victim is lying on one side or face down, turn the client onto the back as a unit, while supporting the head and neck. Kneel beside the head.

2. **Open the airway.**

- Use the head-tilt, chin-lift maneuver, or the jaw-thrust maneuver. A modified jaw thrust is used for victims with suspected neck injury. In unconscious victims, the tongue lacks sufficient muscle tone, falls to the back of the throat, and obstructs the pharynx. *Because the tongue is attached to the lower jaw, moving the lower jaw forward and tilting the head backward lifts the tongue away from the pharynx and opens the airway.* See Figure 47–23.

Head-tilt, chin-lift maneuver:

- Place one hand palm downward on the forehead.

- Place the fingers of the other hand under the bony part of the lower jaw near the chin. The teeth should then be almost closed. The mouth should not be closed completely.

- Simultaneously press down on the forehead with one hand, and lift the victim's chin upward with the other. See Figure 47–24. Avoid pressing the fingers deeply into the soft tissues under the chin, since too much pressure can obstruct the airway.

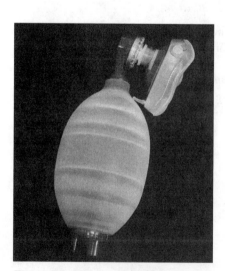

Figure 47–22 An Ambu bag with a face mask.

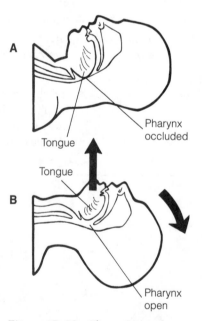

Figure 47–23 The position of an unconscious person's tongue: *A,* pharynx occluded; *B,* pharynx open.

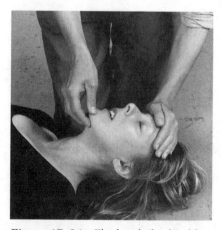

Figure 47–24 The head-tilt, chin-lift maneuver.

▶ **Procedure 47–14** *continued*

- Open the victim's mouth by pressing the lower lip downward with the thumb after tilting the head.

- Remove dentures if they cannot be maintained in place. However, dentures that can be maintained in place make a mouth-to-mouth seal easier should rescue breathing be required.

Jaw-thrust maneuver:

- Kneel at the *top* of the victim's head.

- Grasp the angle of the mandible directly below the earlobe between your thumb and forefinger on each side of the victim's head.

- While tilting the head backward, lift the lower jaw until it juts forward and is higher than the upper jaw. See Figure 47–25.

- Rest your elbows on the surface on which the victim is lying.

- Retract the lower lip with the thumbs prior to giving artificial respiration.

- If the victim is suspected of having a spinal neck injury, *do not hyperextend the neck. Instead, use the modified jaw thrust for a person with a spinal injury:*

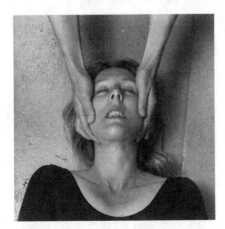

Figure 47–25 The jaw-thrust maneuver.

Modified jaw-thrust maneuver:

- Perform first two steps for jaw-thrust maneuver.

- Do not tilt the head backward while lifting the lower jaw forward.

- Support the head carefully without hyperextending it or moving it from side to side.

3. **Determine the victim's ability to breathe.**

- Place your ear and cheek close to the victim's mouth and nose.

- Look at the chest and abdomen for rising and falling movement.

- Listen for air escaping during exhalation.

- Feel for air escaping against your cheek.

4. **If no breathing is evident, provide rescue breathing if required.**

- Use one of the following methods: mouth-to-mouth, mouth-to-nose, mouth-to-mask, or hand-compressible breathing bag.

5. **Check for a carotid pulse. See step 7.**

- If no pulse is evident, begin cardiac compressions. See Procedure 47–15.

Mouth-to-mouth method:

- Put on a mouth shield.

- Maintain the open airway by using the head-tilt, chin-lift maneuver.

- Pinch the victim's nostrils with the index finger and thumb of the hand on the victim's forehead. *Pinching closes the nostrils and prevents resuscitation air from escaping through them.*

Figure 47–26 Mouth-to-mouth rescue breathing.

- Take a deep breath, and place the mouth, opened widely, around the victim's mouth. Ensure an airtight seal. See Figure 47–26.

- Give two full breaths (1½ seconds per breath). Pause and take a breath after the first ventilation. *The 1½-second time span closely matches the victim's inspiratory time, allows adequate time to provide good chest expansion, and decreases the possibility of gastric distention. Excessive air volumes and rapid inspiratory flow rates can cause pharyngeal pressures that are great enough to open the esophagus, thus allowing air to enter the stomach.*

- Ensure adequate ventilation by observing the victim's chest rise and fall and by assessing the person's breathing as outlined in step 3.

- If the initial ventilation attempt is unsuccessful, reposition the victim's head and repeat the rescue breathing as above. If the victim still cannot be ventilated, proceed to clear the airway of any foreign bodies using the finger sweep, abdominal thrusts, or chest thrusts described earlier. (See Procedure 47–13.)

Mouth-to-nose method:

This method can be used when there is an injury to the mouth or jaw or

▶ Procedure 47–14 Administering Oral Resuscitation *continued*

when the client is edentulous (toothless), making it difficult to achieve a tight seal over the mouth.

- Maintain the head tilt and chin lift.

- Close the victim's mouth by pressing the palm of your hand against the victim's chin. The thumb of the same hand may be used to hold the bottom lip closed.

- Put on a mouth shield.

- Take a deep breath, and seal you lips around the victim's nose. Ensure a tight seal by making contact with the cheeks around the nose.

- Deliver two full breaths of 1½ seconds each, and pause to inhale before delivering the second breath.

- Remove your mouth from the nose, and allow the victim to exhale passively. It may be necessary to separate the victim's lips or to open the mouth for exhaling, since the nasal passages may be obstructed during exhalation.

Mouth-to-mask method:

- Remove the mask from its case and push out the dome.

- Connect the one-way valve to the mask port.

- Position yourself at the top of the victim's head, and open the airway using the jaw-thrust maneuver.

- Place the bottom rim of the mask between the victim's lower lip and chin. Place the rest of the mask over the face using your thumbs on each side of the mask to hold it in place. *This keeps the mouth open under the mask.*

- Perform the jaw-thrust maneuver to tilt the head backward. Use your index, middle, and ring

fingers of both hands behind the angles of the jaw, and grasp the victim's temples with the palms of your hands.

- Maintain this head position while blowing intermittently into the mouthpiece.

Hand-compressible breathing bag method:

- Stand at the victim's head.

- Use one hand to secure the mask at the top and bottom and to hold the victim's jaw forward. Use the other hand to squeeze and release the bag. See Figure 47–27.

- Compress the bag until sufficient elevation of the victim's chest is observed. Then release the bag.

6. **Determine whether the victim's breathing is restored.** See step 3.

7. **Determine the presence of a carotid pulse** (see Figure 47–28).

- Take about 5 to 10 seconds for this pulse check. *Adequate time is needed since the victim's pulse may be very weak and rapid, irregular, or slow.*

- To palpate the carotid artery, first locate the larynx, then slide your

Figure 47–27   An Ambu bag in position.

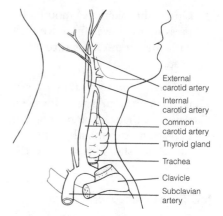

Figure 47–28   Location of the carotid artery.

fingers alongside it into the groove between the larynx and the neck muscles on the same side you are. Use gentle pressure. *This avoids compressing the artery. The carotid pulse site is used because the femoral pulse is difficult to locate on a fully clothed victim and because a carotid pulse can often be palpated when more peripheral pulses, such as the radial, are imperceptible.*

8. **If the carotid pulse is palpable, but breathing is not restored, repeat rescue breathing.**

- Inflate at the rate of 12 breaths per minute (1 breath every 5 seconds).

- Blow forcibly enough to make the victim's chest rise.

- If chest expansion fails to occur, ensure that the head is hyperextended and the jaw lifted upward, or check again for the presence of obstructive material, fluid, or vomitus.

- After each inflation, move your mouth away from the victim's mouth by turning your head toward the victim's chest. *This movement allows the air to escape when the victim exhales. It also gives the nurse time to inhale and to watch for chest expansion.*

► **Procedure 47–14** *continued*

9. **Reassess the carotid pulse after every 12 inflations (after 1 minute).**

- If you cannot locate the pulse, the victim's heart has stopped. Provide cardiac compression. See Procedure 47–15. *Accurate assessment of the victim's pulse is essential because performing external chest compressions on victims who have a pulse can lead to serious medical complications.*

10. **Document relevant information:**

- Document the date and time of resuscitation, including assessment findings prior to the respiratory arrest. Assess events during and after the respiratory arrest and the victim's responses to the intervention.

- Describe the duration of breathlessness.

- Note vital signs, any complications, and type of follow-up care.

EVALUATION FOCUS

Patency of airway; rate, rhythm, and quality of respirations; level of consciousness; breath sounds; vital signs.

SAMPLE RECORDING

Date	Time	Notes
10/3/04	1600	Found breathless and unresponsive. Skin color pale and ashen. Air way opened, two breaths given mouth-to-mask. Carotid pulse 64 and regular. Mouth-to-mask ventilations given at 12 breaths/minute with carotid pulse present and full every 1 minute. Skin color pale, pink. Awake, responsive to painful stimuli. Breath sounds clear to auscultation. Dr. Walker present.————————Deanna Matson, RN
10/3/04	1604	Transferred to CU for mechanical ventilation.————————————Deanna Matson, RN

▶ **Procedure 47–14 Administering Oral Resuscitation** *continued*

LIFESPAN CONSIDERATIONS	HOME CARE CONSIDERATIONS

LIFESPAN CONSIDERATIONS

- Airway obstruction by a foreign body is the most common cause of respiratory arrest in children.

- Acute epiglottitis can lead to upper airway obstruction in children. Symptoms usually occur suddenly and include drooling, difficulty swallowing, and a croaking sound with inspiration.

HOME CARE CONSIDERATIONS

- If a client has cardiac or breathing problems, encourage the caregiver to learn cardiopulmonary resuscitation.

- Carry a pocket mask in the home care nursing bag at all times.

- Activate the emergency medical system and contact the physician. *In most cases of respiratory arrest the client will need oxygen, respiratory support, and ambulance transport to the emergency room.*

- Assist the ambulance crew as needed and provide information about the client's history.

- Once the client is en route to the hospital, call the emergency room and give the report to the nurse in charge, including:

    a. A brief health history.

    b. Medications the client takes at home.

    c. Findings prior to the respiratory arrest.

    d. Duration of respiratory arrest and the client's response to resuscitation.

    e. Vital signs.

- Provide emotional support to family members. If the client lives alone, contact family members, as needed.

47–15 Administering External Cardiac Compressions

PURPOSES
- To provide ventilation and circulation following cardiac arrest
- To provide oxygen to the brain, heart, and vital organs following cardiac arrest
- To increase pressure in the chest causing blood to circulate

ASSESSMENT FOCUS

Level of consciousness, patency of airway, presence/absence of breathing, pulse.

EQUIPMENT
- ❏ A hard surface, such as a cardiac board or the floor, on which to place the victim
- ❏ A face shield or mask with a one-way valve

INTERVENTION

1. **Survey the scene for safety hazards, presence of bystanders, and other victims.**

2. **Assess victim's level of consciousness, patency of airway, presence/absence of pulse.**

- Ask victim, "Are you alright?"

- If victim does not respond, in a health care facility call a "code" or follow agency protocol. If alone outside, call for help and have another person call for EMS or 911.

3. **Position the victim appropriately if not already done.**

- Place the victim supine on a firm surface. *Blood flow to the brain will be inadequate during CPR if the victim's head is positioned higher than the thorax. A hard surface facilitates compression of the heart between the sternum and the hard surface.*

- If the victim is in bed in a health care facility, place a cardiac board—preferably the full width of the bed—under the back. If necessary, place the victim on the floor.

- If the victim must be turned, turn the body as a unit while firmly supporting the head and neck so that the head does not roll, twist, or tilt backward or forward. Turning *the person as a unit prevents further injury (if present) to the neck or spine.*

- Have a bystander elevate the lower extremities (optional). *This may promote venous return and augment circulation during external cardiac compressions.*

4. **Assess responsiveness, airway, breathing, and circulation (see next page).**

5. **Position the hands on the sternum. Proper hand placement is essential for effective cardiac compression. Position the hands as follows:**

- With the hand nearest the victim's legs, use your middle and index fingers to locate the lower margin of the rib cage.

- Move the fingers up the rib cage to the notch where the lower ribs meet the sternum. See Figure 47–29.

- Place the heel of the other hand (nearest the person's head) along

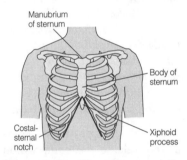

Figure 47–29   The sternum and ribs.

the lower half of the victim's sternum, close to the index finger that is next to the middle finger in the costal-sternal notch. *Proper positioning of the hands during cardiac compression prevents injury to underlying organs and the ribs.* See Figure 47–30. *Compression directly over the xiphoid process can lacerate the victim's liver.*

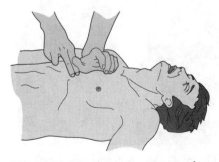

Figure 47–30   Proper positioning of hands during cardiac compression.

▶ Procedure 47–15 Administering External Cardiac Compressions *continued*

- Then place the first hand on top of the second hand so that both hands are parallel. The fingers may be extended or interlaced. *Compression occurs only on the sternum and through the heels of the hands.*

5. **Administer cardiac compression.**

- Lock your elbows into position, straighten your arms, and position your shoulders directly over your hands. See Figure 47–31.

- For each compression, thrust *straight down* on the sternum. For an adult of normal size, depress the sternum 3.8 to 5.0 cm (1.5 to 2 in). *The muscle force of both arms is needed for adequate cardiac compression of an adult. The weight of your shoulders and trunk supplies power for compression. Extension of the elbows ensures an adequate and even force throughout compression.*

- Between compressions, completely release the compression pressure. However, do *not* lift your hands from the chest or change their position. *Releasing the pressure allows the sternum to return to its normal position and allows the heart chambers to fill with blood. Leaving the hands on the chest prevents taking a malposition*

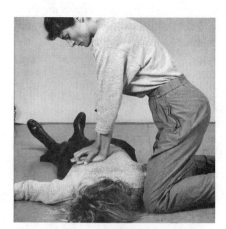

Figure 47–31 Arm and hand position for external cardiac massage.

between compressions and possibly injuring the person.

- Provide external cardiac compressions at the rate of 80 to 100 per minute. Maintain the rhythm by counting "One and, two and," and so on. *The specified compression rate and rhythm stimulate normal heart contractions.*

- Administer 5 or 15 external compressions, depending on the number of rescuers, and coordinate them with rescue breathing. See CPR performed by one rescuer or by two rescuers, next.

VARIATION: CPR performed by one rescuer

- Survey the scene.

- Call for help and have another person call for EMS. In many communities the emergency telephone number is 911. The person who calls the local EMS must be able to impart all of the following information:

  a. Location of the emergency

  b. Telephone number from which the call is being made

  c. What happened

  d. Number of people needing assistance

  e. Condition of the victim(s)

  f. What aid is being given

  g. Any other information that is requested

- If there is no bystander and the rescuer is alone, summon help and then perform CPR.

- Position the victim on the back on a flat, firm surface.

- Kneel beside the victim's chest. If the person is in bed, you may have to kneel on the bed.

6. **Assess responsiveness. If unconscious, open airway, assess breathing and circulation prior to initiating compressions.**

Airway:

- Open the airway with the head tilt, chin-lift maneuver or, if neck injury is suspected, the modified jaw thrust.

- Clear the airway, if you suspect airway obstruction from food or some other foreign object.

Breathing:

- Assess breathing: *Look for* chest movement; *listen for* exhalation; and *feel for* air flow against the cheek.

- Ventilate the victim, if breathing is not present. See Procedure 47–14 for detailed steps.

- Deliver two full breaths into the victim's mouth. Between the breaths, remove your mouth, turn your head to the side, and pause to take a breath.

- If unable to give two breaths, reposition the victim's head, and attempt to ventilate again.

- If still unsuccessful, follow procedures for obstructed airway (Procedure 47–13.)

Circulation:

- Assess for the presence of the carotid pulse for 5–10 seconds.

- If pulse is present:

  a. Continue rescue breathing at 12 times per minute while continuing to monitor the pulse.

- If pulse is absent:

  a. Begin external chest compression.

  b. Perform chest compression: 15 external chest compres-

▶ **Procedure 47–15** *continued*

sions at the rate of 80 to 100 per minute. Count "One and, two and, three and … " up to 15.

c. Open the airway, and give two rescue breaths.

d. Repeat four complete cycles of 15 compressions and two ventilations.

e. Assess the victims carotid pulse. If there is no pulse, continue with CPR and check for the return of the pulse every few minutes.

VARIATION: CPR performed by two rescuers

When help arrives, one rescuer can provide external cardiac compression, and the other can provide pulmonary resuscitation, inflating the lungs once after every five compressions, a 5:1 ratio.

- The second rescuer identifies himself or herself as a trained rescuer and verifies that EMS has been notified. If EMS has been notified, the second rescuer offers to help with CPR.

- The first rescuer completes a cycle of 15 compressions and two breaths, and the second rescuer gets into position to give compression.

- The first rescuer assesses the carotid pulse for 5–10 seconds and if there is no pulse, gives one breath and then states, "No pulse, continue CPR."

- The second rescuer then:

  a. Provides compression.

  b. Sets the pace, counting aloud, "One and, two and, three and, four and, five and, ventilate.'

- The first rescuer:

  a. Provides one ventilation after every five chest compressions.

b. Observes each breath for effectiveness.

c. Assesses the carotid pulse frequently between breaths to assess the effectiveness of cardiac compression.

d. Observes for abdominal (gastric) distention, which can result from overinflation of the lungs. If distention occurs, the rescuer reduces the force of the ventilations, but ensures sufficient ventilation to elevate the ribs.

- When the person compressing the chest becomes fatigued, positions should be changed. To initiate a change in position, the person compressing states, "Change one and, two and, three and, four and, five and"; moves to the person's head; and counts the pulse for 5 seconds.

- The person ventilating gives the breath and moves into position to provide compression.

- If there is no pulse, the original person compressing states, "No pulse—start compression," gives one full breath, and CPR is continued.

When relieved from CPR

- Stand by to assist. Often a person is needed to take notes, document the actions taken, and record the drugs given by the cardiac arrest team.

- Provide emotional support to the victim's family members and any others who may have witnessed the cardiac arrest. This is often a frightening experience for others because it is so sudden and so serious.

VARIATION: CPR for children and infants

Providing CPR for infants and children is similar to CPR for adults.

a. Providing CPR to children

- In children, follow steps 1–3.

- In children, to find the hand position for compressions, run your index and middle fingers up the ribs until you locate the sternal notch. With those two fingers on the lower end of the sternum look at the location of the index finger and lift fingers off sternum and put the heel of the same hand on the sternum just above the location of the index finger. The other hand should remain on the child's forehead so as to maintain an open airway.

- Use the heel of one hand for compressions, keeping the fingers off the chest. Compression depth is 2.5 to 3.8 cm (1 to 1½ in.). Never lift the hand off the chest.

- CPR for a child is given at the following rate: 100 compressions/minute with cycles of five compressions and one breath.

b. Providing CPR to infants

- For infants, follow steps 1–3.

- When ventilating an infant, cover the infant's nose and mouth.

- For pulse checks, use the brachial pulse in the arm.

- To find the position for compressions, place your index finger on the sternum at the nipple line. Place your middle and ring fingers on the sternum next to your index finger, then lift your index finger.

- Compress the chest 1.25 to 2.5 cm (½ to 1 in.) straight down using the pads of two fingers. Keep your fingers in the compression position while the other hand remains on the forehead, maintaining the open airway.

▶ **Procedure 47–15 Administering External Cardiac Compressions** *continued*

- Give compressions at a rate of up to 120 compressions/minute with cycles of five compressions and one breath.

7. Terminating CPR

A rescuer terminates CPR only when one of the following events occurs:

- Another trained individual takes over.

- The victim's heartbeat and breathing are re-established.

- Adjunctive life-support measures are initiated.

- A physician states that the victim is dead and that CPR is to be discontinued.

- The rescuer becomes exhausted, and there is no one to take over.

8. Document relevant information:

- Document the date and time of the arrest and the initiation of CPR, including the events prior to the arrest.

- Note length of resuscitation.

- Record the time, dose, and route of any medications administered.

- Record any advanced cardiac life support interventions such as defibrillation or initiation of IV therapy.

- Include the victim's response to CPR.

- Record the victim's status and outcome of CPR.

- Document vital signs, rhythm strips, any complications, and type of follow-up care.

EVALUATION FOCUS

> Level of consciousness, patency of airway; rate, rhythm, and quality of respirations; pulse rate and blood pressure; breath sounds; cardiac rhythm, if monitored.

SAMPLE RECORDING

Date	Time	Notes
03/23/04	1600	Monitored arrest from ventricular fibrillation. Unresponsive, no respirations or carotid pulse. CPR initiated.—Deborah A. Nathan, RN
03/23/04	1602	Defibrillated with 200 joules with prompt return of sinus rhythm and multifocal premature ventricular beats. Lidocaine 75 mg IV push administered. O_2 at 2L/m via nasal canula. Alert and oriented, B/P 90/50, P 76, R 22. Dr. Peters in to examine. Transferred to CU via bed.————————————————Deborah A. Nathan, RN

▶ **Procedure 47–15** *continued*

LIFESPAN CONSIDERATIONS

- Check carefully for airway obstruction in children with cardiac arrest. *Cardiac arrest in children most often occurs after an initial respiratory arrest.*

- Older clients are most likely to be injured by incorrect placement of the rescuer's hands. *The sternum becomes more brittle with aging.*

- The older client may have an advanced directive, or living will, expressing his wishes for life support.

HOME CARE CONSIDERATIONS

- Encourage caregivers or family members to learn cardioplumonary resuscitation.

- Advise elderly clients to talk with the physician about preparing an advanced directive for life support measures.

- Always carry a pocket mask in the home care nursing bag.

- After activating the emergency response system, continue resuscitation until the ambulance arrives. Be prepared to give report to the ambulance crew and assist them as needed.

- While the client is en route to the hospital, contact the emergency room and report the following to the nurse in charge:

  a. A brief health history

  b. Medications the client takes at home

  c. Findings prior to the cardiopulmonary arrest

  d. Duration of the cardiopulmonary arrest and the client's response to resuscitation

- Provide emotional support to family members. If the client is alone, contact family members or neighbors, as needed.

47–16 Initiating Cardiac Monitoring

PURPOSES
- To continously observe the heart rate and rhythm
- To detect the presence of dysrhythmias and initiate treatment before complications develop

ASSESSMENT FOCUS

Risk factors for developing cardiac dysrhythmias; history of cardiac disease and dysrhythmias; vital signs and level of consciousness as baseline data; allergy to adhesive; ambulation status.

EQUIPMENT

- ❏ Bedside monitor or telemetry unit with fresh battery
- ❏ Electrodes—self-adherent, pregelled, disposable
- ❏ Lead wires
- ❏ Monitor cable
- ❏ Dry gauze pads or ECG prep pads
- ❏ Alcohol prep pads
- ❏ Razor, soap, and water
- ❏ Washcloth and towel

INTERVENTION

1. **Prepare the client.**

- Explain the reason for continuous ECG monitoring to the client. Reassure the client that any changes in heart rhythm can be noted and immediate treatment initiated if necessary.

- Explain that loose or disconnected lead wires, poor electrode contact, excessive movement, electrical interference, or equipment malfunction may trigger alarms and alert the staff, allowing the problem to be corrected.

- Explain that the client may move about within activity restrictions while on the monitor. Explain the skin preparation procedure. Provide for privacy and drape the client appropriately.

2. **Select the appropriate equipment.**

- Assure the presence of a bedside monitor and cable, or, if the client is ambulatory, obtain a telemetry unit and pouch (this may be a specially designed hospital gown or a pouch worn around the neck or waist to hold the transmitter unit).

- Check equipment for damage, such as fraying, bent, or broken

wires. Connect lead wires to cable and secure connections.

3. **Select electrode sites on the chest wall.**

- Choice of sites (Figure 47–32) will depend on the lead to be monitored, the condition of the skin, and any incisions or catheters present.

4. **Prepare the electrode sites.**

- Shave a 4 × 4 inch area for each electrode if the chest is excessively hairy.

- Clean sites with soap and water, and dry thoroughly. Alcohol may be used to remove skin oils; allow to dry for 60 seconds after use.

- Gently abrade the site by rubbing with a dry gauze pad or ECG prep pad to remove dead skin cells, debris, and residue.

5. **Apply the electrodes and connect them to the monitor cable or telemetry unit.**

- Open the electrode package; peel the backing from the electrode and check to assure that the center of the pad is moist with conductive gel.

- Apply electrode pads to the client, pressing firmly to ensure contact.

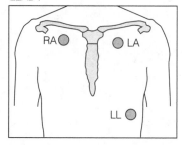

LEAD I

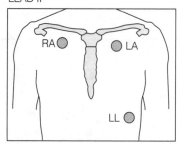

LEAD II

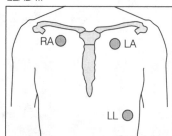

LEAD III

Figure 47–32 The correct electrode positions for a three-leadwire system. Electrode positions are identical for leads I, II, and III. Change lead selector switch to correspond to the lead that is required. LA, left arm; LL, left leg; RA, right arm.

► **Procedure 47–16** *continued*

- Attach leads and position the cable with sufficient slack for the client's comfort. Place the telemetry unit (if used) in the client's gown/pocket.

6. **Assess the monitor tracing and set alarm limits.**

- Assess the ECG tracing on the monitor and adjust settings as needed.

- Set ECG monitor alarm limits for the client, typically at 20 BPM higher and lower than the baseline rate. Turn alarms ON, and leave on at all times.

7. **Ensure client safety.**

- Assess the client immediately if an alarm is triggered.

- Remove and apply new pads every 24 to 48 hours, or if the pad becomes dislodged or nonadherent. Cleanse gel residue from the previous site, and document skin condition under the pads. Choose an alternate site if the skin appears irritated or blistered. Time and date pads with every change.

- Monitor the client periodically for comfort. Assess the electrode and lead wire connections as needed.

8. **Document all relevant information.**

- Record the application of the monitor or telemetry unit and all nursing assessments.

- Document ECG strips according to unit policy and/or physician's order, as well as when the cardiac rhythm or the client's condition changes (especially with complaints of chest pain, decreased level of consciousness, or changes in vital signs).

- The date, time, client identification, monitor lead, and rhythm interpretation should be noted on each ECG strip.

EVALUATION FOCUS

> ECG tracing and cardiac rate and rhythm; presence of arrythmias; vital signs; presence of chest pain or other cardiac symptoms; skin condition at electrode sites.

SAMPLE RECORDING

Date	Time	Notes
05/04/04	1032	Cardiac monitoring initiated. B/P 122/68, R 16, P 76. Denies chest pain or other discomfort. Normal sinus rhythm on monitor.——————————————————————————————Sam Wright, RN

LIFESPAN CONSIDERATIONS

- Older clients need extra skin care to prevent irritation or blistering at the electrode sites. *Skin becomes more fragile with aging.*

- Explain the monitoring procedure in simple terms for children and take time to answer questions.

- Instruct the child to report itching or discomfort from the electrodes, rather than scratching at the sites.

- Active children are best monitored with telemetry. *Lead wires can be easily disconnected as the child moves about and plays.*

48

Fluid, Electrolyte, and Acid-Base Balance

PROCEDURES

48–1 Using a Dial-A-Flo In-Line Device

PURPOSE

- To regulate delivery of the correct amount of intravenous fluid

ASSESSMENT FOCUS

Patency of existing IV line; amount of solution prescribed.

EQUIPMENT

- ❏ Dial-A-Flo in-line device
- ❏ Equipment for an intravenous infusion

INTERVENTION

1. **Attach the Dial-A-Flo device appropriately.**

- Connect the Dial-A-Flo device to the end of the IV tubing.

- Connect the insertion spike of the IV tubing to the solution container.

2. **Prime the tubing.**

- Adjust the regulator on the Dial-A-Flo to the open position.

- Open all clamps and infusion flow regulators on the IV tubing.

- Remove the protective cap at the end of the tubing, and allow the fluid to run through the tubing.

- Reclamp the tubing to prevent continued flow of fluid.

3. **Establish the infusion.**

- Attach the primed tubing to the venipuncture needle or catheter hub.

- Open the IV tubing flow regulator.

- Align the Dial-A-Flo regulator to the arrow indicating the desired volume of fluid to infuse over 1 hour.

4. **Confirm the appropriate drip rate.**

- Count the drip rate for 15 seconds, and multiply by 4. *This ensures that the rate coincides with the calculated drip rate.*

- Recheck the drip rate after 5 minutes and again after 15 minutes. *This detects potential changes in the rate resulting from expansion or contraction of the tubing.*

- If the drip rate does not coincide with that calculated, it may be necessary to adjust the height of the IV pole. *Elevation of the IV pole facilitates flow by gravity.*

5. **Monitor the infusion flow.**

- Check the volume of fluid infused at least every hour, and compare it with the time tape on the IV container.

6. **Document all relevant information.**

- Record the date and time of starting the infusion, the type and amount of fluid infused, the rate at which the IV is being infused, the infusion device used, the status of the IV insertion site, and any adverse responses of the client.

EVALUATION FOCUS

Amount of fluid infused in designated time period; status of IV insertion site; any adverse responses of client.

SAMPLE RECORDING

Date	Time	Notes
12/03/04	1500	1000 mL IV D$_5$W started at 125 mL/hour using Dial-A-Flo. Venipuncture site dry and clean c̄ no signs of infiltration or infection.————————————Carola Brown, SN

▶ **Procedure 48–1 Using a Dial-A-Flo In-Line Device** *continued*

LIFESPAN CONSIDERATIONS	HOME CARE CONSIDERATIONS

- Check the IV flow rate frequently for older clients and children. *Clients in these age groups are most likely to develop fluid volume overload if IV fluid is infused too rapidly.*

- With older clients, check the IV site more often for signs of infiltration (extravasation) of the IV fluid. *Veins become more fragile with aging.*

- Evaluate the home environment and the client or caregiver's ability to use the Dial-A-Flo device.

- Demonstrate use of the Dial-A-Flo device, and have the client or caregiver give a return demonstration.

- Explain the importance of checking the IV flow rate frequently and the actions to take if problems occur (e.g., the solution stops infusing or the IV site becomes swollen or reddened).

Using an Infusion Controller or Pump

PURPOSES
- To maintain the prescribed fluid infusion rate
- To prevent fluid overload

ASSESSMENT FOCUS

Amount and type of IV fluid prescribed; flow rate.

EQUIPMENT

- ❏ Infusion controller or pump
- ❏ The IV solution or medication
- ❏ A volume control chamber (Buretrol or Solu-set) for pediatric clients

- ❏ An IV pole
- ❏ An IV administration set with compatible IV tubing

- ❏ Sterile peristaltic tubing or a cassette if required
- ❏ Alcohol swabs and tape

INTERVENTION

Infusion Controller

1. **Attach the controller to the IV pole.**

- Attach the controller to the IV pole so that it will be below and in line with the IV container.

- Plug the machine into the electric outlet, unless battery power is used.

2. **Set up the IV infusion.**

- Open the IV container, maintaining the sterility of the port, and spike the container with the administration set.

- Place the IV container on the IV pole, and position the drip chamber 76 cm (30 in) above the venipuncture site. *This provides sufficient gravitational pressure for the fluid to flow into the client.*

- Fill the drip chamber of the IV tubing one-third full. *If the drip chamber is filled more than halfway, the drops may be miscounted.*

- Rotate the drip chamber. *This removes vapor that could make the drop count inaccurate.*

- Prime the tubing, and close the clamp. Nonvolumetric controllers (regulators that measure the infusion in drops/minute) use standard tubing that is gravity-primed. *Priming expels all the air from the tubing.*

3. **Attach the IV drop sensor, and insert the IV tubing into the controller.**

- Attach the IV drop sensor (electronic eye) to the drip chamber so that it is below the drip orifice and above the fluid level in the drip chamber. *This placement ensures an accurate drop count. If the sensor is placed too high, it can miss drops; if placed too low it may mistake splashes for drops.*

- Make sure the sensor is plugged into the controller.

- Insert the tubing into the controller according to the manufacturer's instructions.

4. **Initiate the infusion.**

- Perform a venipuncture or connect the tubing to the primary IV tubing or catheter. Don gloves before performing a venipuncture.

- Open the IV control clamp completely.

5. **Set volume dials for the appropriate volume per hour.**

- Close the door to the controller, and ensure that all tubing clamps are wide open. *This enables the controller to regulate the fluid flow.*

- Set the dials on the front of the controller to the appropriate infusion rate and volume. Set the volume at 50 mL less than the required amount, if the controller counts the volume infused. *This will give you time to attach a new container before the present one runs out completely.*

- Press the power button and the start button.

- Count the drops for 15 seconds, and multiply the result by 4. *This verifies that the rate has been correctly set and the controller is operating accurately.*

- Some nurses recommend that all connections be taped. Count the drop rate again after the taping. *Taping could change the drop rate.*

6. **Set the alarm.** *The alarm notifies the nurse when a set volume of fluid has been infused or indicates malfunctioning of the equipment.*

7. **Monitor the infusion.**

- Check the volume of fluid infused at least every hour, and compare it with the time tape on the IV container. *This confirms the actual volume of fluid infused.*

▶ **Procedure 48–2 Using an Infusion Controller or Pump** *continued*

- If the volume infused does not coincide with the time tape or the alarm sounds, check that:

  a. The time tape is accurate.

  b. The rate/volume settings are accurate.

  c. The drip chamber is correctly filled.

  d. The IV tubing clamp is fully open.

  e. The container still has solution.

  f. The drop sensor is correctly placed.

  g. The IV container is correctly placed.

  h. The tubing is not pinched or kinked.

  i. The IV has not infiltrated or clotted at the insertion site.

Infusion Pump

8. **Attach the pump to the IV pole.**

- Attach the pump at eye level on the IV pole. *Because the pump does not depend on gravity pressure, it can be placed at any level. Eye level is convenient for checking its functioning.*

- Plug the machine into the electric outlet, unless battery power is used.

9. **Set up the infusion.**

- Check the manufacturer's directions before using an IV filter or before infusing blood. *Infusion pump pressures may damage filters or cause rate inaccuracies. Certain models may also cause hemolysis of red blood cells.*

- Open the IV container, maintaining the sterility of the port, and spike the container with the administration set.

- Place the IV container on the IV pole above the pump.

- Fill the drip chamber, and rotate it as described in step 2 above.

- Prime the tubing, and close the clamp. Most volumetric chamber pumps, i.e., pumps calibrated to infuse a specific volume of fluid at a specific rate (mL/hour), have a cassette that must also be primed. Manufacturers give instructions for doing this. Often the cassette must be inverted or tilted to be filled with fluid. Some volumetric pumps use special tubing that is gravity-primed.

10. **Attach the IV drop sensor, and insert the IV tubing into the pump.**

- Position the drop sensor, if required, on the drip chamber. See step 3.

- Load the machine according to the manufacturer's instructions.

- Ensure the correct pressure is set.

11. **Initiate the infusion.**

- See step 4.

12. **Set dials for the required drops per minute or milliliters per hour.**

- Close the door to the pump, and ensure that the IV tubing clamps are open.

- Press the power button to the "on" position, and press the start button.

13. **Set the alarm, and monitor the infusion.**

- See steps 6 and 7.

- If the tubing does not contain a regular cassette, slightly change the sections of tubing placed inside the infusion clamp. *This prevents tubing collapse from continual squeezing by the pump.*

14. **Document relevant information.**

- Record the date and time of starting the infusion, the type and amount of fluid being infused, the rate at which it is being infused, the infusion device used, the status of the IV insertion site, and any adverse responses of the client.

EVALUATION FOCUS

> Amount of fluid infused in designated time period; status of IV insertion site, especially the presence of infiltration.

SAMPLE RECORDING

Date	Time	Notes
02/12/04	0900	1000 mL IV D$_5$W started at 125 mL/hour using controller. Venipuncture site clean and dry with no signs of infiltration or infection.————————————————Rodney Stewart, SN

▶ **Procedure 48–2** *continued*

LIFESPAN CONSIDERATIONS	HOME CARE CONSIDERATIONS
• Check the IV flow rate frequently for older adult clients and children. *Persons in these age groups are most likely to develop fluid overload if IV fluid is infused too rapidly.*	• Evaluate the client or caregiver's ability to operate the infusion device at home.
• For older clients, check the IV site often for signs of infiltration. *Veins become more fragile with aging.*	• Emphasize the need for hand washing and clean technique when handling IV equipment. Set aside a clean area in the home to store the IV equipment.
• Emphasize to children that the IV controller or pump is not a toy and shouldn't be touched unless an adult is present. *Children are naturally curious and will want to examine the equipment.*	• Demonstrate the device, and ask for a return demonstration from the client or caregiver.
	• Discuss complications, such as infiltration, power failure, or equipment problems, and the measures to take when they arise.
	• Make certain the client knows how and where to obtain supplies.

48–3 Using an Implantable Venous Access Device (IVAD)

PURPOSES

- To administer intravenous infusions, or medications
- To administer blood and blood products
- To obtain blood samples for laboratory analysis

ASSESSMENT FOCUS

Client's understanding and response to the system; type of therapy prescribed.

EQUIPMENT

- ❏ Priming solution of bacteriostatic saline
- ❏ IV solution container and administration set

or

- ❏ Blood or blood product with transfusion set

or

- ❏ Blood specimen tubes and syringe and needle
- ❏ Sterile gloves
- ❏ 5 mL syringes of normal saline flush and heparinized saline (100 μ/mL of heparin)

- ❏ 2% lidocaine with subcutaneous syringe and needle (optional)
- ❏ Povidone-iodine and alcohol solution and swabs
- ❏ #22-gauge Huber needle
- ❏ Adhesive or nonallergenic tape
- ❏ Occlusive dressing materials
- ❏ Povidone or antibiotic ointment

INTERVENTION

1. **Assemble the equipment.**

- Attach the IV tubing to the infusion or transfusion container.

- Prime the infusion tubing with fluid.

- Prepare syringes of normal saline and heparinized saline. Currently, saline is used to flush the device either before and after medications or just periodically (check agency policy) followed by heparinized saline each time. *Heparinized saline helps prevent clotting.*

2. **Position the client appropriately, and locate the implant port.**

- Position the client in either a supine or sitting position.

- Locate the IVAD device, and grasp it between two fingers of your nondominant hand to stabilize it. IVADs may have top entry or side entry ports, depending on the design. Palpate and locate the septum, the rubber disc at the center of the port where the needle will be inserted.

3. **Prepare the site.**

- Wash hands, and put on sterile gloves.

- *Optional:* Insert 2% lidocaine subcutaneously in the injection site. *This anesthetizes the area for injection.* It may be ordered during the first few weeks after the implant surgery, when the area is tender and swollen and more pain from the needle puncture is felt.

- An ice pack may be placed over the site for several minutes to reduce discomfort from the needle puncture.

- Prepare the skin in accordance with agency policy and let the area dry after applying such solutions as povidone-iodine and alcohol.

4. **Insert the Huber needle.**

- Grasp the device, and again palpate the septum for injection.

Anchor the port with the nondominant hand.

- Insert the needle at a 90° angle to the septum, and push it firmly through the skin and septum until it contacts the base of the IVAD chamber.

- Avoid tilting or moving the needle when the septum is punctured. *Needle movement can damage the septum and cause fluid leakage.*

- When the needle contacts the base of the septum, aspirate for blood to determine correct placement. If no blood is obtained, remove the needle and repeat the procedure after having the client move the arms and change position. *Movement can free the catheter from the vessel wall, where it may be lodged.*

5. **Secure the needle, and ensure proper placement of the IVAD catheter.**

- Support the Huber needle with 2 × 2 dressings and Steristrips.

▶ **Procedure 48–3** *continued*

• Infuse the saline flush and priming solution. There should be no sign of subcutaneous infiltration after infusion of the saline fluid and priming solution.

6. **After use, flush the system with heparinized saline.**

• When flushing, maintain **a positive pressure,** and clamp the tubing as soon as the flush is finished. *These actions avoid reflux of the heparinized saline.*

7. **Attach an IV-lock ("hep-lock" or saline-lock) to the Huber needle.**

• A Huber needle with an IV-lock can remain in place for one week before it needs to be changed. *The IV-lock allows for infusion of medications or fluid without continuous puncturing of the skin covering the IVAD.*

8. **Prevent manipulation or dislodgement of the needle.**

• Apply occlusive transparent dressings to the needle site.

• Apply povidone or antibiotic ointment to the site before dressings are applied as agency protocol dictates.

9. **Document all relevant information.**

• Record the procedure performed and all nursing assessments.

VARIATION: Obtaining a Blood Specimen

To obtain a blood specimen:

• Withdraw 10 mL of blood and discard it. *This initial specimen may be diluted with saline and heparin from previous flushes.*

• Draw up the required amount of blood and transfer it to the appropriate containers (see Procedure 48–5).

• *Slowly* instill 5–20 mL of normal saline, according to agency policy, over a five-minute period. *This thoroughly flushes the catheter and avoids excess pressure.*

• Inject 5 mL of heparin (100 µ/mL) to prevent clotting.

EVALUATION FOCUS

Infusion or transfusion rate; appearance of IVAD site; clinical signs indicating venous thrombosis (pain in the neck, arm, and/or shoulder on the side of the insertion site; neck and/or supraclavicular swelling); infection (redness and swelling at the site); and dislodgement of the needle or catheter (shortness of breath, chest pain, coolness in the chest).

SAMPLE RECORDING

Date	Time	Notes
07/7/04	800	IVAD accessed per protocol. 1000 cc 10% dextrose started at 100 mL/hr via IV pump. IV site clean and dry with no signs of infiltration or infection.————————————————Noah Andrews, RN

▶ Procedure 48–3 Using an Implantable Venous Access Device (IVAD) *continued*

LIFESPAN CONSIDERATIONS

- Explain the access procedure to the young client, encourage questions, and be alert for nonverbal cues. *Children may not understand things that seem obvious to adults. For example, a child may think the IV therapy is a punishment.*

- Let the young client become familiar with the equipment. *Handling the equipment can help resolve fears and misconceptions.*

- Tell the young client the procedure will hurt, but will last only a short time. *Misleading the child about pain will destroy rapport.*

- Allow the young client to make choices whenever possible. *Making choices gives a sense of control.*

HOME CARE CONSIDERATIONS

- Determine home safety and the ability of the client or caregiver to care for the IVAD at home.

- Set aside a clean area in the home to store supplies and equipment.

- Instruct the client and caregiver to report signs of infection (e.g., redness and swelling at the site) and thrombosis (e.g., pain in the neck or shoulder).

- Teach the client how and where to obtain supplies.

48–4 Obtaining a Capillary Blood Specimen and Measuring Blood Glucose

Before obtaining a capillary blood specimen, determine the frequency and type of testing, the client's understanding of the procedure, and the client's response to previous testing.

PURPOSES
- To determine or monitor blood glucose levels of clients at risk for hyperglycemia or hypoglycemia
- To promote blood glucose regulation by the client
- To evaluate the effectiveness of insulin administration

ASSESSMENT FOCUS

Client's learning needs.

EQUIPMENT

- ❏ Blood glucose meter
- ❏ Blood glucose reagent strip compatible with the meter
- ❏ Paper towel
- ❏ Warm cloth or other warming device (optional)
- ❏ Antiseptic swab
- ❏ Disposable gloves
- ❏ Sterile lancet or #19 or #21-gauge needle
- ❏ Cotton ball to wipe the glucose reagent strip (dry wipe method)

INTERVENTION

1. **Prepare the equipment.**

- Obtain a reagent strip from the container and place it on a clean, dry paper towel. *Moisture can change the strip, thereby altering the test results.*

- Calibrate the meter, and run a control sample according to the manufacturer's instructions.

2. **Select and prepare the vascular puncture site.**

- Choose a vascular puncture site (e.g., the side of an adult's finger or the heel, finger, or earlobe of an infant or child). Avoid sites beside bone.

- If either the heel or the finger is used, wrap it first in a warm cloth for 30 to 60 seconds (optional), *or* hold a finger in a dependent position and massage it toward the site. If the earlobe is used, rub it gently with a small piece of gauze. *These actions increase the blood flow to the area, ensure an adequate specimen, and reduce the need for a repeat puncture.*

- Clean the site with the antiseptic swab, and permit it to dry.

3. **Obtain the blood specimen.**

- Don gloves.

- Place the injector, if used, against the site and release the needle, thus permitting it to pierce the skin. Make sure the lancet is perpendicular to the site. *The lancet is designed to pierce the skin at a specific depth when it is in a perpendicular position relative to the skin.*

or

Prick the site with a lancet or needle, using a darting motion.

- Wipe away the first drop of blood with a cotton ball. *The first blood usually contains a greater proportion of serous fluid, which can alter test results.*

- Gently squeeze the site until a large drop of blood forms.

- Hold the reagent strip under the puncture site until blood covers the indicator square. The pad will absorb the blood, and a chemical reaction will occur. Do not smear the blood. *This will cause an inaccurate reading.*

- Ask the client to apply pressure to the skin puncture site with a cotton ball. *Pressure will assist hemostasis.*

4. **Expose the blood to the test strip for the period and in the manner specified by the manufacturer.**

- As soon as the blood is placed on the test strip:

   a. Follow the manufacturer's recommendations on the glucose meter, and monitor the time as indicated by the manufacturer (e.g., 60 seconds). *The blood must remain in contact with the test pad for a prescribed time for accurate results.*

   b. If indicated, lay the glucose strip on a paper towel or on the side of the timer. *The strip should be kept flat so that blood will not pool on only one part of the pad.*

▶ Procedure 48–4 Obtaining a Capillary Blood Specimen *continued*

5. Measure and document the blood glucose.

- Place the strip into the meter according to the manufacturer's instructions. Some devices require that the strip be wiped or blotted after a designated period of time before being inserted in the meter. Other strips do not require blotting or wiping. Refer to the specific manufacturer's recommendations for the specific procedure.

- After the designated time most glucose meters will display the glucose reading automatically.

Correct timing will ensure accurate results.

- Turn off the meter, and discard the test strip and cotton balls.

- Document the method of testing and results on the client's record.

EVALUATION FOCUS

Comparison of glucose meter reading with normal blood glucose levels; status of puncture site; motivation of client to perform the test independently.

SAMPLE RECORDING

Date	Time	Notes
12/04/04	0700	Skin puncture performed on right index finger for blood glucose. Results 82 by glucometer.————————Selena Daznard, RN

LIFESPAN CONSIDERATIONS

Younger Clients

- Allow the younger clients to sit on a parent's lap, if appropriate. However, do not ask a parent to restrain an uncooperative child.

- Use a fingertip for a young client older than age 2, unless contraindicated. For a client less than age 2, use the lower outer aspect of the heel.

- Work quickly to minimize anxiety for the young client.

- Praise the young client for cooperating and assure the child that the procedure is not a punishment.

Older Clients

- Older clients may need assistance using the glucose monitor. *Older clients may have arthritic joint changes, poor vision, or hand tremors.*

- Older clients may have difficulty obtaining diabetic supplies due to financial concerns or homebound status.

HOME CARE CONSIDERATIONS

- Assess the client or caregiver's ability and willingness to perform blood glucose monitoring at home.

- Teach the proper use of the lancet and glucose monitor, and provide written guidelines. Allow time for a return demonstration. *The client may need several visits to completely learn the procedure.*

- Ensure the client's ability to obtain supplies and purchase reagent strips. *The strips are relatively expensive and may not be covered by the client's insurance.*

- Instruct the client how to record the blood glucose levels and when to notify the health care provider.

48–5 Obtaining a Venous Blood Specimen from an Adult by Venipuncture

Before obtaining a venous blood specimen determine specific conditions to be met before obtaining the blood; previous disease, injury, or therapy that places client at risk for a venipuncture, such as bleeding disorder, anticoagulant therapy; presence of IV infusion that can alter test results; and the client's ability to cooperate with procedure.

PURPOSES

- To assess specific elements or constituents of venous blood (e.g., red or white blood cell count, differential white blood cell count, glucose, electrolytes, drugs, bacteria)
- To determine a client's blood type
- To monitor a client's response to specific therapies

ASSESSMENT FOCUS

> Condition of veins and surrounding skin for selected site.

EQUIPMENT

- ❏ Correct test tubes for the tests (Vacuum specimen tubes are required for the vacucontainer method)
- ❏ Disposable gloves
- ❏ Topical antiseptic swab
- ❏ Tourniquet
- ❏ Sterile 1-inch needles, usually #19 or #21 gauge for adults

or

- ❏ Vacucontainer and sterile double-ended needles that screw into the adaptor
- ❏ Sterile syringe of appropriate size for the amount of blood required; sizes 5 to 10 mL are frequently used (optional)

- ❏ 2 × 2 pad
- ❏ Dry sterile sponges
- ❏ Band-Aid
- ❏ Completed labels for each container
- ❏ Completed requisition

INTERVENTION

1. **Verify the physician's orders for the tests to be obtained, and obtain the correct test tubes specific for the tests ordered.**

2. **Identify the client appropriately.**

- Check the client's wristband, and compare the name with the name on the requisition and chart.

- Explain the procedure to the client and enlist cooperation.

3. **Don gloves, and perform venipuncture.**

- See Procedure 48–1 in *Fundamentals of Nursing*.

4. **Obtain the specimen.**

Using Sterile Syringe and Needle

- When the needle is in the vein, gently pull back on the syringe plunger until the appropriate amount of blood is obtained (usually about 5 mL).

- Remove the tourniquet when sufficient blood is obtained, and remove the needle from the vein. Withdraw the needle in line with the vein while placing a 2 × 2 gauze pad over the site without applying pressure. *Removing the tourniquet and applying the gauze pad minimizes bleeding at the site when the needle is withdrawn. Careful removal of the needle reduces vein trauma and client discomfort.*

- Cover the venipuncture site with a sterile gauze pad, and ask the client to hold it firmly in place for

2 to 3 minutes, if able. *This facilitates clotting and minimizes bleeding from the site.*

- Transfer the specimens to the tubes:

  a. Insert the needle directly through the stopper of the blood tube, and allow the vacuum to fill the tube with blood (Figure 48–1). Some nurses change the needle to a sterile #18-gauge needle to facilitate transfer of the blood by this method.

- For all blood tubes containing additives, gently rotate or invert the test tube several times. *This mixes the blood with the tube contents. Shaking is contraindicated because it can cause the erythrocytes to rupture.*

▶Procedure 48–5 Obtaining a Venous Blood Specimen by Venipuncture *continued*

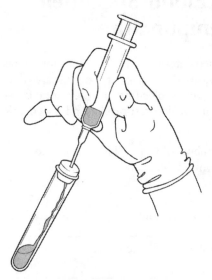

Figure 48–1 Inserting a blood specimen directly through the stopper of the blood tube.

- Ensure that the tubes contain the correct amount of blood. *Each laboratory test requires a specific amount of blood, and tubes with additives must contain the correct ratio of blood to additive.*

Using a Vacucontainer System

- As soon as the venipuncture needle is positioned in the vein, hold the plastic adapter securely, and press the vacuum tube firmly into the short needle until it pierces the top of the tube. Blood will then spurt rapidly into the tube.

- Fill the vacucontainer with blood, release it, and set it aside.

- Insert another vacucontainer if more blood is required.

- Release the tourniquet, and remove the needle from the vein as described above.

- Cover the venipuncture site with a sterile gauze pad as above.

5. Ensure client comfort and safety.

- Assess the client's venipuncture site for oozing. This is especially important for clients who have prolonged blood coagulation times.

- If clots have not begun to form at the site, continue to apply pressure until bleeding has stopped.

- When bleeding is minimized, apply a Band-Aid over the site.

6. Label the test tubes appropriately, and send them to the laboratory.

- Attach labels to all test tubes. Ensure that the information on each label and the laboratory requisition is complete and correct. *Inappropriate identification of specimens can lead to errors of diagnosis or therapy for the client.*

- Arrange for the specimen to be taken to the laboratory or stored appropriately, e.g., in a refrigerator. Blood obtained for culture should be transported immediately and should not be refrigerated. See Variation, next.

7. Document and report relevant information.

- Record the date and time blood is withdrawn, the test(s) to be performed, description of the venipuncture site after specimen collection.

- Report "stat" or any abnormal test results to the physician.

VARIATION: Collecting a Blood Specimen For Culture

In addition to blood withdrawal equipment, two sets of paired culture media bottles (Figure 48–2), a povidone-iodine or alcohol swab, and additional needles are required for this specimen collection.

- Prepare the venipuncture site with povidone-iodine. Use alcohol if the client is allergic to iodine.

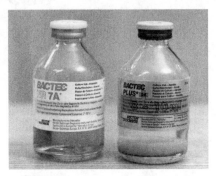

Figure 48–2 Culture bottle set for blood cultures.

- Collect 5 mL of blood from a vein that does not have an IV running into it. *A specimen drawn through an intravenous infusion site will alter the test results.*

- Place a sterile needle on the syringe used to draw blood. *The needle used to puncture the skin may contaminate the specimen and affect culture results.*

- Swab the top(s) of the blood culture blood bottle(s). Insert the needle through the tops, and carefully inject 2½ to 5 mL of blood into one or both bottles, according to agency protocol.

- Use a new sterile needle when puncturing each bottle top. *This will avoid transmitting microorganisms to the blood from the bottle top.*

- Prepare the skin again with povidone-iodine or alcohol solution and collect the second specimen after 15 minutes, or according to agency protocol. Most agencies require each specimen to be collected from a different site.

- Place this second sample in a set of paired culture bottles as above and according to the practice at your agency.

- If a third specimen is needed, follow the above procedure.

- Remove gloves.

- Label the bottles, and transport the specimen to the laboratory *immediately.*

▶ **Procedure 48–5** *continued*

EVALUATION FOCUS

> Site used for venipuncture and appearance of site after the procedure; results of the laboratory tests.

SAMPLE RECORDING

Date	Time	Notes
12/22/04	0700	Venipuncture performed in antecubital vein. Specimen for complete blood count and electrolytes sent to laboratory. Venipuncture site has minimal bleeding. No evidence of hematoma.————————————————————George Sawyers, RN

LIFESPAN CONSIDERATIONS

- A tourniquet may not be appropriate for older clients with fragile veins. *Use of a tourniquet increases venous pressure and can cause veins to leak.*

- If a hematoma occurs after venipuncture, apply warm soaks to the site. *Blood vessel walls become thinner and more delicate with aging.*

- A second person may need to hold the older client's arm in position if contractures or tremors are present.

HOME CARE CONSIDERATIONS

- Use a private area of the home for the procedure and place supplies on a clean towel or cloth.

- Place the specimen in a plastic biohazard bag and store it in a container marked "biohazard."

- Most specimens should be transported in a cooler with ice. Do not expose the specimens to extreme temperatures in the car.

- The specimen must reach the laboratory within a reasonable period of time, usually 1 hour. The time each specimen was drawn must be marked on the tube.

- Ensure that the laboratory knows where the results should be reported. Call the physician immediately with abnormal or critical results.

48–6 Assisting with the Insertion of a Central Venous Catheter

PURPOSE

- To administer nutritional fluids and medications that cannot be given by a peripheral route or when peripheral routes cannot be obtained
- To allow monitoring of central venous pressure
- To provide access for long-term IV therapy
- To provide venous access for blood sampling

ASSESSMENT FOCUS

Baseline vital signs; actual and desired mobility status of the client, which may affect the approach used (supraclavicular or infraclavicular); exit sites for skin integrity and signs of infection; status of antecubital veins if PIC is to be inserted; client's ability to hold breath, maintain the required position, and not move when requested; agency protocol regarding care of central lines and sites.

EQUIPMENT

For insertion

- ❏ Sterile gloves for the physician and the nurse (2 pairs for the nurse)
- ❏ Skin preparation set, if the area needs to be shaved, or soap, water, a washcloth, and a towel
- ❏ Povidone-iodine sponges and ointment, or, if the client is allergic to iodine, 70% alcohol with sterile gauze squares and a combination of antifungal and antimicrobial ointment
- ❏ Masks for the nurse and the physician (in some agencies the client is also required to wear a mask)
- ❏ Bath blanket (if subclavian or jugular insertion is used)
- ❏ Sterile or clean gown for the physician (check agency policy)

- ❏ Subclavian insertion tray
- ❏ Cut-down tray
- ❏ Sterile 3-mL syringe with a 1-in #25 gauge needle
- ❏ Skin anesthetic (e.g., lidocaine 1 or 2% without epinephrine)
- ❏ Radiopaque subclavian catheter of suitable size and length
- ❏ Sterile 4 × 4 gauze squares
- ❏ Moistureproof sterile dressing material
- ❏ Adhesive tape
- ❏ Heparin or normal saline flushes as needed
- ❏ Portable x-ray machine

For establishing the infusion

- ❏ Small IV solution container of normal saline or 5% dextrose in water

- ❏ Sterile TPN tubing or IV administration set with drip chamber and tubing (microdrip tubing is used when less than 100 mL/hour is administered; macrodrip tubing is used when more than 100 mL/hour is given)
- ❏ Extension tubing (30 in)
- ❏ *Optional:* A 0.22-micron cellulose membrane air-eliminating filter
- ❏ Table to secure the tubing connections if Luer-Lok connections are not available
- ❏ IV pole
- ❏ Soft-tipped clamp without teeth to clamp tubing if problems arise

INTERVENTION

1. Prepare the client.

- Describe the procedure, and explain the purpose of the catheter and the procedures involved in care and maintenance of the line.

- Ensure that the client signs a consent form before the procedure begins.

- Instruct the client on how to perform Valsalva's maneuver (forced expiration against a closed glottis), i.e., to take a breath, close the mouth, breathe out, and bear down. Encourage the client to practice this maneuver before the procedure, unless contraindicated by the client's condition.

- If the client is unable to perform Valsalva's maneuver

  a. Ask the client to hold the breath at the end of a deep inspiration or during the expiratory phase of the respiratory cycle, and/or

  b. Have an assistant compress the client's abdomen with both hands.

2. Prepare the IV infusion equipment for attachment to the catheter.

▶ **Procedure 48–6** *continued*

- Connect the infusion tubing spike to the port of the IV solution container using surgical aseptic technique.

- Add the filter to the infusion tubing, then connect the extension tubing below the filter.

- Tape the tubing connections or use Luer-Lok connections. *This will prevent inadvertent separation, which can lead to air embolism, leakage, and contamination.*

- Start the flow of solution, and prime the tubing to remove air. *This dislodges air bubbles and prevents air embolism.*

- Stop the flow of solution, place the tubing protector cap on the end of the tubing, and hang the tubing on the IV pole. *The protector cap maintains the sterility of the open-ended tubing.*

3. **Position the client appropriately.**

- Assist the client to a Trendelenburg position (approximately a 15° to 30° angle). If the client cannot tolerate this position, use a supine position and modified Trendelenburg position with only the feet elevated 45° to 60°. *In Trendelenburg's position, the veins will dilate, and the risk of an air embolism is reduced because slight positive pressure is induced in the central veins.*

- For *subclavian insertion*, place a rolled bath blanket under the client's back between the shoulders. *In this position, venous distention is increased.*

  or

  For jugular insertion:

  a. Place a rolled bath blanket under the opposite shoulder. *The blanket will extend the neck, making anatomic structures more visible for selecting the site.*

  b. Turn the client's head to the opposite side. *This position makes the site more visible and reduces the chance of contamination from microorganisms in the client's respiratory tract.*

  or

  For a *peripheral vein insertion* in the brachiocephalic vein or the superior vena cava, place the client supine with the dominant arm at a 90° angle to the trunk. *This arm position provides the straightest, most direct route to the central venous system. The dominant arm is often used because movement accelerates blood flow and decreases the risk of dependent edema.*

4. **Clean and shave the insertion area.**

- Open skin preparation equipment and don gloves.

- Wash and dry the insertion site with soap and water. *Washing will remove dirt and reduce the number of microorganisms present.*

- Shave the area or clip the hair close to the skin, according to agency policy. *Shaving may cause skin irritation, increasing the risk of infection.*

- Discard the gloves.

- Don a mask and sterile gloves.

- Clean the site with povidone-iodine sponges for 2 minutes or, if using 70% alcohol, for 10 minutes or according to agency protocol. Use a circular motion, working outward. *Working outward prevents reintroducing microorganisms to the site.*

5. **Maintain a sterile field, and assist the physician during catheter insertion.**

- Open sterile packages and hand supplies to the physician as needed, using sterile technique.

6. **Support and monitor the client.**

- Talk to the client during the procedure and explain what is happening. Provide emotional support.

- Monitor the client for signs of respiratory distress, complaints of chest pain, tachycardia, pallor, and cyanosis. *These observations facilitate early detection of pneumothorax and air embolism. An improperly placed catheter may cause pneumothorax, resulting in chest pain and labored breathing.*

7. **Attach the primed IV tubing to the catheter.**

- While the physician removes the stylet from the catheter, quickly attach the IV tubing to the catheter, and simultaneously ask the client to perform Valsalva's maneuver as practiced. *Valsalva's maneuver increases intrathoracic pressure, creating more pressure on the large veins entering the heart and reducing the return of blood to the heart. It therefore reduces the risk of air entering the large heart vein via the opened catheter and the risk of subsequent air embolism.*

- Set the flow at a keep-open rate to maintain venous access until catheter placement is confirmed by x-ray.

8. **After the infusion is attached, apply a temporary dressing to the site.**

- Put on the second pair of sterile gloves.

- Apply povidone-iodine ointment to the site if agency protocol dictates. Many agencies no longer use ointment, believing it causes skin maceration.

- Apply a 4 × 4 sterile gauze dressing or a transparent occlusive

▶ Procedure 48–6 Assisting with the Insertion of a Central Venous Catheter *continued*

dressing according to agency protocol.

9. **After x-ray examination or fluoroscopy confirms the position of the catheter, secure the dressing with tape.**

- See Procedure 48–8.

- Label the dressing with the date and time of insertion and the length of the catheter, if it is not indicated on the catheter.

10. **Establish the appropriate infusion.**

- See Procedure 48–7.

11. **Document all relevant information.**

- Document the time of insertion, the size and length of the catheter, the site of insertion, the name of the physician, the time of the x-ray examination and the results, the kind of infusion, the rate of flow, and all nursing assessments and interventions.

EVALUATION FOCUS

Clinical signs of sepsis and air embolism and pneumothorax.

SAMPLE RECORDING

Date	Time	Notes
12/12/04	1900	16-cm subclavian catheter inserted by Dr. R. Sullivan. 1,000 mL D5W started at 36 mL/hr. Placement confirmed by fluoroscopy at 1850 hr. Vital signs stable. Slight pallor.————Naomi Treasure, NS

LIFESPAN CONSIDERATIONS

- Young clients may need a central venous catheter for long-term IV therapy and blood sampling.

- Explain the procedure beforehand, allowing time for the young client to express thoughts and ask questions. Use play therapy to demonstrate the dressing.

- If possible, allow a parent to stay with the young client during the procedure and provide emotional support.

- Encourage the young client with praise during the procedure.

48–7 Maintaining and Monitoring a CVC System

Before monitoring a CVC system, determine agency policy about central line care, the type of catheter (single- or multiple-lumen) used, and the type and sequence of solutions to be infused.

PURPOSES
- To maintain the prescribed infusion flow rate
- To maintain patency of the central venous system
- To prevent complications associated with central venous lines

ASSESSMENT FOCUS

Appearance of catheter site; rate of flow; any adverse response of the client.

EQUIPMENT
- Tape
- Items for tubing change and dressing change (see Procedure 38–8).
- #21 gauge 1-in needles
- Luer-Lok adapters
- Soft-tipped clamp without teeth
- Alcohol or povidone-iodine wipes
- 10-mL syringe
- Sterile normal saline
- 3-mL syringe
- Heparin flush solution (e.g., 100 units heparin per 1 mL of saline)

INTERVENTION

1. **Label each lumen of multilumen catheters.**

- Mark each lumen or port of the tubing with a description of its purpose (e.g., the distal lumen for CVP monitoring and infusing blood; the middle lumen for TPN; and the proximal lumen for other IV solutions or for blood samples).

or

Use a color code established by the agency to label the proximal, middle, and distal lumens. *Labeling prevents mixing of incompatible medications or infusions and reserves each lumen for specific therapies.*

2. **Monitor tubing connections.**

- Ensure that all tubing connections are taped or secured according to agency protocol.
- Check the connections every 2 hours.
- Tape cap ends if agency protocol indicates.

3. **Change tubing according to agency policy.**

- See Procedure 48–8.
- Some agencies advocate changing TPN tubing every 24 hours and tubing for other infusions every 48 to 72 hours.

4. **Change the catheter site dressing according to agency policy.**

- See Procedure 48–8.
- Most agencies recommend that the dressing be changed every 48 to 72 hours.

5. **Administer all infusions as ordered.**

- Use a controller or pump for all fluids (see Procedure 48–2).
- Prime all tubing to remove air.
- Maintain the fluid flow at the prescribed rate.
- *Optional:* If a *nonviscous* or *intermittent* solution is used, attach a #21 gauge short needle to the infusion tubing, and insert it through a clean Luer-Lok adapter cap. Tape this connection.

- If a *viscous* solution is to be infused, remove the Luer-Lok adapter, and apply the infusion tubing directly to the port or lumen.

- Whenever the line is interrupted for any reason, instruct the client to perform Valsalva's maneuver. If the client is unable to perform Valsalva's maneuver, place the client in a supine position, and clamp the lumen of the catheter with a soft-tipped clamp. Place a strip of tape (about 3 in from the end) over the catheter before applying the clamp. *The clamp is placed over the taped area to prevent damage to the tubing. A clamp without teeth prevents piercing.*

6. **Cap lumens without continuous infusions, and flush them regularly.**

- Cap ports not in use with an intermittent infusion cap to seal the end of a catheter.

▶ **Procedure 48–7 Maintaining and Monitoring a CVC System** *continued*

- Clean the adapter caps with alcohol or povidone-iodine swab before penetration.

- Flush noninfusing tubings with 1 or 2 mL of heparin flush solution every 8 hours or according to agency protocol. *Flushing prevents obstruction of the catheter by a blood clot.*

- Some agencies use normal saline solution instead of heparin solution to flush catheters. *Research indicates that heparin isn't always necessary to keep IV lines open.*

- Always aspirate for blood before flushing tubings (or infusing medications). *This validates that the catheter is appropriately placed in the vein.*

- Use a #25 gauge 5/8-in needle to penetrate the adapter cap when flushing the catheter. *A small gauge needle minimizes the possibility of leakage through the adapter plug, and a short needle minimizes the possibility of damaging the catheter.*

7. **Administer medications as ordered.**

- If a capped port used for medication has been flushed with heparin solution, flush the line with 5 to 10 mL of normal saline according to agency protocol before giving the medication. *Many medications are incompatible with heparin.*

- After the medication is instilled through the port, inject normal saline first and then the heparin flush solution if indicated by agency protocol. *The saline solution flushes the line of the medication. The heparin maintains the patency of the catheter by preventing blood clotting.*

8. **Monitor the client for complications.**

- Assess the client's vital signs, skin color, mental alertness, appearance of the catheter site, and presence of adverse symptoms at least every 4 hours.

- If air embolism is suspected, give the client 100% oxygen by mask, place the person in a left Trendelenburg position (Durant maneuver), and notify the physician.

Lowering the head increases intrathoracic pressure, decreasing the flow of air into the vein during inhalation. A left side-lying position helps prevent the air from moving to the pulmonary artery.

- If sepsis is suspected, replace a TPN, blood, or other infusion with 5% or 10% dextrose solution, change the IV tubing and dressing, save the remaining solution for lab analysis, record the lot number of the solution and any additives, and notify the physician immediately. When changing the dressing, take a culture of the catheter site as ordered by the physician or according to agency protocol.

9. **Document all relevant information.**

- Record the date and time of any infusion started; type of solution, drip rate, and number of milliliters infusing per hour; dressing or tubing changes; appearance of insertion site; and all other nursing assessments.

EVALUATION FOCUS

> Rate of infusion flow; appearance of catheter site; any adverse response of the client.

SAMPLE RECORDING

Date	Time	Notes
12/02/04	1410	Bag #6 of hyperalimentation infusion started and running at 80 mL per hour per infusion pump. Catheter insertion site clean without inflammation or tenderness.————————Carolyn Churchill, RN

▶ **Procedure 48–7** *continued*

LIFESPAN CONSIDERATIONS

- Explain all procedures to the young client beforehand, using play therapy to demonstrate.

- Young clients can help with catheter care procedures by holding nonsterile supplies and handing them to the nurse. *Participating gives the child a sense of control.*

- Tell the young client not to play with the IV tubing, flow clamp, or any other part of the equipment. Encourage the child to decorate the IV tubing with colorful stickers.

HOME CARE CONSIDERATIONS

- When caring for a central catheter in the home, place equipment on a clean towel or nonsterile drape.

- Assess the home environment and help the client choose a clean, dry place to store the IV supplies.

- Evaluate the client or caregiver's ability and willingness to perform catheter care at home. Ask for a return demonstration of all teaching.

- Emphasize the need for hand washing and clean technique when working with the central catheter.

- Ensure that the client knows how and where to obtain supplies.

- Discuss possible complications of a central line, such as phlebitis, sepsis, or thrombus formation, and explain when to notify the health care provider.

48–8 Changing a CVC Tubing and Dressing

PURPOSES
- To prevent excessive growth of microorganisms and infection
- To inspect the catheter insertion site
- To maintain the flow of required fluids

ASSESSMENT FOCUS

Allergy to tape or iodine; infusion rate and amount absorbed; patency of IV system; presence of infiltration at catheter site.

EQUIPMENT

For tubing change
- ❏ New solution container and administration set (tubing)
- ❏ Sterile gloves
- ❏ Mask (especially if the client is immunocompromised)
- ❏ Sterile 2 × 2 gauze squares
- ❏ Antiseptic
- ❏ Tape

For dressing change
- ❏ Central catheter dressing set

or

- ❏ Two face masks (one for the nurse and one for the client)
- ❏ 70% isopropyl alcohol
- ❏ Gloves (2 pairs)
- ❏ 4 × 4 gauze sponges
- ❏ Antiseptic swabs (e.g., 1% iodine tincture or povidone-iodine solutions or, if client is allergic to iodine, 70% alcohol)

- ❏ Povidone-iodine ointment, if indicated by agency protocol, or a combination of antimicrobial and antifungal agents if client is allergic to iodine
- ❏ Precut sterile drain gauze or 2 × 2 gauze and sterile scissors
- ❏ Tincture of benzoin
- ❏ Elastoplast tape or transparent occlusive dressing such as Op-Site
- ❏ Nonallergenic 2.5-cm (1-in) tape

INTERVENTION

Tubing Change

1. Prepare the client.

- Assist the client to the supine position. *This lowers the negative pressure in the vena cava, thus decreasing the risk of air embolism when the catheter is opened.*

2. Prepare the equipment.

- Prepare the solution container, attach the new IV tubing, and prime the tubing as you would for a conventional IV. See Procedure 48–3 in *Fundamentals of Nursing*.

- Don clean gloves and remove the tape securing the tubing to the dressing and the catheter hub connection. Remove and discard the gloves.

- Don sterile gloves and mask.

- Place the sterile gauze underneath the connection site of the

catheter and tubing. Clean the junction of the catheter and tubing with the antiseptic, if required by agency protocol. *This prevents the transfer of microorganisms from the client's skin to the open CVC catheter tip when it is detached; it also decreases the number of microorganisms at the catheter-tubing junction.*

3. Change the tubing.

- Don clean gloves and ask the client to perform Valsalva's maneuver (that is, to take a deep breath and bear down) and to turn the head away while you detach the IV tubing by rotating it out of the hub. *Performance of Valsalva's maneuver reduces the risk of air embolism, and turning the head to the side reduces the chances of contaminating the equipment.*

- Quickly attach the new primed IV tubing to the TPN catheter, ensuring a tight seal.

- Open the clamp on the new tubing, and adjust the flow to the rate ordered.

- Secure the tubing to the catheter with tape if a Luer-Lok connection is not present. *This prevents accidental separation of the tubes and contamination of the system.*

- Loop and tape the tubing over the dressing. *This prevents tension on the catheter and inadvertent separation of the tubing and the catheter.*

4. Label the tubing, and document the tubing change.

- Mark the date and time of the tubing change on the new IV tubing or drip chamber.

- Document the tubing change and all assessments.

Dressing Change

5. Prepare the client.

▶ Procedure 48–8 continued

- Assist the client to a supine or a semi-Fowler's position.

- Don a mask, and have the client don a mask (if tolerated or as agency protocol indicates), and/or ask the client to turn the head away from the insertion site. *This helps protect the insertion site from the nurse's and client's nasal and oral microorganisms. Turning the client's head also makes the site more accessible.*

6. **Prepare the equipment.**

- Wash hands before handling sterile supplies.

- Open the sterile supplies.

7. **Change the dressing.**

- Remove the clean gloves and don sterile gloves. Remove the soiled dressing by pulling the tape slowly and gently from the skin. *This prevents catheter displacement and skin irritation.*

- Inspect the skin for signs of irritation or infection. Inspect the catheter for signs of leakage or other problems. If infection is suspected, take a swab of the drainage for culture, label it, send it to the laboratory, and notify the physician.

- Clean the catheter insertion site with 3 alcohol swabs followed by 3 povodine-iodine swabs. Some agencies require cleaning with iodine first, followed by alcohol.

- Clean in a circular motion, moving from the insertion site outward to the edge of the adhesive border. *Cleaning from the insertion site outward and discarding the sponges after each wipe avoids introducing contaminants from the uncleaned area to the site. Jostling the catheter can cause discomfort to the client and could dislodge the catheter.*

- *Optional:* Apply the povidone-iodine ointment to the insertion site and to the catheter hub. Check agency policy.

- Apply a precut sterile drain gauze around the catheter (Figure 48–3). (If precut gauze is not available, cut a 2 × 2 sterile gauze square, using the sterile scissors.) Apply sufficient sterile gauze dressings to cover the catheter and skin. *This protects the catheter and skin surrounding the insertion site from airborne contaminants.*

or

If using Elastoplast dressing, apply tincture of benzoin to the skin

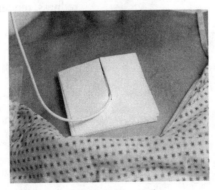

Figure 48–3   A precut sterile gauze placed around a central venous catheter over the insertion site.

surrounding the dressing gauzes, and allow it to air dry about 1 minute. This protects the skin when adhesive tape or Elastoplast is applied and promotes adhesion of the cover dressing. Appropriate drying time is essential to prevent skin breakdown when the dressing is removed.

- Remove your gloves.

8. **Secure the dressing and the tubing.**

- Ask the client to abduct the arm and turn the head away from the dressing site. Tape the dressing securely to the skin with transparent occlusive dressing or Elastoplast. Make sure that the adhesive covering is occlusive. *Arm abduction and head rotation ensure that the client's range of motion is not limited by the dressing and decreases the potential for skin abrasion caused by movement of the adhesive.*

- Loop and tape the IV tubing (not the filter) over the occlusive dressing. *Looping prevents tension on the catheter and its inadvertent detachment if the tubing is pulled.*

- Label the dressing with the date, time, and your initials.

- See Procedure 48–3 in *Fundamentals of Nursing.*

9. **Document the tubing and the dressing change, including all nursing assessments.**

▶ **Procedure 48–8 Changing a CVC Tubing and Dressing** *continued*

EVALUATION FOCUS

Appearance of catheter insertion site; presence of drainage, patency of tubing, infusion rate.

SAMPLE RECORDING

Date	Time	Notes
12/12/04	1805	CVC container and tubing changed. D5W infusing via IVAC pump at 60 mL/hr. Dressing changed at right subclavian triple-lumen catheter site using aseptic technique. No redness, edema or drainage. Povidone-iodine ointment applied.———Evylin Loo, RN

LIFESPAN CONSIDERATIONS

- Use play therapy to demonstrate the dressing change procedure to the young client.

- Allow the young client to help with the procedure if possible. *Participation gives a sense of control.*

- Tell the young client not to handle the IV tubing or the dressing and to notify the nurse if the dressing itches or feels uncomfortable. *Scratching can dislodge the dressing and contaminate the site with microorganisms.*

HOME CARE CONSIDERATIONS

- Evaluate the home environment and help the client choose a clean, dry place to store IV supplies. Supplies should be kept away from pets and children.

- Evaluate the client or caregiver's ability to care for the IV catheter at home. Ask for a return demonstration after each phase of teaching.

- Emphasize the need for hand washing and clean technique when handling the IV line.

- Instruct the client how and where to obtain supplies.

- Teach signs of infection at the catheter site, such as redness, tenderness, drainage, or swelling.

48–9 Removing a Central Venous Catheter

PURPOSES
- To remove a central venous catheter using sterile technique
- To monitor and evaluate the client during the procedure
- To protect the catheter insertion site from infection

ASSESSMENT FOCUS

> Type of catheter; exit site of CV catheter for skin integrity and signs of infection; baseline vital signs.

EQUIPMENT

- ❏ Sterile suture removal set
- ❏ Sterile drape
- ❏ Alcohol sponges
- ❏ Povidone-iodine ointment and 4 × 4 sterile gauze squares, or Vaseline gauze

- ❏ Mask for the nurse; one for the client if an infection is suspected
- ❏ Sterile gloves
- ❏ Sterile moistureproof dressing materials

- ❏ Sterile scissors if culture of catheter tip is needed

INTERVENTION

1. Prepare the equipment.

- Open a sterile suture removal set, and establish a sterile field.
- Open the sterile packages, i.e., sterile gauze squares and alcohol sponges.
- Place some povidone-iodine ointment on one of the sterile gauze squares if this ointment is to be used. Check agency protocol.
- Don a mask, and put one on the client if necessary.
- Close the clamp on the infusion.

2. Position the client appropriately.

- Place the client in a supine or slight Trendelenburg position. *These positions distend the central veins with blood, increase intrathoracic pressure, and limit air entry into the central vein.*
- Don clean gloves and remove the dressing. Remove and discard the gloves.
- Don sterile gloves.
- Remove any sutures that secure the catheter.

3. Remove the catheter.

- Ask the client to perform Valsalva's maneuver during removal. *This maneuver raises intrathoracic pressure and prevents air entry into the central vein.*
- Grasp the catheter hub and carefully withdraw it, maintaining the direction of the vein.
- Inspect the catheter to make sure it is intact. If it is not, immediately place the client in a left lateral Trendelenburg position and notify the nurse in charge or physician. *A piece of the catheter in a vein could cause an embolus*
- If a culture is needed, use sterile scissors to cut approximately 1 inch (2.5 cm) from the distal end of the catheter. Let the cut end drop into a sterile culture container.

4. Immediately after catheter removal, apply pressure with an air-occlusive dressing over the site.

- Use an air-occlusive dressing, such as Vaseline gauze or Telfa covered with antibiotic ointment or plain sterile gauze (check agency policy). *Manual pressure and the occlusive dressing force the tissues together and seal off an air entry path.*

- Completely cover the insertion site with povidone-iodine ointment, if used, sterile gauze pads, and moisture-proof tape. *Nonporous tape helps to ensure impermeability to air.*

or

If agency protocol indicates, use a sterile transparent air-occlusive dressing. *A transparent dressing allows direct observation of the puncture site for signs of infection and bleeding.*

- Label the dressing with the date and time of catheter removal and your initials.
- Leave the air-occlusive dressing in place for 24 to 72 hours or the length of time agency protocol recommends. *The longer the duration of the catheter, the more time required for the subclavian tunnel to seal.*

5. Ensure client safety.

- Ask the client to remain flat and supine for a short time after the subclavian catheter is removed. *This position helps to maintain a positive intrathoracic pressure and allows the tissue tract to begin sealing.*

▶ **Procedure 48–9 Removing a Central Venous Catheter** *continued*

- Observe the client for signs of air embolism.

- If an air embolism is suspected, immediately place the client in a left lateral Trendelenburg position and administer 100% oxygen by face mask. *The left lateral*

Trendelenburg position increases intrathoracic pressure, preventing air entry, and oxygen by mask provides oxygen to poorly perfused tissues.

6. **Document all pertinent information.**

- Document the time of removal; the size, length, and condition of the catheter; and all nursing assessments and interventions.

EVALUATION FOCUS

Appearance of exit site for catheter; comparison of vital signs to baseline data; presence of signs of air embolism.

SAMPLE RECORDING

Date	Time	Notes
01/06/04	1100	18-cm subclavian catheter removed intact. Transparent air occlusive dressing applied. BP 150/90, P 62 and regular, R 15.——————————Rosanna Rodrigues, NS

LIFESPAN CONSIDERATIONS

- Explain to the young client that there may be some pressure as the catheter is removed, but the procedure won't be painful.

- Allow a parent to stay with the young client, if possible.

- Tell the young client not to touch the dressing and to notify the nurse if it itches or feels uncomfortable.

48–10 Measuring Central Venous Pressure

PURPOSES
- To assess hydration status
- To monitor fluid replacement and determine specific fluid requirements
- To evaluate blood volume (e.g., to monitor the degree of hemorrhage in a postoperative client)
- To assess cardiac function and venous return to the heart

ASSESSMENT FOCUS

Patency of CVC line; presence of infection or air embolism; central venous pressure.

EQUIPMENT

- ❏ Intravenous tubing
- ❏ Manometer set, including stopcock
- ❏ Pressure monitoring kit, transducer, and bedside pressure module if continuous monitoring is desired
- ❏ A leveling device, if available
- ❏ Nonallergenic tape or an indelible marker
- ❏ Masks
- ❏ Sterile gloves

INTERVENTION

1. Prepare the client

- Place the client in a supine position without a pillow unless this position is contraindicated. If the client feels breathless, elevate the head of the bed slightly; note the exact position because it must be used for all subsequent CVP readings, and the manometer level must be adjusted accordingly. *The client must always be in the same position to ensure reliable comparative CVP readings.*

- Locate the level of the client's right atrium at the 4th intercostal space on the midaxillary line.

- Mark this site with indelible pen or piece of nonallergenic tape.

2. Prepare the equipment.

- Prepare the IV tubing and infusion, prime the tubing, and then close the clamp on the tubing.

- If you are using a separate manometer and stopcock, attach the manometer to the stopcock. The manometer is attached to the vertical arm of the stopcock.

- If you are using a one-piece manometer and stopcock, attach these to the IV pole.

- Attach the IV tubing to the left side of the three-way stopcock.

3. Flush the manometer and stopcock.

- Do *not* attach the stopcock to the client's catheter until it is flushed free of air. *Air in the line will interfere with the CVP reading and could cause an air embolism.*

- Turn the stopcock to the IV-container-to-manometer postion (Figure 48–4, *A*).

- Open the IV tubing clamp and fill the manometer with the IV solution to a level of about 18 to 20 cm.

- Close the IV tubing clamp.

- Turn the stopcock to the IV-container-to-client position (Figure 48–4, *C*), and flush the stopcock.

- Close the IV tubing clamp.

4. Attach the manometer to the central catheter.

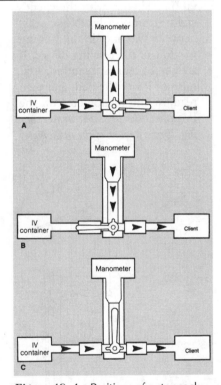

Figure 48–4   Positions of a stopcock; *A*, IV container to manometer; *B*, Manometer to client; *C*, IV container to client.

- Place sterile 4 × 4 gauze under the catheter hub.

- After cleansing the hub with alcohol or povidone-iodine, clamp

▶ Procedure 48–10 Measuring Central Venous Pressure *continued*

the tubing near the insertion site, and attach the manometer tubing to the catheter.

- Turn the stopcock so that the IV runs into the client. (Figure 48–4, *C* on page 207) and open the IV clamp.

5. Measure the central venous pressure.

- Check that the level of the client's right atrium (zero reference point) is aligned with the zero point on the manometer scale. To align them, use the leveling rod on the manometer or a yardstick with a level attached (Figure 48–5). When the rod is horizontal (i.e., aligned with the client's right atrium), a bubble appears between two lines in the viewing window of the leveling device. If an adjustment is required, first raise or lower the bed, and then readjust the manometer on the IV pole. *To ensure an accurate reading, the zero mark of the manometer must correspond with the level of the client's right atrium, and the manometer must be vertical.*

- Adjust the stopcock to the manometer-to-client setting (Figure 48–4, *B* on page 207).

- Observe the fall in fluid level in the manometer tube. Note also the slight fluctuations in the fluid level with the client's inspiration and expiration. If the fluid level does not fluctuate, ask the client to cough. *The fluid level falls with inspiration because of a decrease in intrathoracic pressure. It rises with expiration because of an increase in intrathoracic pressure. No fluctuation may indicate that the 01/P catheter is lodged against the vein wall. Coughing can change the catheter position.*

- Lightly tap the manometer tube with your index finger when the fluid level stabilizes. *This dislodges air bubbles that can distort the reading.*

- Take a reading at the end of an expiration or according to agency protocol. Inspect the column at eye level, and take the CVP reading from the base of the meniscus. If the manometer tube contains a small floating ball, take the reading from its midline.

- Refill the manometer, and take another reading of the CVP. *A repeat measurement ensures accuracy.*

- Readjust the stopcock to the IV-container-to-client position (see Figure 48–4, *C* on page 207) and adjust the infusion to the ordered rate of flow.

6. Obtain continuous CVP readings with a pressure monitoring system.

- Set up a pressure transducer system at the bedside. Attach noncompliant tubing from the catheter to the transducer, following the previous guidelines. Connect the flush solution container to the flush device.

- Position the client as described earlier, so that the right atrium is level with the transducer. Follow manufacturer's instructions to zero the transducer.

- Read the CVP value on the digital display, and observe the waveform. The client must lie quietly while readings are being taken.

7. Return the client to a comfortable position.

8. Document CVP.

- Include the date and time of the CVP reading, the condition and rate of infusion flow, and all assessments.

- Report the changes in CVP as ordered. In many instances a change of 5 cm or more is reported immediately.

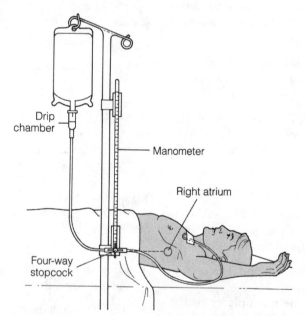

Figure 48–5 The zero point on the manometer scale must be at the level of the client's right atrium.

▶ **Procedure 48–10** *continued*

EVALUATION FOCUS

Central venous pressure; degree of fluctuation of pressure.

SAMPLE RECORDING

Date	Time	Notes
06/06/04	1500	CVP 9. Skin warm and moist. Central line dressing dry. IV infusing at 40 mL/hr.————————————————————————Roberta Smith, SN

LIFESPAN CONSIDERATIONS

- Older clients may need assistance and support to maintain the correct position for the procedure.

- Speak slowly and distinctly to older clients who have a hearing loss. Make eye contact when possible.

- Older clients are at risk for fluid imbalances, which may cause altered central venous pressure.

Procedure Checklists

These Procedure Checklists are intended to be used with the procedures in this manual. Each checklist contains all the essential steps of the procedure. Students may need to adjust the procedures and the checklists in view of the needs of the individual client and according to agency protocol. These checklists can be used in a nursing skills laboratory and in client care areas to facilitate and evaluate learning.

Procedure 15–1
Teaching Progressive Relaxation

PROCEDURE	S	U	COMMENTS
1. Ensure environment is quiet, peaceful, and at a temperature that promotes client comfort.			
2. Tell client how progressive relaxation works.			
Provide rationale for procedure.			
Ask client to identify stressors operating in client's life and reactions to these stressors.			
Demonstrate method of tensing and relaxing muscles.			
3. Assist client to comfortable position.			
Ensure all body parts are supported and joints are slightly flexed, with no strain or pull on muscles.			
4. Encourage client to rest the mind.			
Ask client to gaze slowly across ceiling, down wall, along window curtain, around fabric pattern, and back up wall.			
5. Instruct client to tense and relax each muscle group.			
Progress through each muscle group in order starting with dominant side: a. hand and forearm b. upper arm c. forehead d. central face e. lower face and jaw f. neck g. chest, shoulders, and upper back h. abdomen i. thigh j. calf muscles k. foot			
Encourage client to breathe slowly and deeply during entire procedure.			
Encourage client to focus on each muscle group being tensed and relaxed.			
Speak to client in soothing voice that encourages relaxation.			

	S	U	COMMENTS
6. Ask client to state whether any tension remains after all muscle groups have been tensed and relaxed.			
Repeat procedure for muscle groups not relaxed.			
7. Terminate relaxation exercise slowly by counting backward from 4 to 1.			
Ask client to move body slowly, first hands and feet, then arms and legs, and finally head and neck.			
8. Document client's response to exercise.			

Procedure 15–2
Assisting with Guided Imagery

	S	U	COMMENTS
1. Provide comfortable, quiet environment free of distraction.			
2. Explain rationale and benefits of imagery.			
3. Assist client to reclining position.			
Use touch only if non-threatening to client.			
4. Implement actions to induce relaxation.			
Use client's preferred name.			
Speak clearly in calming and neutral tone of voice.			
Ask client to take slow, deep breaths and to relax all muscles.			
Use progressive relaxation exercises as needed to assist client to achieve total relaxation.			
For pain or stress management, encourage client to "go to a place where you have previously felt very peaceful."			
or			
For internal imagery, encourage client to focus on meaningful image of power and to use it to control specific problem.			
5. Assist client to elaborate on description of image.			
Ask client to use all senses when describing image.			
6. Ask client to describe physical and emotional feelings elicited by image.			

	S	U	COMMENTS
Direct client to explore response to image.			
7. Provide client with continuous feedback.			
Comment on signs of relaxation and peacefulness.			
8. Take client out of image.			
Slowly count backward from 5 to 1. Tell client there will be feelings of restfulness when eyes are opened.			
Remain until client is alert.			
9. Following experience, discuss client's feelings about experience.			
Identify anything that could enhance experience.			
10. Encourage client to practice imagery technique.			

Procedure 28–1
Assessing a Fetal Heart

	S	U	COMMENTS
1. Position client appropriately.			
Assist woman to supine position.			
2. Locate maximum FHR intensity.			
Determine whether area of maximum intensity is recorded on client's chart or marked on client's abdomen.			
or			
Perform Leopold's maneuvers to determine fetal position and locate its posterior.			
3. Auscultate and count FHR.			
Warm hands and head of fetoscope before touching client's abdomen.			
Place fetoscope or stethoscope firmly on maternal abdomen over area of maximum intensity of FHR.			
Listen to and identify fetal heart tone.			
Differentiate fetal heart tone from uterine souffle and from funic souffle.			
Count FHR at least 15 seconds during gestation period before labor.			

During labor, count FHR for 60 seconds in the relaxation period between contractions to determine baseline FHR. Then count FHR for 60 seconds during contraction and for 30 seconds immediately following a contraction.			
4. Assess rhythm and strength of heartbeat.			
Assist woman to listen to FHR if she wishes.			
5. Document and report pertinent assessment data.			
If heart rate or strength is abnormal, or marked changes occur, report immediately to the nurse in charge or physician and initiate electronic fetal monitoring.			
Variation: Using a Doppler stethoscope			
Apply transmission gel to woman's abdomen over area where transducer is to be placed.			
In early pregnancy, ask client to drink plenty of fluids before procedure.			
After determining FHR, remove excess gel from abdomen and transducer.			
Clean transducer with aqueous solution.			

Procedure 28–2
Assessing an Infant's Blood Pressure

1. Prepare and position infant/child appropriately.			
Give explanation of procedure appropriate to child's age.			
Provide calm environment. Allow time for infant to recover from any activity.			
Position infants and children sitting on parent's lap if possible.			
Expose arm and support it comfortably at child's heart level.			
2. Use auscultation method for child over 3 years of age.			
Auscultation method:			
3. Wrap deflated cuff evenly around upper arm.			
Apply center of bladder directly over medial aspect of arm.			

PROCEDURE	S	U	COMMENTS
4. **If client's initial examination, perform preliminary palpatory determination of systolic pressure.**			
Palpate brachial artery with fingertips.			
Close valve on pump and inflate cuff until brachial pulse is no longer felt.			
Note pressure on sphygmomanometer at which pulse is no longer felt.			
Release pressure completely in cuff, and wait 1 to 2 minutes.			
5. **Position stethoscope appropriately.**			
Place bell shaped diaphragm of the stethoscope over brachial pulse.			
6. **Auscultate client's blood pressure.**			
Inflate cuff until sphygmomanometer registers about 30 mm Hg above point where brachial pulse disappears.			
Release valve on cuff so pressure decreases at rate of 2 to 3 mm Hg per second.			
As pressure falls, identify manometer reading at each of five phases.			
Wait 1 to 2 minutes before repeating to confirm accuracy of reading.			
7. **Remove cuff from client's arm.**			
8. **If client's initial examination, repeat procedure on client's other arm.**			
Record two pressures in form 130/80.			
Use abbreviations RA for right arm and LA for left arm.			
9. **Use palpation method, flush technique, or Doppler stethoscope when blood pressure cannot be auscultated.**			
Palpation method:			
Place cuff around the limb so lower edge is about 1 cm (0.4 in) above antecubital space.			
Palpate brachial pulse.			
Inflate cuff to about 30 mm Hg beyond point where brachial pulse disappears.			
Release cuff at rate of 2 to 3 mm Hg per second and identify manometer reading at point where pulse returns to brachial artery.			

PROCEDURE	S	U	COMMENTS
Flush technique (requires two people):			
Place cuff on infant's wrist or ankle.			
Elevate and wrap limb distal to cuff with elastic bandage starting at fingers or toes and working up to blood pressure cuff.			
Lower extremity to heart level.			
Inflate bladder of cuff rapidly to about 200 mm Hg.			
Remove bandage and gradually release pressure at no more than 5 mm Hg per second.			
Record pressure at appearance of a flush.			
Doppler method:			
Plug stethoscope headset into output jack.			
Apply transmission gel to probe or client's skin.			
Hold probe at 45° angle over pulse site.			
Distinguish artery sounds from vein sounds.			
After assessing pulse, remove gel.			
10. Document and report pertinent assessment data.			

Procedure 29–1
Assisting with a Lumbar Puncture

PROCEDURE	S	U	COMMENTS
Preprocedure:			
1. Explain procedure to client and support persons.			
Tell client what to expect during procedure.			
2. Prepare client.			
Have client empty bladder and bowels prior to procedure.			
Position client laterally with head bent toward chest, knees flexed to abdomen, and back to edge of bed or examining table.			
Place small pillow under client's head.			
Drape client, exposing only lumbar spine.			
Open lumbar puncture set if requested to do so by physician.			
During procedure:			
3. Support and monitor client throughout.			

PROCEDURE	S	U	COMMENTS
Stand in front of client, and support back of neck and knees if client needs help in remaining still.			
Reassure client throughout procedure by explaining what is happening. Encourage client to breathe normally and relax as much as possible.			
Observe client's color, respirations, and pulse during lumbar puncture. Ask the client to report headache or persistent pain at the insertion site.			
4. Handle specimen tubes appropriately.			
Don gloves before handling test tubes.			
Label specimen tubes in sequence.			
5. Place small sterile dressing over puncture site.			
Postprocedure:			
6. Ensure client's comfort and safety.			
Assist client to dorsal recumbent position with only one head pillow. The client remains in this position for 1 to 12 hours, depending on physician's orders.			
Determine whether analgesics are ordered and can be given for headaches.			
Offer oral fluids frequently, unless contraindicated.			
7. Monitor client.			
Observe for swelling or bleeding at puncture site.			
Determine whether client feels faint.			
Monitor changes in neurologic status, such as pupillary response, level of consciousness, and muscle strength.			
Determine whether client is experiencing any numbness, tingling, or pain radiating down legs.			
8. Document procedure on client's chart.			

Procedure 29–2
Assisting with an Abdominal Paracentesis

Procedure	S	U	Comments
Preprocedure:			
1. **Prepare client.**			
Explain procedure to client.			
Have client void just before paracentesis. Notify physician if client cannot void.			
Help client assume sitting position in bed or in chair.			
Cover client to expose only necessary area.			
During procedure:			
2. **Assist and monitor client.**			
Support client verbally, and describe steps of procedure as needed.			
Observe client closely for signs of distress and hypovolemic shock.			
Place small sterile dressing over site of incision after cannula or aspirating needle is withdrawn.			
Postprocedure:			
3. **Monitor client closely.**			
Observe for hypovolemic shock.			
Observe client for any scrotal edema.			
Monitor vital signs, urine output, and drainage from puncture every 15 minutes for at least two hours and every hour for four hours thereafter, or as client's condition indicates.			
Measure the abdominal girth at the level of the umbilicus.			
4. **Document all relevant information.**			
5. **Transport labeled specimens to laboratory.**			

Procedure 29–3
Assisting with a Thoracentesis

Procedure	S	U	Comments
Preprocedure:			
1. **Prepare client.**			
Explain procedure to client.			

PROCEDURE	S	U	COMMENTS
Help client assume comfortable position, sitting with arms above head, or arm elevated and stretched forward, or have client lean forward over a pillow.			
Cover client as needed with bath blanket.			

During procedure:

2. **Support and monitor client throughout.**			
Support client verbally and describe steps of procedure as needed.			
Observe client for signs of distress.			
Open the sterile thoracentesis tray and assist the physician as needed.			
3. **Collect drainage and laboratory specimens.**			
4. **Place small sterile dressing over site of puncture.**			

Postprocedure:

5. **Monitor client.**			
Assess pulse rate, respiratory rate, and skin color.			
Observe changes in client's cough, sputum, respiratory depth, breath sounds, and note complaints of chest pain.			
6. **Position client in accordance with agency protocol.**			
7. **Document all relevant information.**			
8. **Transport specimens to laboratory.**			

Procedure 29–4
Assisting with a Bone Marrow Biopsy

Preprocedure:

1. **Prepare client.**			
Explain procedure.			
Help client assume supine position for biopsy of sternum, or prone position for biopsy of either iliac crest. Expose biopsy site.			
Administer a sedative as ordered.			

During procedure:

2. **Monitor and support client throughout.**			

PROCEDURE	S	U	COMMENTS
Describe steps of procedure as needed, and provide verbal support.			
Observe client for pallor, diaphoresis, and faintness due to bleeding or pain.			
3. **Place small dressing over site of puncture after needle is withdrawn. Apply direct pressure per agency protocol.**			
4. **Assist with preparing specimens as needed.**			
Postprocedure:			
5. **Monitor client.**			
Assess for discomfort and bleeding from site. Report any bleeding to nurse in charge.			
Provide analgesic as needed and ordered.			
6. **Document all relevant information.**			
7. **Transport specimens to laboratory.**			

Procedure 29–5
Assisting with a Liver Biopsy

	S	U	
Preprocedure:			
1. **Prepare client.**			
Give preprocedural medications as ordered.			
Explain procedure to client.			
Ensure that client fasts for at least 2 hours before procedure.			
Administer appropriate sedative about 30 minutes prior or at specified time.			
Help client assume supine position, with upper right quadrant of abdomen exposed, keeping all other areas covered with bedclothes.			
During procedure:			
2. **Monitor and support client throughout.**			
Support client in supine position.			
Instruct client to take a few deep inhalations and exhalations and to hold breath after final exhalation for up to 10 seconds while needle is inserted, biopsy obtained, and needle is withdrawn.			
Instruct client to resume breathing when needle is withdrawn.			
Apply pressure to site of puncture.			

PROCEDURE	S	U	COMMENTS
3. Apply small dressing to site of puncture.			

Postprocedure:

PROCEDURE	S	U	COMMENTS
4. **Position client appropriately.**			
Assist client to right side-lying position with small pillow or folded towel under biopsy site. Instruct client to remain in position for several hours.			
5. **Monitor client.**			
Assess client's vital signs every 15 minutes for first hour following test or until vital signs are stable. Then monitor vital signs every hour for 24 hours or as needed.			
Determine whether client is experiencing abdominal pain.			
Check biopsy site for localized bleeding.			
6. **Document all relevant information.**			
7. **Transport specimens to laboratory.**			

Procedure 30–1
Performing a Surgical Hand Scrub

PROCEDURE	S	U	COMMENTS
1. **Prepare for surgical hand scrub.**			
Remove wristwatch and all rings.			
Check hands and arms for abnormal skin conditions.			
Sleeves pushed above elbows.			
Uniform is well tucked in at waist.			
Apply cap and face mask.			
Adjust water temperature to lukewarm.			
2. **Scrub hands.**			
Hold hands above level of elbows.			
Apply antimicrobial solution to hands.			
Use firm, rubbing, and circular movements to wash palms and backs of hands, wrists, and forearms.			
Interlace fingers and thumbs, and move hands back and forth.			
Hold hands and arms under running water to rinse thoroughly, keeping hands higher than elbows.			

PROCEDURE	S	U	COMMENTS
Check nails, and clean with file or orange stick if necessary.			
Apply antimicrobial solution and lather hands again. Using scrub brush, scrub each hand for 45 seconds.			
Using scrub brush, scrub from wrists to 5 cm (2 in) above each elbow.			
Continue to hold hands higher than elbows.			
Rinse hands and arms thoroughly so that water flows from hands to elbows.			
Turn off water with foot pedal.			
If hands touch sink, use extra 10 strokes to decontaminate.			
3. Dry hands and arms.			
Use one sterile towel for each hand and arm. Keep hands in front and above waist.			

Procedure 32–1
Giving an Infant Sponge Bath

PROCEDURE	S	U	COMMENTS
1. Prepare environment.			
Wash hands before handling a newborn.			
Ensure that the room is warm.			
Measure temperature of water.			
2. Prepare infant.			
Undress infant, and bundle in supine position.			
Ascertain infant's weight and vital signs.			
3. Wash infant's head.			
Clean infant's eyes with water only, wiping from inner to outer canthus.			
Wash and dry infant's face using water only.			
Lift infant using football hold, and position infant's head over washbasin. Lather scalp with mild soap.			
Rinse and dry scalp well.			
Place infant in supine position.			
4. Wash infant's body.			
Wash, rinse, and dry each arm, hand and axilla.			

PROCEDURE	S	U	COMMENTS
Wash, rinse, and dry infant's chest and abdomen.			
Keep infant covered with bath blanket or towel between washing and rinsing.			
Clean base of umbilical cord with cotton ball dipped in 70% isopropyl alcohol.			
Wash, rinse, and dry infant's legs and feet.			
Turn infant on stomach or side. Wash, rinse, and dry back.			
5. Clean genitals and anterior perineum.			
Place infant on back. Clean and dry genitals and anterior perineal area from front to back.			
Clean folds at groin.			
For females:			
Separate labia, and using a clean moistened cotton ball for each stroke, clean between them wiping from front to back.			
For males:			
If infant is uncircumcised, retract foreskin if possible, and clean glans penis, using moistened cotton ball. After swabbing, replace foreskin.			
In infant has been recently circumcised, clean glans penis by gently squeezing cotton ball moistened with clear water over site. Note signs of bleeding or infection.			
Clean shaft of penis and scrotum.			
Apply A and D Ointment to perineum.			
6. Clean posterior perineum and buttocks.			
Grasp infant's ankles, raise feet, and elevate buttocks.			
Wash and rinse area with washcloth.			
Dry area, and apply ointment.			
7. Check for dry, cracked, or peeling skin, and apply mild baby oil or lotion.			
8. Dress and position infant.			
Diaper and clothe infant. Cover and bundle infant with blanket.			
9. Record any significant assessments.			

Procedure 32–2
Giving an Infant Tub Bath

Procedure	S	U	Comments
1. **Prepare bath area.**			
Prepare flat, padded surface in bath area to dress and undress infant. Cover surface with a towel.			
Place tub or basin near dressing surface.			
Measure temperature of water.			
2. **Clean infant's eyes and face before placing infant in tub.**			
Follow Procedure 32–1, step 3.			
3. **Place infant into tub.**			
Gradually immerse infant into tub.			
4. **Wash infant.**			
Keeping infant's head and back supported on forearm, lather scalp with mild soap. Rinse scalp well.			
Soap and rinse infant's trunk, extremities, genitals, and perineal area with free hand.			
5. **Remove infant from tub, and dry infant well.**			
Remove infant from tub, and quickly bundle baby in a towel.			
Gently pat infant dry, giving special attention to body creases and folds.			
6. **Ensure infant's comfort and safety.**			
Diaper and clothe infant. Cover and bundle infant with blanket.			
7. **Document all pertinent information.**			

Procedure 32–3
Changing a Diaper

Procedure	S	U	Comments
1. **If using cloth diaper, fold diaper using one of three methods: rectangular, triangular, or kite.**			
2. **Position and handle infant appropriately.**			
Place infant in supine position on clean, flat surface near assembled supplies.			
3. **Remove soiled diaper.**			

PROCEDURE	S	U	COMMENTS
Place fingers between infant's skin and diaper, and unpin diaper on each side. Close pins, and place them out of reach of infant.			
Pull front of diaper down between infant's legs.			
Grasp infant's ankles with one hand, and lift buttocks.			
Use clean portion of diaper to wipe any excess urine or feces from buttocks. Wipe from front to back.			
Remove diaper and lower infant's buttocks.			
4. Clean buttocks and anal-genital area.			
Use warm water and soap or commercial cleansing tissues.			
Clean toward posterior. Rinse and dry area well with towel.			
Apply protective ointment or lotion to perineum, buttocks, and skin creases.			
5. Apply clean diaper, and fasten it securely.			
Grasp infant's ankles with one hand and raise infant's legs and buttocks. Place diaper under infant so back edge is at waist level.			
Draw diaper up between infant's legs to waist in front.			
Fasten diaper at waist with tape provided. If using safety pins for cloth diapers, hold fingers between baby and diaper while pinning.			
Position pins vertically or horizontally, and facing upward or outward.			
6. Ensure infant comfort and safety.			
Clothe and return infant to crib.			
7. Document all pertinent information.			
Record stool and/or urine observations.			

Procedure 32–4
Care of the Client with Pediculosis

	S	U	COMMENTS
1. Remove head lice.			
Don gown, gloves, and surgical cap before procedure.			
Place a small damp or dry washcloth over client's eyes.			

PROCEDURE	S	U	COMMENTS
Check scalp for rawness or excoriation. Don't apply shampoo if skin is inflamed.			
Apply medicated shampoo and work into hair and scalp thoroughly.			
Rinse hair and scalp thoroughly.			
Optional:			
Remove dead lice and nits with fine-toothed comb or brush dipped in hot vinegar.			
Disinfect comb or brush with medicated shampoo.			
Repeat shampoo if indicated.			
2. Remove body and pubic lice.			
Don gown and gloves.			
Have client bathe in soap and water.			
Apply medicated topical cream or lotion to infested areas and allow to remain for prescribed time period.			
Clean treated areas with soap and water to remove dead lice and medication.			
If eyelashes are involved, use a prescribed opthalmic ointment as ordered. Remove nits manually.			
3. Dispose of linens and clothing appropriately.			
Place used towel, gowns, and bed linens into label isolation bag.			
Provide clean gown and bed linens for client.			
4. Document any pertinent information.			

Procedure 32–5
Inserting Contact Lenses

PROCEDURE	S	U	COMMENTS
1. Take client's lens storage case, and select correct lens for eye.			
Start with right eye.			
Hard lenses:			
2. Lubricate lens.			
Put a few drops of sterile wetting solution on right lens.			
Spread wetting solution on both surfaces of lens by using thumb and index finger.			

PROCEDURE	S	U	COMMENTS
3. Insert lens.			
Ask client to tilt head backward.			
Place lens convex side down on tip of dominant index finger.			
Ask client to gaze slightly upward.			
Separate upper and lower eyelids of right eye with thumb and index finger of nondominant hand.			
Place lens gently on cornea, directly over iris and pupil.			
Repeat above steps for left lens.			
4. If lens is off center, center lens.			
Soft lenses:			
5. Keep dominant finger dry for insertion.			
Remove lens from saline-filled storage case with nondominate hand.			
6. Position lens correctly for insertion.			
For a regular soft lens:			
Hold lens at edge between thumb and index finger.			
Flex lens slightly, edges point inward.			
For an ultrathin soft lens:			
Put lens on placement finger and allow it to dry for a few seconds.			
Inspect lens to see whether edges turn upward.			
7. Wet lens with saline solution using nondominant fingers.			
8. Insert lens.			
Ensure placement finger is dry.			
Insert lens in same manner as hard lenses.			
9. Document pertinent information.			

Procedure 32–6
Removing Contact Lenses

PROCEDURE	S	U	COMMENTS
1. Locate position of lens.			
Ask client to tilt head backward.			
Retract upper eyelid with index finger, and ask client to look up, down, and from side to side.			

PROCEDURE	S	U	COMMENTS
Repeat with lower eyelid.			
2. Reposition displaced lens.			
Lens may pop out on its own if client pulls eyelid up and out toward ear. Ask client to blink to release lens. If lens remains, go to step 3.			
Hard lenses:			
3. Separate upper and lower eyelids.			
Use both thumbs or index fingers to separate upper and lower eyelids of one eye until they are beyond edges of lens.			
or			
Use middle finger to retract upper eyelid and thumb of same hand to retract lower lid.			
4. Remove lens.			
Gently move margins of both lower and upper eyelid toward lens.			
Hold top eyelid stationary at edge of lens, and lift bottom edge of lens by pressing lower lid at its margin firmly under lens.			
After lens is slightly tipped, slide lens off and out of eye by moving both eyelids toward each other.			
Grasp lens with index finger and thumb, and place in palm of hand.			
Place first lens in its designated cup in storage case.			
Repeat above steps for other lens.			
Soft lenses:			
5. Separate upper and lower eyelids.			
Ask client to look upward and keep eye opened wide.			
Retract lower or upper lid with one or two fingers of nondominant hand.			
Using index finger of dominant hand, move lens down to inferior part of sclera.			
6. Remove lens.			
Gently pinch lens between pads of thumb and index finger of dominant hand.			
Place lens in palm of hand.			
Repeat above step for other lens.			

PROCEDURE	S	U	COMMENTS
7. Clean and store lenses appropriately.			
Place lens in correct slot in its storage case.			
8. Document all relevant information.			

Procedure 32–7
Removing, Cleaning, and Inserting an Artificial Eye

PROCEDURE	S	U	COMMENTS
1. Remove eye.			
Assist client to a sitting or supine position.			
Pull lower eyelid down over infraorbital bone with dominant thumb, and exert slight pressure below eyelid.			
Compress small rubber bulb, and apply tip directly on eye. Gradually decrease finger pressure on bulb, and draw eye out of socket.			
Grasp eye and place it carefully in lined container.			
2. Clean eye and socket.			
Clean socket with soft gauze or cotton wipes and normal saline. Pat area dry.			
Wash and dry tissue around eye, stroking from inner to outer canthus using fresh gauze for each wipe.			
Wash artificial eye gently with warm normal saline. Dry it with dry wipes.			
If eye is not to be reinserted, place it in lined container filled with water or saline, close lid, label container with client's name and room number.			
3. Reinsert eye.			
Ensure eye is moistened with water or saline.			
Using thumb and index finger, retract eyelids, exerting pressure on supraorbital and infraorbital bones.			
With thumb and index finger of other hand, hold eye so front of it is toward palm of hand. Slip eye gently into socket, and release lids.			
Moisten prosthesis with eye irrigation solution once it is in place.			
4. Document pertinent information.			

Procedure 33–1
Administering Dermatologic Medications

Procedure	S	U	COMMENTS
1. Verify order.			
Compare medication record with most recent order.			
Determine label on medication tube or jar with medication record.			
2. Prepare client.			
Provide privacy and expose area of skin to be treated.			
3. Prepare area for medication.			
Wash hands and don gloves.			
Determine whether area is to be washed before applying medication. If it is, wash it gently, and pat it dry with gauze pads.			
4. Apply medication and dressing as ordered.			
Place small amount of cream on tongue blade, and spread it evenly on skin.			
or			
Pour some lotion on gauze, and pat skin area with it.			
or			
If a liniment is used, rub it into skin with hands using long, smooth strokes.			
Repeat application until area is completely covered.			
Apply sterile dressing as necessary.			
or			
Apply prepackaged transdermal patch as directed.			
Apply medicated products only to area being treated.			
5. Provide client comfort.			
Provide clean gown or pajamas after application if medication will come in contact with clothing.			
6. Document all relevant assessments and interventions.			

Procedure 33–2
Administering Nasal Instillations

PROCEDURE	S	U	COMMENTS
1. Verify medication or irrigation order.			
2. Prepare client.			
If secretions are excessive, ask client to blow nose to clear nasal passages.			
Inspect discharge on tissues for color, odor, and thickness.			
3. Assess client.			
Assess congestion of mucous membranes and any obstruction to breathing. Ask client to hold one nostril closed and blow out gently through other nostril. Listen for any sound of obstruction to air. Repeat for other nostril.			
Assess signs of distress when nares are occluded. Block each naris of an infant or young child and observe for signs of greater distress when naris is obstructed.			
Assess facial discomfort.			
Using nasal speculum, assess any crusting, redness, bleeding, or discharge of mucous membranes of nostrils.			
4. Position client appropriately.			
Eustachian tube:			
Have client assume back-lying position.			
Ethmoid and sphenoid sinuses:			
Have client take a back-lying position with head over edge of bed or a pillow under shoulders so head is tipped backward.			
Maxillary and frontal sinuses:			
Have client assume back-lying position with head over edge of bed or a pillow under shoulders and head turned toward side to be treated.			
5. Administer medication.			
Draw up required amount of solution into dropper.			
Hold tip of dropper just above nostril, and direct solution laterally toward middle of the nose as client breathes through mouth.			
Repeat for other nostril if indicated.			

PROCEDURE	S	U	COMMENTS
Ask client to remain in position for 5 minutes and breath through the mouth.			
Wipe excess medication from client's face.			
Discard any remaining solution in dropper, clean dropper, and dispose of soiled supplies appropriately.			
6. **Document all relevant information.**			

Procedure 33–3
Administering an Intradermal Injection

PROCEDURE	S	U	COMMENTS
1. **Verify order.**			
Check physician's order for medication, dosage, and route.			
2. **Prepare medication from ampule or vial.**			
3. **Identify and prepare client for injection.**			
Check client's arm band and ask client's name.			
Explain that medication will produce small bleb.			
4. **Select and clean site.**			
Don gloves and clean site with swab moistened with alcohol or other colorless antiseptic. Start at center of site and widen circle outward.			
5. **Prepare syringe for injection.**			
Remove needle cap while waiting for site to dry.			
Expel any bubbles from syringe.			
Grasp syringe in dominant hand, holding it between thumb and four fingers, with palm upward. Hold needle at 15° angle to skin surface, with bevel of needle up.			
6. **Inject fluid.**			
With nondominant hand, pull skin taut, and thrust needle tip firmly through epidermis. Do not aspirate.			
Inject medication carefully so it produces small bleb on skin.			
Withdraw needle quickly while providing countertraction on skin, and apply Band-Aid if indicated. Do not massage area.			
Dispose of syringe and needle safely in *sharps* container.			

	PROCEDURE	S	U	COMMENTS
7.	Document all relevant information.			
8.	Assess client's response to testing substance in 24 or 48 hours, depending on test.			

Procedure 34–1
Basic Bandaging

1.	**Position and prepare client.**			
	Provide client with chair or bed, and arrange support for area to be bandaged.			
	Make sure area to be bandaged is clean and dry.			
	Align part to be bandaged with slight flexion of joint, unless contraindicated.			
2.	**Apply bandage.**			
Circular turns:				
	Hold bandage in dominant hand, keeping roll uppermost, and unroll bandage about 8 cm (3 in).			
	Apply end of bandage to part of body to be bandaged.			
	Encircle body part a few times with each turn overlapping one-half to two-thirds of previous turn.			
	Check that bandage is firm, but not too tight. Ask client if bandage is comfortable.			
	Secure end of bandage with tape or safety pin over uninjured area.			
Spiral turns:				
	Make two circular turns.			
	Continue spiral turns at 30° angle, each overlapping preceeding one by two-thirds width of bandage.			
	Terminate bandage with two circular turns, and secure ends.			
Spiral reverse turns:				
	Anchor bandage with two circular turns, bring bandage upward at 30° angle.			
	Place thumb of free hand on upper edge of bandage.			
	Unroll bandage about 15 cm (6 in), turn hand so that bandage falls over itself.			

PROCEDURE	S	U	COMMENTS
Continue bandage around limb, overlapping each previous turn by two-thirds width of bandage.			
Terminate bandage with two circular turns and secure end.			
Recurrent turns:			
Anchor bandage with two circular turns.			
Fold bandage back on itself, and bring it centrally over distal end to be bandaged.			
Holding it with other hand, bring bandage back over end to right of center bandage but overlapping it by two-thirds width of bandage.			
Bring bandage back on left side, overlapping first turn by two-thirds width of bandage.			
Continue pattern of alternating right and left until area is covered.			
Terminate bandage with two circular turns and secure.			
Figure-eight turns:			
Anchor bandage with two circular turns.			
Carry bandage above joint, around it, and below it, making a figure-eight.			
Continue above and below joint, overlapping previous turn by two-thirds width of bandage.			
Terminate bandage above joint with two circular turns and secure end.			
Thumb spica:			
Anchor bandage with two circular turns around wrist.			
Bring bandage down to distal aspect of thumb, and encircle thumb. Leave tip of thumb exposed if possible.			
Bring bandage back up and around wrist, then back down and around thumb, overlapping previous turn by two-thirds width of bandage.			
Repeat last two steps, working up thumb and hand until thumb is covered.			
Anchor bandage with two circular turns around wrist and secure.			
3. Document all relevant information.			

Procedure 34–2
Applying a Stump Bandage

	S	U	COMMENTS
1. Position client appropriately.			
Assist client to semi-Fowler's position in bed or to sitting position on edge of bed.			
Clean skin or stump wound and apply sterile dressing as needed.			
2. Apply bandage.			
Figure-eight bandage:			
Anchor bandage with two circular turns around hips.			
Bring bandage down over stump and then back up and around hips.			
Bring bandage down again, overlapping previous turn, and making figure-eight around stump and back up around hips.			
Repeat, working bandage up stump.			
Anchor bandage around hips with two circular turns.			
Secure bandage with tape or safety pins.			
or			
Place end of elastic bandage at top of anterior surface of leg and have client hold it in place. Bring bandage diagonally down toward end of stump.			
Applying even pressure, bring bandage diagonally upward toward groin area.			
Make figure-eight turn behind top of leg, downward again over and under stump, and back up to groin area.			
Repeat figure-eight turns at least twice.			
Anchor bandage around hips with two circular turns, and secure.			
Recurrent bandage:			
Anchor bandage with two circular turns around stump.			
Cover stump with recurrent turns.			
Anchor recurrent bandage with two circular turns, and secure.			

PROCEDURE	S	U	COMMENTS

Spiral bandage:

    Make recurrent turns to cover end of stump.

    Apply spiral turns from distal aspect of stump toward body.

    Anchor bandage with two circular turns and hips, and secure.

3. **Document all relevant information.**

Procedure 34–3
Applying an Infant Radiant Warmer

1. **Prepare warmer.**

    Using manual control setting, turn on radiant warmer.

    Warm the blankets, towels, and washcloths.

2. **Assess and prepare infant for treatment.**

    Wipe blood and vernix from newborn's head and body using prewarmed towels.

    Wrap infant in preheated blankets, transfer infant to mother (parents), and return infant to warmer.

    Remove blankets, apply diaper and head cover.

    Apply temperature sensor to infant's abdomen between umbilicus and xiphoid process.

    Cover temperature sensor with reflective covering.

    Turn warmer control device to automatic setting.

3. **Initiate warming process.**

    Adjust temperature setting control to desired goal temperature.

    Turn warmer on and set temperature sensor alarm at upper limit of desired temperature range.

4. **Monitor warming process.**

    Check infant's temperature sensor reading every 15 to 30 minutes.

    Check infant's axillary temperature every 15 to 30 minutes until stable, then every 2 to 4 hours.

PROCEDURE	S	U	COMMENTS
Monitor sensor probe site and surrounding skin for irritation or breakdown.			
5. Terminate warming process.			
When infant's temperature reaches desired level, dress infant in T-shirt, diaper, and head cover. Wrap infant in two blankets, and transfer infant from warmer to an open crib.			
Check infant's axillary temperature every 2 to 4 hours.			
If infant's temperature drops below 36.1C (97.0F), return infant to warmer, remove clothing, and reinitiate warming procedure.			
6. Document all relevant information.			

Procedure 34–4
Managing Clients with Hyperthermia and Hypothermia Blankets

PROCEDURE	S	U	COMMENTS
1. Prepare client.			
Assess vital signs, and explain procedure.			
Place blanket covered with sheet under client and pillow under client's head.			
Insert or place thermistor probe and tape in place.			
Place second blanket over client, if indicated.			
2. Prepare equipment.			
Connect blanket pad to modular unit and inspect for adequate functioning.			
Inspect pad and cords for frays or exposed wires.			
Twist male tubing connectors of coil blanket tubing into connectors on modular unit.			
Check solution level in module and fill with distilled water if necessary.			
Turn on unit, and check for adequate filling of coils throughout blanket as solution circulates.			
Turn client temperature control knob to desired temperature and determine whether temperature gauge is functioning.			
Set modular control knob or master switch to either manual or automatic mode, and note accuracy of temperature settings.			

PROCEDURE	S	U	COMMENTS
If using automatic mode:			
Insert thermistor probe plug into thermistor probe jack on modular unit.			
Check automatic mode light.			
Set machine to desired temperature.			
Set limits for pad temperature.			
If using manual mode:			
Set master temperature control knob to desired temperature.			
Check manual mode light.			
If blanket is nondisposable, cover it with plastic cover or thin sheet.			
3. Monitor client closely.			
Take vital signs every 15 minutes for first hour, every 30 minutes for second hour, and every hour thereafter.			
Determine client's neurological status regularly as needed.			
Observe skin for indications of burns, intactness, and color.			
Turn client every 30 minutes to 1 hour and determine any intolerance to blanket.			
4. Maintain therapy as required.			
Check probe position or remove and clean rectal probe every 3 to 4 hours or when client has bowel movement.			

Procedure 34–5
Administering Hot Soaks and Sitz Baths

	S	U	
Hand or foot soak:			
1. Prepare soak.			
Fill container half full and test temperature of solution with thermometer.			
Pad edge of container with towel.			
Use sterile solution and sterile thermometer if client has an open wound.			
2. Prepare and assess client.			
Assist client to well-aligned, comfortable position.			

PROCEDURE	S	U	COMMENTS
Don disposable gloves as required, remove dressings, and discard them in bag. Assess amount, color, odor, and consistency of drainage on removed dressings.			
Inspect appearance of area to be soaked.			
3. Commence soak.			
Immerse body part completely in solution.			
If soak is sterile, cover open container with sterile drape or container wrapper.			
Place large sheet or blanket over soak. Proceed to step 7.			
Sitz bath:			
4. Prepare bath.			
Fill sitz bath with water at 40C (105F).			
Pad tub or chair with towel as required.			
5. Prepare client.			
Have client void. Remove gown, or fasten it above waist.			
Don gloves if an open area or drainage are present.			
Remove T-binder and perineal dressings if present, and note amount, color, odor, and consistency of any drainage.			
Assess appearance of area to be soaked for redness, swelling, odor, breaks in skin, and drainage.			
Wrap blanket around client's shoulders and over legs as needed.			
6. Begin sitz bath.			
Assist client into bath and provide support for client as needed.			
Leave signal light within reach. Stay with client if warranted, and terminate bath if necessary.			
7. Monitor client.			
Soak:			
Assess client and test temperature of solution at least once per soak. Assess for discomfort, need for additional support, and any reactions to soak.			

PROCEDURE	S	U	COMMENTS
If solution has cooled, remove body part, empty solution, add newly heated solution, and reimmerse body part.			
Sitz bath:			
Assess client's comfort level, color, and pulse rate.			
Immediately report any unexpected or adverse responses to nurse in charge.			
Test temperature of solution at least once during bath. Adjust temperature as needed.			
8. **Discontinue soak or bath.**			
At completion of soak, remove body part from basin, and dry it thoroughly and carefully. If soak was sterile, don sterile gloves and dry wound with sterile gauze pads.			
Assess appearance of affected area carefully, and reapply dressing if required.			
or			
At completion of sitz bath, assist client out of bath and dry area with towel.			
Assess perineal area and reapply dressings and garments as required.			
9. **Document all relevant information.**			

Procedure 34–6
Administering a Cooling Sponge Bath

PROCEDURE	S	U	COMMENTS
1. **Obtain all relevant baseline data.**			
Assess client for other signs of fever.			
2. **Prepare client.**			
Remove gown and assist client to comfortable supine position.			
Place bath blanket over client.			
If ice bags or cold packs are not used, place bath towels under each axilla and shoulder.			
3. **Sponge face with plain water and dry it.**			
Apply ice bag or cold pack to head for comfort.			
4. **Place cold applications in axillae and groins.**			

PROCEDURE	S	U	COMMENTS
Wet four washcloths, wring them out so they are very damp, but not dripping.			
Place washcloths, ice bags or cold packs in axillae and groins.			
Leave washcloths in place for about five minutes, or until they feel warm. Rewet and replace as required.			
5. Sponge arms and legs.			
Place bath towel under one arm and sponge arm for about 5 minutes.			
or			
Place saturated towel over extremity rewetting as necessary.			
Pat arm dry and repeat steps for other arm and legs.			
When sponging extremities, hold washcloth briefly over wrists and ankles.			
6. Reassess client's vital signs after 15 minutes.			
Compare findings and evaluate effectiveness of sponge bath.			
Continue sponge bath if client's temperature is above 37.7C (100F), discontinue if below, or if pulse rate is significantly increased and remains so after five minutes.			
7. (Optional) Sponge chest and abdomen for 3 to 5 minutes and pat areas dry.			
8. Sponge back and buttocks 3 to 5 minutes and pat areas dry.			
9. Remove cold applications from axillae and groins.			
Reassess vital signs.			
Document assessments, including all vital signs, and type of sponge bath given.			
Variation: Pediatric bathing			
Cooling baths for children can be given in tub, bed, or crib.			
Tub:			
Immerse child in tepid water for 20 to 30 minutes.			

PROCEDURE	S	U	COMMENTS
Firmly support child's head and shoulders. Gently squeeze water over back and chest or spray water from sprayer over body.			
Use a floating toy or other distraction for conscious child.			
Discontinue bath if there is evidence of chilling.			
Dry and dress child in light-weight clothing or diaper and cover with light cotton blanket.			
Take temperature 30 minutes after bath.			
Bed or crib sponge:			
Place undressed child on absorbent towel.			
Follow adult sponge bath method or use following towel method: a. Apply cool bath or icebag to forehead. b. Wrap each extremity in towel moistened with tepid water. c. Place one towel under back and another over neck and torso. d. Change towels as they warm. e. Continue procedure for about 30 minutes.			

Procedure 34–7
Cleaning a Drain Site and Shortening a Penrose Drain

PROCEDURE	S	U	COMMENTS
1. **Verify physician's order.**			
Confirm drain is to be shortened by nurse and length it is to be shortened.			
2. **Prepare client.**			
Explain procedure to client and that there may be a pulling sensation for a few seconds when drain is being drawn out, but this procedure should not be painful.			
Position client for dressing change.			
3. **Remove dressings and clean incision and drain site.**			
Clean incision site first, wearing sterile gloves.			
Clean skin around drain site by swabbing in half or full circles from drain site outward, using separate swabs for each wipe. Clean until all drainage is removed.			
Assess amount, odor, thickness, and color of drainage.			

	S	U	
4. **Clean and assess the drain site.**			
Clean skin around drain site by swabbing in half or full circles outward from drain site.			
Assess amount and character of drainage.			
5. **Shorten drain.**			
If drain has not been shortened before, remove suture.			
With hemostat, grasp drain by its full width, and pull out required length.			
Wearing sterile gloves, insert sterile safety pin through base of drain as close to skin as possible.			
With sterile scissors, cut off excess drain leaving 2.5 cm (1 in) above skin.			
6. **Apply dressings to drain site and incision.**			
Apply sterile dressings one at a time using sterile gloved hands or sterile forceps.			
Apply final surgipad by hand. Remove gloves and secure dressing with tape or tie.			
7. **Document procedure and nursing assessments.**			

Procedure 34–8
Establishing and Maintaining a Closed Wound Drainage System

	S	U	
1. **Establish suction if it has not been already initiated.**			
Place evacuator unit on solid, flat surface and don gloves.			
Open drainage plug on top of unit.			
Compress unit; while it is compressed, close drainage plug.			
2. **Empty evacuator unit.**			
When drainage fluid reaches "Full" line. Don gloves and open drainage plug.			
Invert unit and empty into collecting receptacle.			
Reestablish suction.			
Measure amount of drainage, and note characteristics.			
3. **Document all relevant information.**			

Procedure 34–9
Applying Moist Sterile Compresses

	S	U	Comments
1. **Prepare client.**			
Assist client to comfortable position.			
Expose area for compress or pack.			
Provide support for body part requiring compress or pack.			
Don disposable gloves and remove wound dressing, if present.			
2. **Moisten compress or pack.**			
Place gauze in solution.			
or			
Heat flannel towel in steamer, or chill it in basin of water and ice.			
3. **Protect surrounding skin as indicated.**			
With cotton swab or applicator stick, apply petrolatum jelly to skin surrounding wound.			
4. **Apply moist heat.**			
Wring out gauze compress and apply gauze lightly to designated area, and if tolerated by client, mold compress close to body. Pack gauze snugly against all wound surfaces.			
or			
Wring out flannel and apply to body area, molding it closely to body part.			
For sterile pack, use sterile gloves.			
5. **Immediately insulate and secure application.**			
Cover gauze or flannel with dry towel and piece of plastic.			
Secure compress or pack in place with gauze ties or tape.			
6. **Monitor client.**			
Assess client for discomfort at 5 to 10 minute intervals. If client feels any discomfort, assess for erythema, numbness, maceration, or blistering.			

PROCEDURE	S	U	COMMENTS
For applications over large body areas, note any change in pulse, respirations, and blood pressure. With unexpected reaction, terminate treatment and report to nurse in charge.			
7. **Remove compress or pack at specified time.**			
Apply sterile dressing if one is required.			
8. **Document relevant information.**			

Procedure 34–10
Removing Skin Sutures

PROCEDURE	S	U	COMMENTS
1. **Prepare client.**			
Inform client suture removal may produce slight discomfort, such as pulling or stinging, but should not be painful.			
2. **Remove dressings and clean incision.**			
Don sterile gloves and clean suture line with antimicrobial solution before and after suture removal.			
3. **Remove sutures.**			
Plain interrupted sutures:			
Grasp sutures at knot with forceps.			
Place curved tip of suture scissors under suture as close to skin as possible and cut suture.			
With forceps, pull suture out in one piece, Inspect carefully to make sure all suture material is removed.			
Discard suture onto piece of sterile gauze or into moisture-proof bag. Do not contaminate forcep tips.			
Continue to remove alternate sutures.			
If no dehiscence occurs, remove remaining sutures. If dehiscence does occur, do not remove remaining sutures. Report to nurse in charge.			
With small dehiscence, apply sterile butterfly tape over gap, after pressing wound edges together.			
With large dehiscence, cover wound with sterile gauze and immediately report to nurse in charge or physician.			

Mattress interrupted sutures:

    Cut visible part of suture close to skin opposite knot, and remove small piece.

    Grasp knot with forceps and pull.

Plain continuous sutures:

    Cut thread of first suture opposite knot. Then cut thread of second suture on same side as first thread.

    Grasp knot with forceps and pull.

    Cut off visible part left on second suture.

    Grasp third suture next to skin opposite beginning knot side and pull underlying thread out between second and third suture.

    Cut remaining thread from third suture.

    Repeat last two steps for remaining sutures until last knot is reached. After first stitch is removed, each thread is cut down same side, below original knot.

    Cut last suture opposite ending knot and pull out last suture.

Blanket continuous sutures:

    Cut threads that are opposite looped blanket edge.

    Pull each stitch out at looped edge.

Mattress continuous sutures:

    Cut visible suture at both skin edges opposite beginning knot and next suture opposite knot. Remove visible portions of sutures.

    Pull first suture out by knot.

    Lift second suture on beginning knot side to pull out underlying suture in center.

    Go to third suture opposite beginning knot side, lift out suture, and cut off all visible parts close to skin.

    Go to knot side of third suture, pull out underlying center thread, and cut remaining portion of third suture thread close to skin.

    Repeat last two steps, working from side to side of incision, until last suture is reached.

    Cut visible suture opposite knot. Go to knot and pull out remaining pieces.

4.   Clean and cover incision.

PROCEDURE	S	U	COMMENTS
Clean incision with antimicrobial solution.			
Apply small, light, sterile dressing.			
5. Instruct client about follow-up wound care.			
If wound is dry and healing well, client can usually take a shower in a day or two.			
Instruct client to contact physician if increased redness, drainage, or open areas are present.			
6. Document suture removal and assessment data on appropriate records.			

Procedure 35–1
Preparing the Operative Site

PROCEDURE	S	U	COMMENTS
1. Drape client appropriately.			
Expose only area to be prepared.			
2. If depilatory is to be used, test client's reaction to it.			
Apply small amount of depilatory on small part of area where hair is to removed.			
Apply cream to test area smoothly and thickly. Do not rub in.			
Leave cream on specified time.			
Remove depilatory by rinsing with lukewarm water and washcloth. Do not use soap.			
Pat area dry with gauze squares.			
Wait for 24 hours, and assess client's skin for redness or other responses.			
3. Remove hair.			
Depilatory:			
If client's skin remains normal after skin test, apply depilatory and follow above steps for hair removal.			
Clipping:			
Make sure area is dry.			
Remove hair with clippers; do not apply pressure.			
Wet shave:			
Don gloves and place moisture-proof towel under area to be prepared.			
Lather skin well with soap solution.			

PROCEDURE	S	U	COMMENTS
Stretch skin taut, and hold razor at about 45° angle to skin.			
Shave in direction in which hair grows.			
Rinse soap solution and loose hair from skin with sponges.			
4. Clean and disinfect surgical area according to agency practice.			
Clean any body crevices with applicators and solutions. Dry with swabs.			
If antimicrobial solution is used, apply to area immediately after it is clipped. Check agency policy as to how long to leave on.			
5. Inspect skin after hair removal.			
Closely observe for reddened or broken areas. Report any skin lesions to the nurse in charge.			
6. Dispose of used equipment appropriately.			
7. Document all relevant information.			

Procedure 35–2
Applying Antiemboli Stockings

PROCEDURE	S	U	COMMENTS
1. Select an appropriate time to apply stockings.			
Apply in morning or remove and replace at least twice a day if possible.			
Wash legs and feet daily.			
Assist client who has been ambulating to lie down for 15 to 30 minutes before applying stockings.			
2. Apply elastic stocking to foot.			
Assist client to lying position in bed.			
Dust ankle with talcum powder, and ask client to point toes.			
Turn stocking inside out by inserting hand into stocking from top and grabbing heel pocket from inside. Foot portion should now be inside stocking leg.			
Remove hand, and with heel pocket downward, hook index and middle fingers of both hands into foot section.			

	S	U	
Face client, and slip foot portion of stocking over client's foot, toes, and heel. Move up foot, stretching stocking sideways.			
Support client's ankle with one hand while using other hand to pull heel pocket under heel.			
Center heel in pocket.			
3. Apply remaining inverted portion of stocking.			
Gather remaining portion of stocking up to toes, and pull only this part over heel.			
At ankle, grasp gathered portion between index and middle fingers, and pull stocking up leg to knee.			
For thigh- or waist-length stocking, ask client to straighten leg while stretching rest of stocking over knee.			
Ask client to flex knee while pulling stocking over thigh. Stretch stocking from top to distribute evenly over thigh. Top should rest 2.5 to 7.5 cm (1 to 3 in) below gluteal fold.			
For waist-length stocking, ask client to stand and continue extending stocking up to top of gluteal fold.			
Apply adjustable belt and adjust foot section to ensure toe comfort.			
4. Document application of antiemboli stockings.			

Procedure 41–1
Using a Hydraulic Lift

	S	U	
1. Prepare client.			
Explain procedure, and demonstrate lift.			
2. Prepare equipment.			
Lock wheels of client's bed.			
Raise bed to high position, put up side rail on opposite side of bed, and lower side rail on near side.			
Position lift close to client.			
Place chair that is to receive client beside bed.			
Lock wheels of chair.			

PROCEDURE	S	U	COMMENTS
3. Position client on sling.			
Roll client on side.			
Place canvas seat or sling under client, with wide lower edge under client's thighs and the narrow edge up under client's shoulders.			
Raise bed rail on near side of bed, and lower opposite side rail.			
Roll client to opposite side, and pull canvas sling through.			
Roll client to supine position in the center of the sling.			
4. Attach sling to swivel bar.			
Wheel lift into position, on side where chair is positioned. Set base at widest position and lock wheels.			
Lower side rail.			
Lower horizontal bar or mast boom to sling level.			
Attach lifter straps or hooks. Face hooks away from the client.			
5. Lift client gradually.			
Elevate head of bed to place client in sitting position.			
Nurse 1:			
Close pressure valve, and gradually pump jack handle until client is above bed surface.			
Nurse 2:			
Assume broad stance, and guide client with hands as client is lifted.			
Check placement of sling before moving client away from bed.			
6. Move client over chair.			
Nurse 1:			
With pressure valve securely closed, slowly roll lift until client is over chair.			
Nurse 2:			
Guide movement with hands until client is directly over chair.			
7. Lower client into chair.			

PROCEDURE	S	U	COMMENTS

Nurse 1:

    Release pressure valve gradually.

Nurse 2:

    Guide client into chair.

8. Ensure client comfort and safety.

    Remove hooks from canvas seat. Leave seat in place.

    Align client appropriately in sitting position.

    Apply seatbelt or other restraint as needed.

    Place call bell within reach.

Procedure 41–2
Providing Passive Range-of-Motion Exercises

1. Prior to initiating exercises, review any possible restrictions with physician or physical therapist. Also refer to agency protocol.

2. Assist client to supine position and expose body parts requiring exercise.

    Place client's feet together, place arms at sides, and leave space around head and feet.

3. Follow a repetitive pattern and return to starting position after each motion. Repeat each motion three times on affected limb.

Shoulder and elbow movement:

    Begin each exercise with client's arm at client's side. Grasp arm beneath elbow with one hand and beneath wrist with other hand.

4. Flex, externally rotate, and extend shoulder.

    Move arm up to ceiling and toward head of bed.

5. Abduct and externally rotate shoulder.

    Move arm away from body and toward client's head until hand is under head.

6. Abduct shoulder.

    Move arm over body until hand touches client's other hand.

7. Rotate shoulder internally and externally.

Place arm out to side at shoulder level (90° abduction) and bend elbow so forearm is at right angle to mattress.

Move forearm down until palm touches mattress and then up until back of hand touches bed.

8. Flex and extend elbow.

Bend elbow until fingers touch chin, then straighten arm.

9. Pronate and supinate forearm.

Grasp client's hand as for handshake, turn palm downward and upward, ensuring only forearm moves.

Wrist and hand movement:

Flex client's arm at elbow until forearm is at right angle to mattress. Support wrist joint with one hand while other hand manipulates joint and fingers.

10. Hyperextend wrist and flex fingers.

Bend wrist backward, and at same time, flex fingers, moving tips of fingers to palm of hand.

Align wrist in straight line with arm, place fingers over client's fingers to make fist.

11. Flex wrist and extend fingers.

Bend wrist forward, and at same time extend fingers.

12. Abduct and oppose thumb.

Move thumb away from fingers and then across hand toward base of little finger.

Leg and hip movement:

During leg and hip exercises, place one hand under client's knee and other under ankle.

13. Flex and extend knee and hip.

Lift leg and bend knee, moving knee up toward chest as far as possible. Bring leg down, straighten knee, and lower leg to bed.

14. Abduct and adduct leg.

Move leg to side, away from client and back across in front of other leg.

15. Rotate hip internally and externally.

Roll leg inward, then outward.			
Ankle and foot movement:			
Place hands in positions described, depending on motion to be achieved.			
16. Dorsiflex foot and stretch Achilles tendon.			
Place one hand under client's heel, resting inner forearm against bottom of client's foot.			
Place other hand under knee to support it.			
Press forearm against foot to move it upward toward leg.			
17. Invert and evert foot.			
Place one hand under client's ankle and one hand over arch of foot.			
Turn foot inward, then turn it outward.			
18. Plantar flex foot, and extend and flex toes.			
Place one hand over arch of foot to push foot away from leg.			
Place fingers of other hand under toes to bend toes upward, and then over toes to push toes downward.			
Neck movement:			
Remove client's pillow.			
19. Flex and extend neck.			
Place palm of hand under client's head and palm of other hand on client's chin.			
Move head forward until chin rests on chest, then back to resting supine position without head pillow.			
20. Laterally flex neck.			
Place heels of hands on each side of client's cheeks.			
Move top of head to right and to left.			
Hyperextension movements:			
21. Assist client to prone or lateral position on closest side of bed, but facing away.			
22. Hyperextend shoulder.			
Place one hand on shoulder and other under client's elbow.			
Pull upper arm up and backward.			

PROCEDURE	S	U	COMMENTS
23. Hyperextend hip.			
Place one hand on hip. With other hand, cradle lower leg in forearm, and cup knee joint with hand.			
Move leg backward from hip joint.			
24. Hyperextend neck.			
Remove pillow. With client's face down, place one hand on forehead and other on back of skull.			
Move head backward.			
Following exercise:			
25. Assess client's pulse and endurance of exercise.			
26. Report to nurse in charge any unexpected problems or notable changes in client's movements.			
27. Document exercise and assessments.			

Procedure 41–3
Applying a Continuous Passive Motion Device to the Knee

PROCEDURE	S	U	COMMENTS
1. Check safety test date.			
2. Verify physician's orders and agency protocol.			
Determine degrees of flexion, extension, and speed initially prescribed.			
3. Set up machine.			
Remove egg crate mattress if indicated, and place machine on bed.			
Apply supportive sling to movable cradle.			
Attach machine to Balkan frame using traction equipment.			
Connect control box to machine.			
4. Set prescribed levels of flexion, extension, and speed.			
Check that machine is functioning properly by running it through complete cycle.			
5. Position client and place leg in machine.			
Place client in supine position, with head of bed slightly elevated.			

Support leg, and with client's help, lift leg and place it in padded cradle.			
Lengthen or shorten appropriate sections of frame to fit machine to client. The knee joint should correspond with the goniometer on the machine.			
Adjust footplate so foot is supported in neutral position or slight dorsiflexion.			
Ensure leg is neither internally nor externally rotated.			
Apply restraining straps around thigh, top of foot, and cradle, allowing enough space to fit several fingers under it.			
6. **Start machine.**			
When machine reaches fully extended position, stop machine, and verify degree of flexion with goniometer.			
Restart machine, and observe a few cycles of flexion and extension to ensure proper functioning.			
7. **Ensure continued client safety and comfort.**			
Make sure client is comfortable. Observe for nonverbal signs of discomfort.			
Raise side rails.			
Stay with confused or sedated client while machine is on.			
Instruct mentally alert client how to operate on/off switch.			
Loosen straps and check client's skin at least twice per shift.			
Wash perineal area at least once per shift, and keep it dry.			
Drape towel over groin of a male client.			
8. **Document all relevant information.**			

Procedure 43–1
Managing Pain with a Transcutaneous Electric Nerve Stimulation Unit (TENS)

1. **Explain purpose and application procedure to client and family.**			
2. **Prepare equipment.**			

PROCEDURE	S	U	COMMENTS
Insert battery into TENS unit to test status of functioning.			
With TENS unit off, plug in lead wires.			
3. Clean application area.			
Wash, rinse, and dry designated area with soap and water.			
4. Apply electrodes to client.			
If electrodes are not prejelled, moisten with small amount of water or apply gel.			
Place electrodes on clean, unbroken skin area. Choose area according to location, nature and origin of pain.			
Ensure electrodes make full surface contact with skin.			
Tape all sides evenly with hypoallergenic tape.			
5. Turn unit on.			
Ascertain amplitude control is set at 0.			
Slowly increase intensity of amplitude until client notes slight increase in discomfort, then slowly decrease until client notes a pleasant sensation.			
6. Monitor client for discomfort.			
7. After the treatment:			
Turn off the controls and unplug the lead wires.			
Clean the electrodes and wash the client's skin with soap and water.			
Replace the used battery pack with a charged battery.			
8. Provide client teaching.			
Review with client instructions for use, and verify that client understands.			
Have client demonstrate use of TENS unit.			
Instruct client not to submerge unit in water.			
9. Document all relevant information.			

Procedure 44–1
Assisting an Adult to Eat

	S	U	COMMENTS
1. Check client's chart or plan of care for diet order.			

PROCEDURE	S	U	COMMENTS
2. Prepare client and overbed table.			
Assist client in washing hands prior to meal. Assist with oral hygiene as needed.			
Clear and arrange overbed table close to the bedside to allow client to see food.			
3. Position client and self appropriately.			
Assist client to comfortable position.			
Assume sitting position, if possible, beside client.			
4. Assist client as required.			
Check tray for client's name, type of diet, and completeness. Confirm client's name by checking wristband before leaving tray.			
Encourage client to eat independently, assisting as needed.			
Remove food covers, pour liquids, cut foods into smaller pieces, and butter bread if needed.			
For blind client, identify placement of food by using a clock system.			
5. After meal, ensure client comfort.			
Assist client to clean mouth and hands.			
Reposition client.			
Replace food covers, and remove food tray from bedside.			
6. Document all relevant information.			
Note how much and what type of food was eaten, and amount of fluid intake. If client is not eating, notify nurse in charge.			

Procedure 44–2
Bottle-Feeding an Infant

PROCEDURE	S	U	COMMENTS
1. Obtain and verify orders before feeding.			
2. Prepare bottle, nipple, and formula.			
If formula is refrigerated, warm to room temperature.			
Test size of nipple holes by turning bottle upside down.			
3. Ensure infant comfort.			
Change infant's diaper, if needed			

Procedure	S	U	Comments
Sit comfortably in chair with infant.			
Tuck bib or clean cloth under infant's chin.			
4. Position infant appropriately.			
Cradle baby in arms, with head slightly elevated. Support head and neck.			
5. Insert nipple, and feed baby.			
Insert nipple gently along infant's tongue and hold bottle at 45° angle.			
6. Remove bottle periodically and burp baby.			
Place baby either over shoulder, in supported sitting position on lap, or in prone position on lap.			
Rub or pat infant's back gently.			
7. Continue with feeding until formula is finished and/or baby is satisfied.			
8. Ensure infant safety and comfort after feeding. Return infant to crib or isolate.			
Check whether diaper needs changing, and change if necessary.			
Position infant on side.			
Ensure crib sides are elevated before leaving infant.			
Assess infant for signs of allergic reaction.			
9. Document all relevant information.			

Procedure 44–3
Feeding Solid Foods to an Infant

Procedure	S	U	Comments
1. Prepare infant for meal.			
Change diaper if damp or soiled.			
Put bib on infant, and place infant on lap, in infant seat or highchair.			
2. Promote acceptance and digestion of food.			
Gently hold infant's arms or give infant something to hold to control infant's hands.			
Offer plain foods before sweet ones.			
Place small spoonfuls of food well back on infant's tongue.			
Scrape up any food that is pushed back out of mouth, and refeed it.			

	S	U	COMMENTS
Talk to infant throughout meal.			
3. Provide follow-up care as needed.			
Wash and dry infant's face and hands.			
Change diaper, if needed.			
Place infant in safe position in crib. Ensure crib sides are elevated before leaving infant.			
4. Document all relevant information.			

Procedure 45–1
Obtaining and Testing a Specimen of Feces

	S	U	COMMENTS
1. Give clients the following information and instructions.			
Purpose of stool specimen and how client can assist collecting it.			
Defecate in clean or sterile bedpan or bedside commode.			
Do not contaminate specimen with urine or menstrual discharge. Void before specimen collection.			
Do not place toilet tissue in bedpan after defecation.			
Notify nurse as soon as possible after defecation.			
2. Assist clients who need help.			
Assist client to use bedside commode or bedpan placed on bedside chair or under toilet seat in bathroom.			
After client has defecated, cover bedpan or commode.			
Don gloves and clean client as required. Inspect skin around anus.			
3. Transfer required amount of stool to stool specimen container.			
Use one or two tongue blades to transfer some or all stool to specimen container.			
or			
For a culture, dip sterile swab into specimen and place swab in sterile test tube using sterile technique.			
or			

260

PROCEDURE	S	U	COMMENTS
For an occult blood test, see step 5.			
Wrap used tongue blades in paper towel before disposing of them in plastic-lined waste container.			
Place lid on container as soon as specimen is in container.			
4. Ensure client comfort.			
Empty and clean bedpan or commode, and return it to its place.			
Remove and discard gloves.			
Provide air freshener for any odors if needed.			
5. Label and send specimen to laboratory.			
Ensure specimen label and requisition form have correct information and are securely attached to specimen container.			
Arrange for specimen to be taken to laboratory immediately or follow instructions on specimen container.			
To test stool for oocult blood, follow manufacturer's directions. Put on gloves. a. For Guaiac test, smear thin layer of feces on paper towel or filter paper with tongue blade. Drop reagents onto smear as directed. b. For Hematest, smear thin layer of feces on filter paper, place tablet in middle of specimen, and add two drops of water as directed. c. For Hemoccult slide, smear thin layer of feces over circle inside envelope, and drop reagent solution onto smear.			
Note reaction. For all tests, blue color indicates positive result.			
6. Document all relevant information.			

Procedure 45–2
Removing a Fecal Impaction Digitally

1. Prepare client			
Explain procedure to client.			
Assist client to right or left lateral or Sims' position.			
Cover client with bath blanket.			

PROCEDURE	S	U	COMMENTS
2. **Prepare equipment.**			
Place linen-saver pad under client's hips, and arrange top bedclothing so it falls obliquely over hips, exposing only buttocks.			
Place bedpan and toilet tissue nearby on bed or bedside chair.			
Don gloves and lubricate gloved index finger.			
3. **Remove impaction.**			
Gently insert index finger into rectum, moving toward umbilicus.			
Gently massage around stool.			
Work finger into hardened mass of stool to break it up.			
Work stool down to anus, remove it in small pieces, and place them in bedpan.			
Assess client for signs of pallor, feelings of faintness, shortness of breath, and perspiration. Stop procedure if these occur.			
Assist client to position on clean bedpan, commode, or toilet.			
4. **Assist client with hygienic measures as needed.**			
Wash rectal area with soap and water and dry gently.			
Remove and discard gloves.			
5. **Teach client measures to promote normal elimination, if appropriate.**			
6. **Document procedure and all assessments.**			

Procedure 45–3
Irrigating a Colostomy

PROCEDURE	S	U	COMMENTS
1. **Prepare client.**			
Assist client who must remain in bed to side-lying position. Place disposable bedpad on bed in front of client, and place bedpan on top of pad beneath stoma.			
Assist ambulatory client to sit on toilet or commode. Ensure client is not unduly exposed.			
Throughout procedure, provide explanations and encourage client to participate.			

2. **Prepare equipment.**

    Fill solution bag with 500 mL warm tap water or other solution as ordered.

    Hang solution bag on IV pole, bottom level with client's shoulder, or 12 to 18 inches above stoma.

    Attach colon catheter securely to tubing.

    Open regulator clamp and run fluid through tubing to expel all air. Close clamp until ready for irrigation.

3. **Remove colostomy bag and position irrigation drainage sleeve.**

    Remove soiled colostomy bag and place in moisture-resistant bag.

    Center irrigation drainage sleeve over stoma and attach snugly.

    Direct lower, open end of drainage sleeve into bedpan or between client's legs into toilet.

4. **If ordered, dilate stoma.**

    Don gloves and lubricate tip of little finger.

    Gently insert finger into stoma, using a massaging motion.

    Repeat, using progressively larger fingers until maximum dilation is achieved.

5. **Insert stoma cone or colon catheter.**

    Lubricate tip of stoma cone or colon catheter.

    Using rotating motion, insert through opening in top of irrigation drainage sleeve and gently through stoma.

    Insert catheter 7 cm (3 in) or stoma cone until it fits snugly. Do not apply force.

6. **Irrigate colon.**

    Open tubing clamp and allow fluid to flow. If cramping occurs, stop flow until cramping subsides, then resume flow.

    After fluid is instilled, remove catheter or cone and allow colon to empty.

7. **Seal drainage sleeve and allow complete emptying of colon.**

Procedure	S	U	Comments
Clean base of irrigation drainage sleeve and seal bottom with drainage clamp.			
Encourage ambulatory client to ambulate for about 30 minutes.			
8. Empty and remove irrigation sleeve.			
9. Ensure client comfort.			
Clean area around stoma and dry thoroughly.			
Put colostomy appliance on client as needed.			
10. Document and report relevant information.			

Procedure 46–1
Collecting a Routine Urine Specimen from an Adult or Child Who Has Urinary Control

Procedure	S	U	Comments
1. Give ambulatory clients information and instructions.			
Explain purpose and how client can assist.			
Explain all specimens must be free of fecal contamination.			
Instruct all female clients to discard toilet tissue in toilet or waste bag rather than in bedpan.			
Give client specimen container and direct client to void 120 mL (4 oz) in bathroom.			
2. Assist clients who are seriously ill, physically incapacitated, or disoriented.			
Provide required assistance in bathroom, or help client use bedpan or urinal.			
Wear gloves when assisting client to void in bedpan or urinal, and when transferring urine to specimen container.			
Empty bedpan or urinal.			
Remove gloves and wash hands.			
3. Ensure specimen is sealed and container clean.			
4. Label and transport specimen to laboratory immediately or refrigerate.			
5. Document all relevant information.			

Procedure 46–2
Collecting a Timed Urine Specimen

Procedure	S	U	Comments
1. Give client procedure information and instructions.			
2. Start collection period.			
Ask client to void in toilet, bedpan, or urinal. Discard urine and document time test starts with discarded specimen. Collect all subsequent urine specimens, including one at end of period.			
Ask client to ingest required amount of liquid for certain tests or restrict fluid intake. Follow test instructions.			
Instruct client to void all subsequent urine into bedpan or urinal and to notify nursing staff when each specimen is provided.			
Number specimen containers sequentially.			
Place alert signs in client's unit.			
3. Collect all required specimens.			
Place each specimen into appropriately labeled container.			
If outside of specimen container is contaminated with urine, clean it with soap and water.			
Ensure each specimen is refrigerated throughout timed collection period.			
Measure amount of each specimen.			
Ask client to provide last specimen 5 to 10 minutes before end of collection period.			
Inform client that test is completed.			
Remove alert signs and specimen equipment from bathroom.			
4. Document all relevant information.			

Procedure 46–3
Collecting a Urine Specimen from an Infant

Procedure	S	U	Comments
1. Prepare parents and infant.			
Explain procedure to parents.			
Handle infant gently, and talk in soothing tones.			

PROCEDURE	S	U	COMMENTS
Remove infant's diaper and clean perineal-genital area with soap and water and then with an antiseptic.			
For girls:			
Separate labia and wash, rinse, and dry perineal area from front to back on each side of urinary meatus, and then over meatus. Repeat, using antiseptic solution to clean, sterile water to rinse, and dry cotton balls to dry.			
For boys:			
Clean and disinfect both penis and scrotum. Wash penis in circular motion from tip toward scrotum, and wash scrotum last. Retract foreskin of an uncircumcised boy.			
2. Apply specimen bag.			
Remove protective paper from bottom half of adhesive backing of collection bag.			
Spread infant's legs apart.			
Place opening of collection bag over urethra or penis and scrotum. Base of opening needs to cover vagina or to fit well up under scrotum.			
Press adhesive portion firmly against infant's skin, starting at perineum.			
Remove protective paper from top half of adhesive backing, and press it firmly in place, working from top center outward.			
Apply a loose-fitting diaper.			
Elevate head of crib mattress to semi-Fowler's position.			
3. Remove bag, and transfer specimen.			
After child has voided desired amount, gently remove bag from skin.			
Empty urine from bag through opening at its base into specimen container.			
Discard urine bag.			
If outside of container is contaminated, disinfect it.			
4. Ensure client comfort.			
Apply infant's diaper.			
Leave infant in comfortable and safe position held by parent or in a crib.			

PROCEDURE	S	U	COMMENTS
5. Transport specimen.			
Ensure specimen label and laboratory requisition have correct information. Attach them securely to specimen.			
Arrange for specimen to be sent to laboratory immediately or refrigerate it.			
6. Document all relevant information.			

Procedure 46–4
Changing a Urinary Diversion Ostomy Appliance

PROCEDURE	S	U	COMMENTS
1. Determine need for appliance change.			
Assess appliance for leakage of urine.			
Ask client about any discomfort at or around stoma.			
Drain pouch into graduated cylinder when one-third to one-half full and prior to removing pouch.			
With evidence of leakage or discomfort at or around stoma, change appliance.			
2. Communicate acceptance and support of client throughout procedure.			
3. Select appropriate time.			
4. Prepare client and support persons.			
Explain procedure to client and support persons.			
Change appliance quickly, and provide privacy, preferably in bathroom.			
Assist client into comfortable standing, sitting, or lying position.			
Don gloves and unfasten belt, if worn.			
5. Shave peristomal skin of well-established ostomies as needed.			
6. Remove emptied ostomy appliance.			
Assess volume and character of output.			
Peel bag off slowly while holding client's skin taut.			
If disposable, discard appliance in moisture-proof bag.			
7. Clean and dry peristomal skin and stoma.			

PROCEDURE	S	U	COMMENTS
Using tampon or rolled piece of cotton-free gauze to wick urine from stoma until appliance is reapplied.			
Using cotton balls, wash peristomal skin with warm water and mild soap if needed.			
Pat dry skin with towel or cotton balls.			
8. Assess stoma and peristomal skin.			
Inspect color, size, and shape. Note any bleeding.			
Inspect peristomal skin for redness, ulcerations, or irritation.			
9. If using Skin Prep liquid or wipes:			
Cover stoma with gauze pad.			
Wipe Skin Prep evenly around peristomal skin, or use an applicator to apply thin layer of liquid to area.			
Allow Skin Prep to dry.			
10. If using wafer- or disc-type barrier:			
Use according to manufacturer's directions.			
Use stoma measuring device and trace a circle on backing of skin barrier.			
Make a template of stoma pattern and cut out traced pattern.			
Remove backing on one side of skin barrier and apply to faceplate of ostomy appliance.			
11. Prepare clean appliance.			
For disposable pouch with adhesive square, trace and cut a circle no larger than 2–3 cm (1/8 in) stoma size on appliance adhesive square. Peel off backing, and attach seal to disc-type skin barrier or, if liquid product was used, apply to client's peristomal skin.			
For reusable pouch with faceplate attached, apply either adhesive cement or double-faced adhesive disc to faceplate.			
For reusable pouch with detachable faceplate, remove protective paper strip from one side of disc, and apply to back of faceplate. Remove remaining protective paper strip from other side, and attach faceplate to disc-type skin barrier or, if liquid product was used, apply to client's peristomal skin.			

12. **Apply clean appliance.**			
For a disposable pouch, remove gauze pad or tampon over stoma, and gently press adhesive backing onto skin and smooth out wrinkles. Remove air from pouch, and attach spout to urinary drainage system or cap.			
For a reusable pouch with faceplate attached, insert coiled paper guidestrip into faceplate opening leaving strip protruding slightly. Using guidestrip, center faceplate over stoma, and firmly press adhesive seal to peristomal skin. Place deodorant in bag if desired, and close spout with cap.			
For reusable pouch with detachable faceplate, press and hold faceplate against client's skin for a few minutes, and tape to client's abdomen using four or eight 7.5 cm (3 in) strips of tape. Stretch opening on back of pouch and position it over base of faceplate, easing over faceplate flange. Place lock ring between pouch and back of pouch and faceplate flange, and close spout of pouch with cap.			
13. **Document relevant information.**			
14. **Adjust client's teaching plan and nursing care plan as needed.**			

Procedure 47–1
Collecting a Sputum Specimen

1. **Give client following information and instructions:**			
Purpose of test and how to provide sputum specimen.			
Not to touch inside of sputum container.			
To expectorate sputum directly into sputum container.			
To keep outside of container free of sputum, if possible.			
How to hold pillow firmly against abdominal incision if client finds it painful to cough.			
Amount of sputum required.			
2. **Provide necessary assistance to collect specimen.**			
Assist client to standing or sitting position.			

PROCEDURE	S	U	COMMENTS
Ask client to hold sputum cup on outside. For client who is not able to do so, don gloves and hold cup for client.			
Ask client to breathe deeply and then cough up secretions.			
Hold cup so that client can expectorate into it, making sure sputum does not come into contact with outside of container.			
Assist client to repeat coughing until sufficient amount of sputum has been collected.			
Cover container with lid immediately after sputum is in container.			
If spillage occurs on outside of container, clean outer surface with disinfectant.			
Remove and discard gloves.			
3. **Ensure client comfort.**			
Assist client to rinse mouth with mouthwash as needed.			
Assist client to position of comfort that allows maximum lung expansion as required.			
4. **Label and transport specimen to laboratory.**			
Ensure specimen label and laboratory requisition carry correct information. Attach securely to specimen.			
Arrange for specimen to be sent to laboratory immediately or refrigerated.			
5. **Document all relevant information.**			

Procedure 47–2
Obtaining Nose and Throat Specimens

1. **Prepare client and equipment.**			
Assist client into sitting position.			
Don gloves in case client's mucosa is touched.			
Open culture tube and place on sterile wrapper.			
Remove one sterile applicator, and hold by stick end, keeping remainder sterile.			
2. **Collect specimen.**			
For throat specimen:			
Ask client to open mouth, extend tongue, and say "ah."			

	S	U	
Use penlight to illuminate posterior pharynx while depressing tongue with tongue blades. Depress tongue firmly without touching throat.			
Insert swab into mouth without touching the mouth or tongue.			
Run swab along tonsils, contacting any areas on pharynx that are erythematous or contain exudate.			
Remove swab without touching mouth or lips.			
Insert swab into correctly labeled sterile tube without allowing it to touch outside of container.			
Crush culture medium at bottom of tube, and push swab into medium.			
Place top securely on tube.			
Repeat above steps with second swab.			
Discard tongue blade in waste container, and discard gloves.			
For nasal specimen:			
If using nasal speculum, gently insert lighted speculum in one nostril.			
Insert sterile swab through speculum without touching edges. When working without speculum, pass swab along septum and floor of nose.			
After passing swab about 3 to 4 inches into nasopharynx, rotate swab.			
Remove swab without touching speculum and place it into sterile tube.			
Repeat steps for other nostril.			
3. **Label and transport specimens to laboratory.**			
4. **Document all relevant information.**			

Procedure 47–3
Assisting a Client to Use a Sustained Maximal Inspiration (SMI) Device

	S	U	
1. **Prepare client.**			
Explain procedure.			
Assist client into upright position in bed or chair.			

PROCEDURE	S	U	COMMENTS
For Flow-Oriented SMI:			
2. Set spirometer.			
If spirometer has inspiratory volume-level pointer, set pointer at prescribed level.			
3. Instruct client to use spirometer as follows:			
Hold spirometer in upright position.			
Exhale normally.			
Seal lips tightly around mouthpiece and take in slow, deep breath to elevate balls. Then, hold breath for 2 seconds initially, increasing to 6 seconds keeping balls elevated if possible. Instruct client to avoid brisk, low-volume breaths that snap balls to top of chamber.			
Remove mouthpiece and exhale normally.			
Cough productively, if possible, after using spirometer.			
Relax, and take several deep breaths before using spirometer again.			
Repeat procedure several times, and then, one or two times hourly.			
For Volume-Oriented SMI:			
4. Set spirometer to predetermined volume. Check physician's or respiratory therapist's order.			
5. Instruct client to use spirometer as follows:			
Exhale normally.			
Seal lips tightly around mouthpiece, and take slow, deep breath until piston is elevated to predetermined level.			
Hold breath for 6 seconds.			
Remove mouthpiece, and exhale normally.			
Cough productively, if possible, after using spirometer.			
Relax, and take several normal breaths before using spirometer again.			
Repeat procedure several times, then one or two times hourly.			
For all devices:			
6. Clean equipment.			

Clean mouthpiece with water, and shake dry. Label mouthpiece and disposable SMI with client's name. Leave disposable SMI at bedside for client to use as prescribed. Change disposable mouthpiece every 24 hours.

7. **Document all relevant information.**

Procedure 47–4
Administering Percussion, Vibration, and Postural Drainage (PVD) to Adults

1. **Prepare client.**

   Provide visual and auditory privacy.

   Explain positions client will need to assume, as well as percussion and vibration techniques.

2. **Assist client to appropriate position for postural drainage.**

   Use pillows to support client comfortably in required positions.

3. **Percuss affected area.**

   Ensure area to be percussed is covered by towel or gown.

   Ask client to breathe slowly and deeply.

   Cup hands, relax wrist, and flex elbows.

   With both hands cupped, alternately flex and extend wrists rapidly to slap chest.

   Percuss each affected lung segment for 1 to 2 minutes. Percussing action should produce hollow, popping sound.

4. **Vibrate affected area.**

   Place flattened hands, one over other (or side by side) against affected chest area.

   Ask client to inhale deeply through mouth and exhale slowly through pursed lips or nose.

   During exhalation, straighten elbows, lean slightly against client's chest while tensing arm and shoulder muscles in isometric contractions.

   Vibrate during five exhalations over one affected lung segment.

   Encourage client to cough and expectorate secretions into sputum container. Offer client tissues and mouthwash.

PROCEDURE	S	U	COMMENTS
Auscultate client's lungs, and compare findings to baseline data.			
5. Label and transport specimen, if obtained.			
Arrange for specimen to be sent to laboratory immediately, or refrigerate.			
6. Document percussion, vibration, and postural drainage and assessments.			

Procedure 47–5
Administering Percussion, Vibration, and Postural Drainage (PVD) to Infants and Children

PROCEDURE	S	U	COMMENTS
1. Prepare infant or child.			
Provide explanation suitable to child's age.			
Assist child to appropriate position for postural drainage.			
Use pillows to support client comfortably in required positions.			
2. Percuss affected area using percussion device if appropriate, or three fingertips flexed and held together.			
Vibrate affected area as appropriate, using vibrator appropriate to child's age.			
Instruct child to sit up, and encourage deep breathing and coughing to remove loosened secretions.			
or			
Suction airway.			
Repeat percussion, vibration, deep breathing, and coughing for each lobe requiring drainage.			
3. Document PVD and all assessments.			

Procedure 47–6
Bulb Suctioning an Infant

PROCEDURE	S	U	COMMENTS
1. Position infant appropriately for procedure.			
Bundle infant in large towel or blanket to restrain arms, or cradle child in your arm, tucking infant's near arm behind your back and holding other arm securely with your hand.			
Put bib or towel under infant's chin.			
2. Suction oral and nasal cavities.			

PROCEDURE	S	U	COMMENTS
Compress bulb of syringe with thumb before inserting syringe.			
Keeping bulb compressed, insert tip of syringe into infant's nose or mouth.			
Release bulb compression gradually, and slowly move it outward to aspirate secretions.			
Remove syringe, hold tip over waste receptacle, and compress bulb again.			
Repeat until infant's nares and mouth are clear of secretions and breathing sounds are clear.			
3. Ensure infant comfort and safety.			
Cuddle and soothe infant as necessary. Place infant in side-lying or prone position.			
4. Ensure availability of equipment for next suction.			
Rinse syringe and waste receptacle.			
Place syringe in clean folded towel at cribside.			
5. Document all relevant information.			
Variation:			
Use DeLee suction Device (Mucus Trap).			

Procedure 47–7
Administering Oxygen by Humidity Tent

PROCEDURE	S	U	COMMENTS
1. Verify physician's order.			
2. Prepare child.			
Provide explanation appropriate to age of child.			
Cover child with gown or cotton blanket.			
3. Prepare humidity tent.			
Close zippers on each side of tent.			
Fanfold front part of canopy into bedclothes or into an overlying drawsheet, and ensure all sides of canopy are tucked well under mattress.			
If cool mist is ordered, fill trough with ice to depth indicated by line.			
Ensure drainage tube for trough is in place.			
Fill water jar with sterile distilled water.			
Connect tent to wall oxygen or compressed air.			

PROCEDURE	S	U	COMMENTS
Flood tent with oxygen by setting flow meter at 15 liters per minute for about 5 minutes. Adjust flow meter according to orders.			
Open damper valve for about 5 minutes to increase humidity.			
4. Place child in tent and assess child's respiratory status.			
Assess vital signs, skin color, breathing, and chest movements frequently.			
5. Provide required care for child.			
Change bedding and clothing when damp.			
Encourage parents to stay with child. Allow parents to comfort child outside tent if child becomes fussy.			
Monitor child frequently for condition changes.			
Allow toys in tent, but not stuffed toys.			
6. Monitor functioning of humidity tent.			
Monitor air flows.			
Minimize opening tent.			
Monitor concentration of oxygen.			
Maintain tent temperature at 20 to 21C (68 to 70F).			
7. Document relevant data.			

Procedure 47–8
Inserting and Maintaining a Pharyngeal Airway

PROCEDURE	S	U	COMMENTS
1. Insert airway.			
Oropharyngeal airway:			
Explain procedure. Check for and remove dentures.			
Place client in supine position with neck hyperextended or with pillow placed under shoulders.			
Don disposable gloves, open client's mouth, and place tongue depressor on anterior half of tongue.			
Lubricate airway with water-soluble lubricant or with cool water.			

PROCEDURE	S	U	COMMENTS
Turn airway upside down, with curved end upwards or sideways, and advance it along roof of mouth.			
When airway passes uvula, rotate airway until curve of airway follows natural curve of tongue.			
Remove excess lubricant from client's lips.			
Nasopharyngeal airway:			
Determine size of airway needed.			
Assess patency of each naris.			
Ask client, if conscious, to blow nose.			
Lubricate entire tube with a topical anesthetic, if ordered.			
Hold airway by wide end and insert narrow end into naris, applying gentle inward and downward pressure when advancing airway.			
Advance airway until external horn fits against outer naris.			
Remove excess lubricant from nares.			
2. Tape airway in position, if required.			
3. Ensure client's comfort and safety.			
Oropharyngeal tube:			
Maintain client in lateral or semiprone position.			
Suction secretions as required.			
Provide mouth care at least every 4 hours, and check mucous membranes for ulceration.			
Remove airway once client has regained consciousness and has swallow, gag, and cough reflexes.			
Nasopharyngeal tube:			
Remove tube, clean it with warm, soapy water, and insert in other nostril at least every 8 hours, or as ordered.			
Provide nasal hygiene every 4 hours or more often if needed.			
4. Document all relevant information.			

Procedure 47–9
Plugging a Tracheostomy Tube

PROCEDURE	S	U	COMMENTS
1. Position client.			

PROCEDURE	S	U	COMMENTS
Assist client into semi-Fowler's position unless contraindicated.			
2. Suction airways.			
Suction client's nasopharynx and oropharynx if there are any secretions present.			
Change suction catheters and suction tracheostomy.			
3. Deflate tracheal cuff if ordered.			
Suction tracheostomy tube again if secretions are present.			
4. Insert tracheostomy plug.			
Using sterile gloves, fit tracheostomy plug into either inner or outer cannula, depending on whether tracheostomy tube has double or single cannula.			
Monitor client closely for 10 minutes for signs of respiratory distress. At first signs of respiratory distress, remove plug, and suction tracheostomy if necessary.			
Clean inner cannula, if removed.			
Observe client frequently while tube is plugged.			
5. Remove plug at designated time.			
After removing plug, suction tracheostomy if indicated, and replace inner cannula if removed.			
Reinflate cuff if ordered.			
6. Document all relevant information.			

Procedure 47–10
Assisting with the Insertion of a Chest Tube

PROCEDURE	S	U	COMMENTS
1. Prepare client.			
Explain procedure.			
Explain placement and rationale for chest tube(s) to client and family.			
Position client as directed by physician, with area to receive tube facing upward. Determine from physician whether to have bed in supine position or semi-Fowler's.			
2. Prepare equipment.			

PROCEDURE	S	U	COMMENTS
Open chest tube tray and sterile gloves on overbed table.			
Assist with cleaning the insertion site.			
Cleanse stopper of local anesthetic with alcohol swab and invert vial and hold it for physician to aspirate medication.			
Assist with clamping tube or connecting to drainage system.			
Maintain sterile technique.			
3. Provide emotional support and monitor client as required.			
4. Provide airtight dressing.			
After tube insertion: Don sterile gloves and wrap piece of sterile petrolatum gauze around chest tube. Place drain gauzes around insertion site. Place several 4 × 4 gauze squares over them.			
Tape dressings, covering them completely.			
5. Secure chest tube appropriately.			
Tape chest tube to client's skin away from insertion site.			
Tape connections of chest tube to drainage tube and to drainage system.			
Coil drainage tubing and secure it to bed linen, ensuring enough slack for client movement.			
6. When all drainage connections are completed, ask client to:			
Take deep breath and hold it for a few seconds and then slowly exhale.			
7. Prepare client for portable chest x-ray to check placement of tube.			
8. Ensure client safety.			
Place rubber-tipped chest tube clamps at bedside.			
Assess client regularly for signs of pneumothorax and subcutaneous emphysema.			
Assess client's vital signs every 15 minutes for first hour, then as ordered.			
Auscultate lungs every 4 hours.			

Check for intermittent bubbling in water-seal bottle or chamber.			
Check for gentle bubbling in suction-control chamber.			
Inspect drainage in collection container at least every 30 minutes during first 2 hours, then every 2 hours.			
9. Document all relevant information.			

Procedure 47–11
Monitoring a Client with Chest Drainage

1. Assess client.			
Assess vital signs every 4 hours or more often, as indicated.			
Determine ease of respirations, breath sounds, respiratory rate, and chest movement.			
Monitor client for signs of pneumothorax.			
Inspect dressing for excessive and abnormal drainage. Palpate around dressing site, and listen for crackling sound.			
Assess level of discomfort.			
2. Implement all necessary safety precautions.			
Keep two 15- to 18-cm (6- to 7-in) Kelly clamps within reach at bedside.			
Keep one sterile petrolatum gauze within reach at bedside.			
Keep extra drainage system available in client's room. To change drainage system: a. Clamp chest tube close to insertion site with two rubber-tipped clamps placed in opposite directions. b. Reestablish water-sealed drainage system and remove the clamps.			
Keep drainage system below chest level and upright at all times, unless chest tubes are clamped.			
3. Maintain patency of drainage system.			
Check that all connections are secured with tape.			

PROCEDURE	S	U	COMMENTS
Inspect drainage tubing for kinks or loops dangling below entry level of drainage system.			
Coil drainage tubing and secure to bed linen, ensuring enough slack for client movement.			
Inspect air vent in system periodically for occlusions.			
Milk or strip chest tubing as ordered and only in accordance with agency protocol.			
To milk chest tube, follow these steps: a. Lubricate about 10 to 20 cm (4 to 8 in) of drainage tubing. b. With one hand, securely stabilize and pinch tube at insertion site. c. Compress tube with thumb and forefinger of hand and milk it by sliding down tube, moving away from insertion site. d. If entire tube is to be milked, reposition hands farther along tubing, and repeat steps a through c in progressive overlapping steps, until end of tubing is reached.			
4. Assess any fluid level fluctuation and bubbling in drainage system.			
In gravity drainage systems, check for fluctuation (tidaling) of fluid level in water-seal glass tube in bottle system or water-seal chamber in commercial system as client breathes.			
To check for fluctuation in suction systems, temporarily turn off suction and observe fluctuation.			
Check for intermittent bubbling in water of water-seal bottle or chamber.			
Check for gentle bubbling in suction-control bottle or chamber.			
5. Assess drainage.			
Inspect drainage in collection container at least every 30 minutes during first two hours after chest tube insertion, and every 2 hours thereafter.			
Every 8 hours mark time, date, and drainage level on adhesive tape and affix to container, or mark it directly on disposable container.			
Note any sudden change in amount or color of drainage. If drainage exceeds 100 mL per hour or if color change indicates hemorrhage, notify physician immediately.			

6. Watch for dislodgement of tubes and remedy problem promptly.

If chest tube become disconnected from drainage system:

a. Have client exhale fully.

b. Clamp chest tube close to insertion site with two rubber-tipped clamps in opposite direction.

c. Quickly clean ends of tubing with an antiseptic, reconnect, and tape securely.

d. Unclamp tube as soon as possible.

e. Assess client closely for respiratory distress.

f. Check vital signs every 10 minutes.

If chest tube becomes dislodged from insertion site:

a. Remove dressing, and immediately apply pressure with petrolatum gauze, hand or towel.

b. Cover site with petrolatum gauze and sterile 4 × 4 dressing.

c. Tape dressing with air-occlusive tape.

d. Notify physician immediately.

e. Assess client for respiratory distress every 10 to 15 minutes or as client condition indicates.

If drainage system is accidentally tipped over:

a. Immediately return it to upright position.

b. Ask client to take several deep breaths.

c. Notify nurse in charge.

d. Assess client for respiratory distress.

7. If continuous bubbling persists in water-seal collection chamber, indicating an air leak, determine its source.

To detect an air leak, follow next steps sequentially:

a. Check tubing connection sites. Tighten and retape any that appear loose.

b. If bubbling continues, clamp chest tube near insertion site and determine if bubbling stops while client takes several deep breaths.

c. If bubbling stops, proceed with next step. Source of air leak is above clamp. It may be at insertion site or inside client.

d. If bubbling continues, source of air leak is below clamp. See next step below.

To determine if air leak is at insertion site or inside of client:

a. Unclamp tube and palpate gently around insertion site. If bubbling stops, leak is at insertion site. Apply a petrolatum gauze and 4 x 4 gauze around insertion site, and secure dressings with adhesive tape.

b. If leak is not at insertion site, it is inside client. Leave tube unclamped, notify physician, and monitor client for signs of respiratory distress.

To locate air leak below chest tube clamp:

a. Move clamp a few inches down and keep moving it downward a few inches at a time. Each time clamp is moved, check water-seal collection chamber for bubbling.

b. When leak is located, seal leak by applying tape to that portion of drainage tube.

c. If bubbling continues after entire length of tube is clamped, air leak is in drainage device. Replace drainage system according to agency protocol.

8. **Take specimen of chest drainage as required.**

Specimens of chest drainage are taken from disposable systems through self-sealing port. If specimen is required:

a. Use a povidone-iodine swab to wipe self-sealing diaphragm on back of drainage collection chamber. Allow to dry.

b. Attach sterile #18 or #20 gauge needle to 3- or 5-mL syringe and insert needle into diaphragm.

c. Aspirate specimen, transfer fluid to sterile specimen container, label container, and send to laboratory.

9. **Ensure essential client care.**

Encourage deep-breathing and coughing exercises every 2 hours if indicated. Have client sit upright to perform exercises, and splint tube insertion site with pillow or hand. Provide pain medication, as ordered, before the exercise.

While client takes deep breaths, palpate chest for thoracic expansion. Note whether chest expansion is symmetric.

Reposition client every 2 hours. When client is lying down on affected side, place rolled towels beside tubing.

Assist client with range-of-motion exercises of affected shoulder three times per day.			
When transporting and ambulating client: a. Attach rubber-tipped forceps to client's gown. b. Keep water-seal unit below chest level and upright. c. Disconnect drainage system from suction apparatus before moving client and make sure air vent is open.			
10. Document all relevant information.			

Procedure 47–12
Assisting with the Removal of a Chest Tube

1. Prepare client.			
Administer analgesic, if ordered, 30 minutes before tube is removed.			
Ensure chest tube is securely clamped.			
Assist client into semi-Fowler's position or to lateral position on unaffected side.			
Put absorbent pad under client beneath chest tube.			
Instruct client how to perform Valsalva's maneuver when physician removes chest tube.			
2. Prepare sterile field and sterile air-tight gauze.			
Open sterile packages and prepare sterile field.			
Don sterile gloves and place sterile petrolatum gauze on 4 x 4 gauze square.			
3. Remove soiled dressing.			
While wearing gloves, be careful not to dislodge tube when removing underlying gauzes.			
Discard soiled dressing in moisture-resistant bag.			
4. Assist with removal of tube.			
While physician removes tube, assist client to perform Valsalva's maneuver, and provide emotional support.			
Immediately apply petrolatum gauze dressing to insertion site and cover with air-occlusive tape.			

5. Continue to provide emotional support and monitor client's response to chest tube removal.

6. Assess client.

Monitor vital signs and assess quality of respirations as ordered or as needed.

Auscultate client's lungs every 4 hours.

Assess client regularly for signs of pneumothorax, subcutaneous emphysema, and infection.

7. Prepare client for chest x-ray if ordered.

8. Document relevant information.

Procedure 47–13
Clearing an Obstructed Airway

Abdominal thrusts—standing or sitting victim:

1. Identify yourself as a trained rescuer.

Stand behind victim and wrap arms around person's waist.

Direct bystander to call EMS.

2. Give abdominal thrusts.

Make fist with one hand, tuck thumb inside of fist, place flexed thumb just above victim's navel and below xiphoid process.

With other hand, grasp fist and press it into person's abdomen with firm, quick upward thrust.

Deliver successive thrusts as separate and complete movements until victim's airway clears or victim becomes unconscious.

If victim becomes unconscious, lower person carefully to floor, supporting head and neck.

Abdominal thrusts—unconscious victim lying on ground:

1. Direct bystander to call EMS.

2. Airway management.

Tilt victim's head back, lift chin, and pinch nose shut. Put on mouth shield, if available.

Give two slow breaths. If unable to ventilate, re-tilt head and repeat breaths.

3. Give abdominal thrusts.

PROCEDURE	S	U	COMMENTS
Straddle one or both of victim's legs.			
Place heel of one hand slightly above victim's navel and well below xiphoid process.			
Place other hand directly on top of first; keep your shoulders over victim's abdomen and your elbows straight.			
Point fingers of both hands toward victim's head and give five quick abdominal thrusts to middle of abdomen.			
4. Foreign object check.			
Using fingers and thumb, lift victim's lower jaw and tongue. Slide one finger down inside cheek and attempt to hook object out. In children, perform finger sweep only if object can be seen.			
5. Repeat abdominal thrusts, airway maneuvers, and foreign object checks until airway is clear or victim breathes.			
Chest thrusts—conscious standing or sitting person:			
1. Identify yourself as a trained rescuer.			
Stand behind victim with arms under victim's armpits and encircling victim's chest.			
Direct bystander to call EMS.			
Place thumb side of fist on middle of victim's breastbone.			
2. Deliver thrusts.			
Grab fist with other hand and deliver quick backward thrust.			
Repeat thrusts until obstruction is relieved or victim become unconscious.			
Chest thrusts—unconscious victim lying flat:			
1. Airway management.			
Tilt victim's head back, lift chin, and pinch nose shut. Put on mouth shield, if available.			
Give two slow breaths. If unable to ventilate, re-tilt head and repeat breaths.			
2. Deliver thrusts.			
Position victim supine and kneel close to side of victim's trunk.			
Position hands as for cardiac compression with heel of hand on lower half of sternum.			

3. Foreign object check.

Using fingers and thumb, lift victim's lower jaw and tongue. Slide one finger down inside cheek and attempt to hook object out. In children, perform finger sweep only if object can be seen.

4. Repeat chest thrusts, airway maneuvers, and foreign object checks until airway is clear or victim breathes.

Back blows and chest thrusts for infants:

1. Deliver back blows.

Straddle infant over forearm with head lower than trunk.

Support head by firmly holding jaw in hand.

With heel of free hand, deliver five sharp blows to infant's back over spine between shoulder blades.

2. Deliver chest thrusts.

Turn infant as a unit to supine position.

Place free hand on infant's back.

While continuing to support jaw, neck, and chest with other hand, turn and place infant on thigh with head lower than trunk.

Using two fingers, administer five chest thrusts over sternum, one finger width below nipple line.

For conscious infant, continue chest thrusts and back blows until airway is cleared or infant becomes unconscious.

If infant is unconscious, assess airway and give two breaths. If unable to ventilate, re-tilt infant's head and give two breaths. If air does not go in, give back blows and chest thrusts.

Lift jaw and tongue and check for foreign object. If object is seen, sweep it out with finger.

Repeat sequence of foreign object checks, breaths, back blows, and chest thrusts until airway clears or infant begins to breathe.

Finger sweep:

1. Prepare victim.

Don disposable gloves.

Open victim's mouth by grasping tongue and lower jaw between thumb and fingers, and lifting jaw upward.			
2. **Perform finger sweep.**			
Insert index finger of free hand along inside of victim's cheek and deep into throat.			
With finger hooked, use sweeping motion to try to dislodge and lift out foreign object.			
If measures fail, try abdominal thrusts in adults and children. With infant, give back blows and chest thrusts.			
After removing foreign object, clear out liquid material with a scooping motion using two fingers wrapped with tissue or cloth.			
3. **After maneuver, assess air exchange.**			
4. **Document relevant information.**			

Procedure 47–14
Administering Oral Resuscitation

1. **Clear mouth and throat of obstructive material and position victim appropriately.**			
Clear mouth and throat using finger sweep.			
If victim is lying on one side or face down, turn victim onto back as a unit, while supporting head and neck. Kneel beside head.			
2. **Open airway.**			
Use head-tilt, chin-lift maneuver or jaw-thrust maneuver. Use modified jaw-thrust for persons with suspected neck injury.			
Head-tilt, chin-lift maneuver:			
Place one hand palm down on forehead.			
Place fingers of other hand on bony part of lower jaw near chin.			
Simultaneously press down on forehead and lift victim's chin.			
Open victim's mouth by pressing lower lip downward with thumb after tilting head.			
Remove dentures if they cannot be maintained in place.			

PROCEDURE	S	U	COMMENTS
Jaw-thrust maneuver:			
Kneel at *top* of victim's head.			
Grasp angle of mandible directly below earlobe between thumb and forefinger on each side of victim's head.			
While tilting head backward, lift lower jaw until it juts forward and is higher that upper jaw.			
Rest elbows on surface which victim is lying.			
Retract lower lip with thumbs prior to giving artificial respiration.			
If spinal neck injury is suspected, do not hyperextend victim's neck. Use modified jaw-thrust maneuver instead.			
Modified jaw-thrust maneuver:			
Perform first two steps for jaw-thrust maneuver.			
Do not tilt head backward while lifting lower jaw forward.			
Support head carefully without hyperextending it or moving it from side to side.			
3. Determine victim's ability to breathe.			
Place ear and cheek to victim's mouth and nose.			
Look at chest and abdomen for rising and falling movement.			
Listen for air escaping during exhalation.			
Feel for air escaping against cheek.			
4. If no breathing is evident, provide rescue breathing if required.			
Use mouth-to-mouth, mouth-to-nose, mouth-to-mask, or hand-compressible breathing bag method. If no pulse is evident, begin cardiac compressions. See Procedure 47–15.			
5. Check for carotid pulse. See step 7.			
Mouth-to-mouth:			
Put on mouth shield.			
Maintain open airway.			
Pinch victim's nostrils with index finger and thumb.			

PROCEDURE	S	U	COMMENTS
Take deep breath, and place mouth opened widely around victim's mouth. Ensure air-tight seal.			
Deliver two full breaths of 1-1/2 seconds each into victim's mouth.			
Ensure adequate ventilation by observing victim's chest rise and fall.			
If initial ventilation attempt is unsucessful, reposition victim's head and repeat rescue breathing. If victim still cannot be ventilated, proceed to clear airway of any foreign objects by using finger sweep, abdominal thrusts, or chest thrusts.			
Mouth-to-nose:			
Maintain head-tilt and chin-lift.			
Close victim's mouth by pressing hand against victim's chin.			
Put on mouth shield.			
Take deep breath, seal lips around victim's nose.			
Deliver two full breaths of 1-1/2 seconds each.			
Remove mouth from victim's nose and allow victim to exhale passively.			
Mouth-to-mask:			
Remove mask from case and push out dome.			
Connect one-way valve to mask.			
Kneel at top of victim's head, and open airway using jaw-thrust maneuver.			
Place bottom rim of mask between victim's lower lip and chin. Place rest of mask over face using thumbs on each side to hold mask in place.			
Perform jaw-thrust manuever to tilt head backward. Use three fingers of both hands behind angles of jaw, and grasp victim's temples with palm of hands.			
Maintain head position while blowing intermittently into mouth piece.			
Hand-compressible breathing bag:			
Stand at victim's head.			
Use one hand to secure mask and to hold victim's jaw forward. Use other hand to squeeze and release bag.			

PROCEDURE	S	U	COMMENTS
Compress bag until sufficient elevation of chest is observed, and then release bag.			
6. Determine whether victim's breathing is restored.			
7. Determine presence of carotid pulse.			
Take about 5 to 10 seconds for this pulse check.			
To palpate carotid artery, locate larynx, then slide fingers alongside it into groove between larynx and neck muscles.			
8. If carotid pulse is palpable, but breathing is not restored, repeat rescue breathing.			
Blow forcibly enough to make victim's chest rise.			
If chest expansion fails to occur, ensure that head is hyperextended and jaw lifted upward, or check again for the presence of obstructive material, fluid, or vomitus.			
After each inflation, move your mouth away from victim's.			
9. Reassess carotid pulse after every 12 inflations (after 1 minute).			
If you cannot locate pulse, the victim's heart has stopped. Provide cardiac compression. See Procedure 47–15.			
10. Document relevant information.			

Procedure 47–15
Administering External Cardiac Compressions

PROCEDURE	S	U	COMMENTS
1. Survey scene for safety hazards, presence of bystanders, and other victims.			
2. Assess victim's level of consciousness, patency of airway, presence/absence of breathing, and pulse.			
Ask victim, "Are you alright?"			
If victim does not respond, in a health care facility call a "code" or follow agency protocol. If alone outside of health care facility, call for help and have another person call for EMS or 911.			
3. Position victim appropriately.			
Place victim in supine position.			

Procedure	S	U	Comments
If in a health care facility, place cardiac board under victim's back, or place victim on floor if necessary.			
If victim must be turned, turn body as a unit while supporting head and neck.			
Have a bystander elevate lower extremities, if possible.			
4. Assess responsiveness, airway, breathing, and circulation.			
Responsiveness:			
Assess responsiveness. If unconscious, open airway, assess breathing and circulation prior to initiating compressions.			
Airway:			
Open airway with head-tilt, chin-lift maneuver or, if neck injury is suspected, the modified jaw-thrust.			
Breathing:			
Assess breathing: look, listen, and feel for air flow.			
Ventilate victim if breathing is not restored.			
Deliver two full breaths into victim's mouth.			
If unable to ventilate, reposition victim's head and repeat two breaths.			
If still unsuccessful, follow procedures for obstructed airway (see Procedure 47–13).			
Circulation:			
Assess carotid pulse for 5 to 10 seconds.			
If pulse is present, continue rescue breathing at 12 breaths per minute while monitoring pulse.			
If pulse is absent, begin external chest compressions and rescue breathing.			
5. Position hands on sternum.			
With hand nearest victim's legs, use middle and index fingers to locate lower margin of rib cage.			
Move fingers up rib cage to notch where lower ribs meet sternum.			
Place heel of other hand along lower half of victim's sternum.			
Place first hand on top of second hand, and extend or interlace fingers.			

PROCEDURE	S	U	COMMENTS
6. Administer cardiac compressions.			
Lock elbows, straighten arms, and position shoulders directly over hands.			
For each compression, thrust straight down on sternum. For adult, depress sternum 3.8 to 5.0 cm (1.5 to 2 in).			
Between compressions, completely release compression pressure, but do not lift or move hands.			
Provide external cardiac compressions at rate of 80 to 100 per minute. Count "one and, two and," and so on.			
Administer 5 or 15 external compressions depending on number of rescuers, and coordinate with rescue breathing.			
CPR performed by one rescuer:			
Survey the scene.			
Call for help and have another person call for EMS (911).			
If there is no bystander, and rescuer is alone, summon help and then perform CPR.			
7. Assess responsiveness. If unconscious, open airway, assess breathing and circulation prior to initiating compressions. Follow steps 4 and 5.			
Perform two rescue breaths.			
Perform 15 external chest compressions at rate of 80 to 100 per minute. Counting "one and, two and," up to 15.			
Alternate rescue breathing and external compressions for four complete cycles.			
Assess victim's carotid pulse after four cycles. If there is no pulse, continue CPR, checking pulse every few minutes.			
CPR performed by two rescuers:			
One rescuer provides external cardiac compression and the other provides pulmonary resuscitation.			
Second rescuer, identified as a trained rescuer, verifies that EMS has been notified.			
First rescuer completes cycle of fifteen compressions with two breaths. Second rescuer gets into position to give compressions.			

PROCEDURE	S	U	COMMENTS
First rescuer assesses carotid pulse for five seconds, and if pulse is absent, gives one breath and then states, "No pulse, continue CPR."			
Second rescuer then provides compressions, and paces by counting aloud, "one and, two and, three and, four and, five and, ventilate."			
First rescuer provides one ventilation after every five chest compressions, and observes each breath for effectiveness.			
First rescuer assesses carotid pulse frequently between breaths for effectiveness of cardiac compressions. Also observes for overinflation of lungs by watching for abdominal distention.			
When second rescuer becomes fatigued, position change is indicated by stating, "Change one and, two and, three and, four and, five and . . . " Then person compressing moves to victim's head and counts pulse for 5 seconds.			
Person ventilating gives breath and moves into position to provide compressions.			
If no pulse is present, original person compressing states, "No pulse, start compression," gives one full breath, and CPR is again initiated.			
When relieved from CPR:			
Stand by to assist cardiac arrest team.			
Provide emotional support to victim's family and bystanders.			
Variation: CPR for children			
For children, follow steps 1 through 3.			
In children, find hand position for compression by running index and middle finger up ribs to sternal notch. Look at location of index finger and lift fingers off sternum and put heel of same hand just above location of index finger.			
Other hand remains on child's forehead to keep airway open.			
Use heel of one hand for compressions, keeping fingers off chest. Compression depth is 2.5 to 3.8 cm (1 to 1-1/2 in).			
Give compressions at rate of 100 per minute with cycles of five compressions to one breath.			

Variation: CPR for infants

For infants, when ventilating, cover infant's mouth and nose.			
For pulse checks, use brachial pulse site.			
Find position for compressions, place index finger on sternum at nipple line. Place middle and ring fingers on sternum next to index finger, then lift index finger.			
Compress chest 1.25 to 2.5 cm (1/2 to 1 in) straight down using two fingers while other hand remains on forehead to maintain open airway.			
Give compressions at a rate of up to 120 per minute, with cycles of five compressions and one breath.			

8. Terminating CPR

Terminate CPR only when another trained individual takes over, when heartbeat and breathing have been reestablished, when adjunctive life-support measures are initiated, when a physician states victim is dead and to discontinue CPR, or when rescuer is exhausted and there is no one else to take over.			

9. Document relevant information.

Procedure 47–16
Initiating Cardiac Monitoring

1. Prepare the client.

Explain reason for continuous ECG monitoring to the client.			
Explain that loose or disconnected lead wires, poor electrode contact, excessive movement, electrical interference, or equipment malfunction may trigger alarms and alert staff.			
Explain that client may move about within activity restrictions while on monitor. Explain skin preparation procedure. Provide for privacy and drape client appropriately.			

2. Select appropriate equipment.

Assure presence of bedside monitor and cable, or, if client is ambulatory, obtain telemetry unit and pouch. Check equipment for damage. Connect lead wires to cable and secure connections.			

PROCEDURE	S	U	COMMENTS
3. Select electrode sites on chest wall.			
Sites depend on lead to be monitored, condition of skin, and any incisions or catheters present.			
4. Prepare electrode sites.			
Shave 4 × 4 inch area for each electrode if chest is excessively hairy.			
Clean sites with soap and water; dry thoroughly. Alcohol may be used to remove skin oils; allow to dry for 60 seconds after use.			
Genly abrade site by rubbing with dry gauze pad or ECG prep pad.			
5. Apply electrodes and connect them to monitor cable or telemetry unit.			
Open electrode package; peel backing from electrode and check that center of pad is moist with conductive gel.			
Apply electrode pads to client, pressing firmly to ensure contact.			
Attach leads and position cable with sufficient slack for client's comfort. Place telemetry unit (if used) in client's gown pocket.			
6. Assess monitor tracing and set alarm limits.			
Assess ECG tracing on monitor, adjusting settings as needed.			
Set ECG monitor alarm limits for client, typically at 20 bpm higher and lower than baseline rate. Turn alarms ON, and leave on at all times.			
7. Ensure client safety.			
Assess client immediately if alarm is triggered. Remove and apply new pads every 24 to 48 hours, of if pad becomes dislodged or nonadherent. Cleanse gel residue from previous site, and document skin condition under pads. Choose alternate site if skin appears irritated or blistered. Time and date pads with every change.			
Monitor client periodically for comfort. Assess electrode and lead wire connections as needed.			
8. Document all relevant information.			

Procedure 48–1
Using a Dial-A-Flo In-line Device

1. Attach Dial-A-Flo device appropriately.			
Connect Dial-A-Flo device to end of tubing.			
Connect insertion spike of IV tubing to solution container.			
2. Prime tubing.			
Adjust regulator on Dial-A-Flo to open position.			
Open all clamps and infusion flow regulators on IV tubing.			
Remove protective cap at end of tubing, and allow fluid to run through tubing.			
Reclamp tubing to prevent continued flow.			
3. Establish infusion.			
Attach primed tubing to venipuncture needle or catheter hub.			
Open IV tubing flow regulator.			
Align Dial-A-Flo regulator to arrow indicating desired volume of fluid to infuse over 1 hour.			
4. Confirm appropriate drip rate.			
Count drip rate for 15 seconds and multiply by 4.			
Recheck after 5 minutes and again after 15 minutes.			
If drip rate does not coincide with that calculated, adjust height of IV pole.			
5. Monitor volume of fluid infused at least every hour, and compare it with time tape on IV container.			
6. Document all relevant information.			

Procedure 48–2
Using an Infusion Controller or Pump

Infusion controller:			
1. Attach controller to IV pole below and in line with IV container. Plug machine into electrical outlet.			
2. Set up IV infusion.			

PROCEDURE	S	U	COMMENTS
Open IV container, maintaining sterility of port, and spike container with administration set			
Place IV container on pole, and position drip chamber 76 cm (30 in) above venipuncture site.			
Fill drip chamber of IV tubing one-third full.			
Rotate drip chamber.			
Prime tubing, and close clamp.			
3. **Attach IV drop sensor, and insert IV tubing into controller.**			
Attach IV drop sensor to drip chamber below drip orifice and above fluid level in drip chamber.			
Make sure sensor is plugged into controller.			
Insert tubing into controller.			
4. **Initiate infusion.**			
Perform a venipuncture or connect tubing to primary IV tubing and catheter. Don gloves.			
Open IV control clamp completely.			
5. **Set volume dials for appropriate volume per hour.**			
Close door, and ensure that all tubing clamps are wide open.			
Set dials on front of controller to appropriate infusion rate and volume.			
Press power and start button.			
Count drops for 15 seconds and multiply result by 4.			
6. **Set alarm.**			
7. **Monitor infusion.**			
Check volume of fluid infused at least every hour, and compare it with time tape on IV container.			
Infusion pump:			
8. **Attach pump at eye level on IV pole.**			
9. **Set up infusion.**			
Check manufacturer's directions before using filter or infusing blood.			

Open IV container, maintaining sterility of port, and spike container with administration set.			
Place IV container on IV pole above pump.			
Fill drip chamber, and rotate it.			
Prime tubing, and close clamp.			
10. Attach IV drop sensor and insert IV tubing into pump.			
Position drop sensor, if required, on drip chamber. See step 3.			
Load machine and ensure correct pressure is set.			
11. Initiate infusion.			
12. Set dials for required drops per minute or millimeters per hour.			
Close door to pump and ensure IV tubing clamps are open.			
Press power button to "on," and press start button.			
13. Set alarm and monitor infusion.			
14. Document relevant information.			

Procedure 48–3
Using an Implantable Venous Access Device (IVAD)

1. Assemble equipment.			
Attach IV tubing to infusion or transfusion container.			
Prime infusion tubing with saline.			
Prepare syringes of normal saline and heparinized saline.			
2. Position client appropriately and locate implant port.			
Position client in either a supine or sitting position.			
Locate IVAD, and grasp it between two fingers of nondominant hand to stabilize it. Palpate and locate septum.			
3. Prepare site.			
Wash hands, and don sterile gloves.			

PROCEDURE	S	U	COMMENTS
Optional:			
Insert 2% lidocaine subcutaneously in injection site.			
Place ice pack on site to reduce discomfort from puncture.			
Prepare skin and let area dry.			
4. Insert Huber needle.			
Grasp device and palpate septum for injection. Anchor the port with the nondominant hand.			
Insert needle at a 90° angle to septum, and push firmly through skin and septum until it contacts base of IVAD chamber.			
When needle contacts base of septum, aspirate for blood to determine placement.			
5. Secure needle and ensure proper placement of IVAD catheter.			
Support Huber needle with 2 × 2 dressing and Steristrips.			
Infuse saline flush and priming solution.			
6. After use, flush system with heparinized saline.			
When flushing, maintain positive pressure, and clamp tubing as soon as flush is finished.			
7. Attach IV-lock to Huber needle.			
8. Prevent manipulation or dislodgment of needle.			
Apply occlusive transparent dressing to needle sit.			
Apply povidone or antibiotic ointment to site before dressings are applied.			
9. Document all relevant information.			
Variation: Obtaining a blood specimen			
Withdraw 10 mL of blood and discard it.			
Draw up required amount of blood and transfer it to appropriate containers.			
Slowly instill 20 mL of normal saline over a 5 minute period.			
Inject 5 mL of heparinized saline.			

Procedure 48–4
Obtaining a Capillary Blood Specimen and Measuring Blood Glucose

PROCEDURE	S	U	COMMENTS
1. **Prepare equipment.**			
Obtain reagent strip from container and place on clean, dry paper towel.			
Calibrate meter and run a control sample according to manufacturer's instructions.			
2. **Select and prepare puncture site.**			
Choose a vascular puncture site.			
Clean site with antiseptic swab, and permit it to dry.			
3. **Obtain blood specimen.**			
Don gloves.			
Place injector, if used, against site and release needle, permitting it to pierce skin. Make sure lancet is perpendicular to site.			
or			
Prick site with a lancet or needle, using a darting motion.			
Wipe away first drop of blood with cotton ball.			
Gently squeeze site until large drop of blood forms.			
Hold reagent strip under puncture site until enough blood covers indicator squares.			
Ask client to apply pressure to skin puncture site with cotton ball.			
4. **Expose blood to test strip for period of time and in manner specified by manufacturer.**			
Press timer on glucose meter and monitor time.			
5. **Measure and document blood glucose.**			
Place strip into meter according to manufacturer's instructions.			
At desired time, activate meter to display glucose reading.			
Turn off meter and discard test strip and cotton balls.			

PROCEDURE	S	U	COMMENTS
Document method of testing and results on client's record.			

Procedure 48–5
Obtaining a Venous Blood Specimen from an Adult by Venipuncture

	PROCEDURE	S	U	COMMENTS
1.	Verify physician's orders for tests to be obtained, and obtain correct test tubes for specific test ordered.			
2.	Identify client appropriately.			
	Check client's wristband.			
	Explain procedure and enlist client's cooperation.			
3.	Don gloves and perform venipuncture.			
4.	Obtain specimen.			

Using sterile syringe and needle:

PROCEDURE	S	U	COMMENTS
When needle is in vein, gently pull back on syringe plunger until appropriate amount of blood is obtained.			
Remove tourniquet when sufficient blood is obtained, and remove needle from vein. Place a sterile 2 × 2 gauze pad over site and ask client to firmly hold it in place 2 to 3 minutes, if able.			
Transfer specimens to tubes by inserting needle directly through stopper of blood tube, allowing vacuum to fill tube with blood. Ensure that each tube contains the correct amount of blood.			
For all blood tubes containing additives, gently rotate or invert test tube several times.			

Using a vacucontainer system:

PROCEDURE	S	U	COMMENTS
Once venipuncture needle is positioned in vein, hold plastic adapter securely, and press vacuum tube firmly into short needle until it pierces top of tube.			
Fill vacucontainer with blood, release it, and set it aside.			
Insert another vacucontainer if more blood is required.			
Release tourniquet and remove needle from vein.			
Cover site with sterile gauze pad.			

PROCEDURE	S	U	COMMENTS
5. Ensure client comfort and safety.			
Assess client's venipuncture site.			
Apply pressure until bleeding has stopped.			
When bleeding is minimized, apply a Band-Aid over site.			
6. Label test tubes appropriately and send them to laboratory.			
7. Document and report relevant information.			
Variation: Collecting a blood specimen for culture			
Gather equipment, including two paired sets of culture media bottles with povidone-iodine.			
Prepare site with povidone-iodine.			
Collect 5 mL of blood from vein that does not have an IV running into it.			
Place sterile needle on syringe used to draw blood.			
Swab tops of blood culture bottles. Insert needle through tops, and carefully inject 2.5 to 5 mL of blood into one or both bottles. Use a new sterile needle when puncturing each bottle top.			
Prepare skin and collect second specimen after 15 minutes.			
Place second sample in set of paired culture bottles. Most agencies require that each specimen be collected from a different site.			
If a third specimen is needed, follow above procedure.			
Remove gloves.			
Label bottles, and transport to laboratory *immediately*.			

Procedure 48–6
Assisting with the Insertion of a Central Venous Catheter

PROCEDURE	S	U	COMMENTS
1. Prepare client.			
Describe procedure and explain purpose of catheter and procedures involved in care and maintenance of line.			
Ensure client has signed a consent form before beginning.			

PROCEDURE	S	U	COMMENTS
Instruct client on how to perform Valsalva's maneuver. Encourage client to practice before procedure, unless contraindicated by client's condition.			
If client is unable to perform Valsalva's maneuver: a. Ask client to hold breath at end of deep inspiration or during expiratory phase of respiratory cycle and/or b. Have assistant compress client's abdomen with both hands.			
2. Prepare IV infusion equipment for attachment to catheter.			
Connect infusion tubing spike to port of IV solution container using surgical aseptic technique.			
Add filter to the infusion tubing, then connect extension tubing below the filter.			
Tape tubing connections or use Leur-Lok connections..			
Start flow of solution, place tubing protector cap on end of tubing and hang tubing on IV pole.			
3. Position client appropriately.			
Assist client to a Trendelenburg position. If client cannot tolerate this position, use supine or modified Trendelenburg position with only feet elevated 45° to 60°.			
For *subclavian insertion*, place rolled bath blanket under client's back between shoulders.			
For *jugular insertion*, place rolled bath blanket under opposite shoulder, turning client's head to opposite side.			
For *peripheral vein insertion* in brachiocephalic vein or superior vena cava, place client supine with dominant arm at 90° angle to trunk.			
4. Clean and shave insertion area.			
Open skin preparation equipment and don gloves.			
Wash and dry insertion site with soap and water.			
Shave area or clip hair close to skin if indicated by agency policy.			

PROCEDURE	S	U	COMMENTS
Discard gloves.			
Don mask and sterile gloves.			
Clean site with povidone-iodine sponges for 2 minutes or, if using 70% alcohol, for 10 minutes or according to agency protocol. Use circular motion, working outward.			
5. Maintain a sterile field, and assist the physician during catheter insertion.			
Open sterile packages and hand supplies to physician as needed.			
6. Support and monitor client.			
Explain procedure to client, and provide support.			
Maintain client in position.			
Monitior client for signs of respiratory distress, complaints of chest pain, tachycardia, pallor, or cyanosis.			
7. Attach primed IV tubing to catheter.			
While physician removes stylet from catheter, quickly attach IV tubing to catheter, and simultaneously ask client to perform Valsalva's maneuver as practiced.			
Set flow at keep-open rate until catheter placement is confirmed by x-ray.			
8. After infusion is attached, apply temporary dressing to site.			
Put on second pair of sterile gloves.			
Apply povidone-iodine ointment to site if agency protocol dictates.			
Apply 4 × 4 sterile gauze dressing or transparent occulsive dressing according to agency protocol.			
9. After x-ray examination or fluoroscopy confirms position of catheter, secure dressing with tape.			
See Procedure 48–8.			
Label dressing with date and time of insertion and length of catheter.			
10. Establish appropriate infusion.			
See Procedure 48–7.			
11. Document all relevant information.			

Procedure 48–7
Maintaining and Monitoring a CVC System

PROCEDURE	S	U	COMMENTS
1. **Label each lumen of multilumen catheters.**			
Mark each lumen or port with description of its purpose, or use color code established by agency.			
2. **Monitor tubing connections.**			
Ensure all tubing connections are taped or secured according to agency protocol.			
Check connections every 2 hours.			
Tape cap ends if agency protocol indicates.			
3. **Change tubing according to agency policy.**			
4. **Change catheter site dressing according to agency policy.**			
5. **Administer all infusions as ordered.**			
Use controller or pump for all fluids.			
Prime all tubing to remove air.			
Maintain fluid flow at prescribed rate.			
When line is opened for any reason, instruct client to perform Valsalva's maneuver or clamp the lumen of the catheter with a soft-tipped clamp.			
6. **Cap lumens without continuous infusions, and flush regularly.**			
Cap ports not in use with an intermittent infusion cap.			
Clean adapter caps with alcohol or povidone-iodine swab before penetration.			
Flush noninfusing tubings with 1 or 2 mL of heparin flush solution every eight hours or according to agency protocol. Some catheters require only normal saline flushes.			
Aspirate for blood before flushing tubings.			
Use #25 gauge 5/8-inch needle to penetrate adapter cap when flushing catheter.			
7. **Administer medications as ordered.**			
If a capped medication port is flushed with heparin solution, flush the line with 5 to 10 mL of normal saline according to agency protocol before infusing the medication.			

PROCEDURE	S	U	COMMENTS
After medication is instilled through port, inject normal saline, then heparin flush solution if indicated by agency protocol.			
8. Monitor client for complications.			
Assess client's vital signs, skin color, mental alertness, appearance of catheter site, and presence of adverse symptoms at least every 4 hours.			
If air embolism is suspected, give client 100% oxygen by mask, place person in left Trendelenburg position, and notify physician.			
If sepsis is suspected, replace infusion with 5% or 10% dextrose solution, and change IV tubing and dressing. Save remaining solution for lab analysis, record lot number of solution and any additives, and notify physician immediately. When changing dressing, take culture of catheter site as ordered by physician or according to agency protocol.			
9. Document all relevant information.			

Procedure 48–8
Changing a CVC Tubing and Dressing

PROCEDURE	S	U	COMMENTS
Tubing change:			
1. Prepare client.			
Assist client to supine position.			
2. Prepare equipment.			
Prepare solution container, attach new IV tubing, and prime tubing.			
Don clean gloves and remove tape securing tubing to dressing and catheter hub connection. Remove and discard the gloves.			
Don clean sterile gloves and mask.			
Place sterile gauze underneath connection site of catheter and tubing. Clean junction of catheter and tubing with antiseptic, if required by agency protocol.			
3. Change tubing.			
Don clean gloves and ask client to perform Valsalva's maneuver and to turn head away while you detach IV tubing by rotating it out of hub.			
Quickly attach new primed IV tubing to the TPN catheter, ensuring tight seal.			

PROCEDURE	S	U	COMMENTS
Open clamp on new tubing and adjust flow to rate ordered.			
Secure tubing to catheter with tape if Luer-Lok connection is not present.			
Loop and tape tubing over dressing.			
4. Label tubing, and document tubing change.			
Mark date and time of tubing change on new IV tubing or drip chamber.			
Document tubing change and all assessments.			
Dressing change:			
5. Prepare client.			
Assist client to supine or semi-Fowler's position.			
Don mask, have client don mask (if tolerated or as agency protocol), and/or ask client to turn head away from insertion site.			
6. Prepare equipment.			
Wash hands before handling sterile supplies.			
Open sterile supplies.			
7. Change dressing.			
Remove clean gloves and don sterile gloves.			
Remove soiled dressing by pulling tape slowly and gently from skin.			
Inspect skin for signs of irritation or infection. Inspect catheter for signs of leakage or other problems. If infection is suspected, take swab of drainage for culture, label it, send it to laboratory, and notify physician.			
Clean the catheter insertion site with 3 alcohol swabs followed by 3 povidone-iodine swabs. Some agencies require cleaning with iodine first, followed by alcohol.			
Clean in circular motion, moving from insertion site outward to edge of adhesive border.			
Apply precut sterile drain gauze around catheter or cut sterile 2 × 2 with sterile scissors. Apply sufficient sterile gauze dressings to cover catheter and skin.			
or			
If using Elastoplast dressing, apply tincture of benzoin to skin surrounding dressing gauzes, and allow it to air dry about 1 minute.			

Remove gloves.			
8. Secure dressing and tubing.			
Ask client to abduct arm and turn head away from dressing site. Tape dressing securely to skin with transparent occlusive dressing or Elastoplast.			
Loop and tape IV tubing over occlusive dressing.			
Label dressing with date, time, and initials.			
9. Document tubing and dressing change, including all nursing assessments.			

Procedure 48–9
Removing a Central Venous Catheter

1. Prepare equipment.			
Open sterile suture removal set, and establish sterile field.			
Open sterile packages.			
Place some povidone-iodine ointment on one sterile gauze square if ointment is to be used. Check agency protocol.			
Don mask, and put one on client if necessary.			
Close clamp on infusion.			
2. Position client appropriately.			
Place client in supine or slight Trendelenberg position.			
Don clean gloves and remove dressing. Remove and discard gloves.			
Don sterile gloves.			
Remove any sutures that secure catheter.			
3. Remove catheter.			
Ask client to perform Valsalva's maneuver during removal.			
Grasp catheter hub and carefully withdraw it, maintaining direction of vein.			
Inspect catheter to make sure it is intact. If it is not, immediately place client in left lateral Trendelenburg position and notify nurse in charge or physician.			

4. Immediately after catheter removal, apply pressure with an air-occlusve dressing over site.

Use air-occlusive dressing, such as Vaseline gauze or Telfa covered with antiobiotic ointment or plain sterile gauze (check agency policy).

Completely cover insertion site with povidone-iodine ointment, if used, sterile pads, and moisture-proof tape.

or

If agency protocol indicates, use sterile transparent air-occlusive dressing.

Label dressing with date and time of catheter removal and your initials.

Leave air-occlusive dressing in place for 24 to 72 hours or length of time agency protocol recommends.

5. Ensure client safety.

Ask client to remain flat and supine for a short time after subclavian catheter is removed.

Observe client for signs of air embolism.

If air embolism is suspected, immediately place client in left lateral Trendelenburg position and administer 100% oxygen by face mask.

6. Document all pertinent information, including time of removal; size, length, and condition of catheter; and all nuring assessments and interventions.

Procedure 48–10
Measuring Central Venous Pressure

1. Prepare client.

Place client in supine position without pillow unless this position is contraindicated. If client feels breathless, elevate head of bed slightly; note exact position.

Locate level of client's right atrium at fourth intercostal space on midaxillary line.

Mark site with indelible pen or piece of nonallergenic tape.

PROCEDURE	S	U	COMMENTS
2. Prepare equipment.			
Prepare IV tubing and infusion, prime tubing, and then close clamp on tubing.			
When using separate manometer and stopcock, attach manometer to stopcock. Manometer is attached to vertical arm of stopcock.			
If using one-piece manometer and stopcock, attach them to IV pole.			
Attach IV tubing to left side of three-way stopcock.			
3. Flush manometer and stopcock.			
Do *not* attach stopcock to client's catheter until it is flushed free of air.			
Turn stopcock to IV-container-to-manometer position.			
Open IV tubing clamp and fill manometer with IV solution to level of about 18 to 20 cm.			
Close IV tubing clamp.			
Turn stopcock to IV-container-to-client position and flush stopcock.			
Close IV tubing clamp.			
4. Attach manometer to central catheter.			
Place sterile 4 × 4 gauze under catheter hub.			
After cleansing hub with alcohol or povidone-iodine, clamp tubing near insertion site, and attach manometer tubing to catheter.			
Turn stopcock so that IV runs into client.			
5. Measure central venous pressure.			
Check that level of client's right atrium is aligned with zero point on manometer scale. If adjustment is required, first raise or lower bed, then readjust manometer on IV pole.			
Adjust stopcock to manometer-to-client setting.			
Observe fall in fluid level in manometer tube. Also, note slight fluctuations in fluid level with client's inspiration and expiration. If fluid level does not fluctuate, ask client to cough.			
Lightly tap manometer tube with index finger when fluid level stablizes.			

PROCEDURE	S	U	COMMENTS
Take reading at end of an expiration or according to agency protocol. Inspect column at eye level, and take CVP reading from base of meniscus. If manometer contains small floating ball, take reading from its midline.			
Refill manometer, and take another reading of CVP.			
Readjust stopcock to IV-container-to-client position, and adjust infusion to ordered rate of flow.			
6. Obtain continuous CVP readings with pressure monitoring system.			
Set up a pressure transducer system at bedside. Attach noncompliant tubing from the catheter to transducer, and connect flush solution to flush device.			
Position client so that right atrium is level with transducer. Zero transducer according to manufacturer's instructions.			
Read CVP value on digital display, and observe waveform.			
7. Return client to a comfortable position.			
8. Document CVP.			
Report changes in CVP as ordered.			

References Cited in Text*

American Red Cross CPR for the Professional Rescuer, 1993, American National Red Cross.

Guidelines for Cardiopulmonary Resuscitation and Emergency Cardiac Care. 1992. *Journal of the American Medical Association* 286(16): 2171–97.

Hogan, L., and Beland, I. July 1976. Cervical neck syndrome. *American Journal of Nursing* 76:1104–7.

Holder, G., Alexander, J. February 1990. A new and improved guide to I.V. therapy . . . protocols for intravenous therapy. *American Journal of Nursing* 90:43–47.

Luce, J.M.; Tyler, M.L.; and Pierson, D.J. 1984. *Intensive respiratory care*. Philadelphia: W.B. Saunders Co.

Maier, P. September 1986. Take the work out of range-of-motion exercises with continuous passive motion machine. *RN* 49: 46–49.

Olds, S.B.; London, M.L.; and P.W. Ladewig. 1992. *Maternal-newborn nursing: A family centered approach*, 4th ed. Redwood City, CA: Addison-Wesley Nursing.

Palau, D. and Jones, S. October 1986. Test your skill at trouble shooting chest tubes. *RN* 49:43–45.

Quinn, A. September 1986. Thora-Drain III: Closed chest drainage made simpler and safer. *Nursing 86* 16: 46–51.

Smith, A.J., and Johnson, J.Y. 1990. *Nurses guide to clinical procedures*. Philadelphia: J.B. Lippincott Co.

*Additional references can be found in the corresponding chapter of *Fundamentals of Nursing*, sixth edition.

Appendix: Standard Precautions for All Client Care

These precautions are used in the care of all hospitalized persons regardless of their diagnosis or possible infection status. They apply to blood, all body fluids, secretions, and excretions *except sweat* (whether or not blood is present or visible), nonintact skin, and mucous membranes.

Thus they combine the major features of UP (Universal Precautions) and BSI (Body Substance Isolation). Recommended practices for Standard Precautions are shown in the following table.

Transmission-Based Precautions

These precautions are used in addition to Standard Precautions for clients with known or suspected infection that are spread in one of three ways: by airborne or droplet transmission, or by contact. The three types of transmission-based precautions may be used alone or in combination, but always **in addition** to Standard Precautions. They encompass all the conditions or diseases previously listed in the category-specific or disease-specific classifications devleoped by the CDC in 1983.

Recommended Isolation Precautions in Hospitals (HICPAC 1996, revised February 17, 1997)

Standard Precautions (Tier One)

- Designed for *all* clients in hospital.

- These precautions apply to (1) blood; (2) all body fluids, excretions, and secretions except sweat; (3) nonintact (broken) skin; and (4) mucous membranes.

- Designed to reduce risk of transmission of microorganisms from recognized and unrecognized sources.

1. Wash hands after contact with blood, body fluids, secretions, excretions, and contaminated objects whether or not gloves are worn.

   a. Wash hands immediately after removing gloves.

   b. Use a nonantimicrobial soap for routine handwashing.

   c. Use an antimicrobial agent or an antiseptic agent for the control of specific outbreaks of infection.

2. Wear clean gloves when touching blood, body fluids, secretions, excretions, and contaminated items (for example, soiled gowns).

   a. Clean gloves can be unsterile unless they are intended to prevent the entrance of microorganisms into the body.

   b. Remove gloves before touching noncontaminated items and surfaces.

   c. Wash hands immediately after removing gloves.

3. Wear a mask, eye protection, or a face shield if splashes or sprays of blood, body fluids, secretions, or excretions can be expected.

4. Wear a clean, nonsterile gown if client care is likely to result in splashes or sprays of blood, body fluids, secretions, or excretions. The gown is intended to protect clothing.

   a. Remove a soiled gown carefully to avoid the transfer of microorganisms to others (for example, clients or other health care workers).

   b. Wash hands after removing gown.

5. Handle client care equipment that is soiled with blood, body fluids, secretions, or excretions carefully to prevent the transfer of microorganisms to others and to the environment.

   a. Make sure reusable equipment is cleaned and reprocessed correctly.

   b. Dispose of single-use equipment correctly.

6. Handle, transport, and process linen that is soiled with blood, body fluids, secretions, or excretions in a manner to prevent contamination of clothing and the transfer of microorganisms to others and to the environment.

7. Prevent injuries from used equipment such as scalpels or needles, and place them in puncture-resistant containers.

Transmission-Based Precautions (Tier Two)

Airborne Precautions

Use the Tier One precautions as well as the following:

1. Place client in a private room that has negative air pressure, 6 to 12 air changes per hour and discharge of air to the outside or a filtration system for the room air.

2. If a private room is not available, place client with another client who is infected with the same microorganism.

3. Wear a respiratory device (N95 respirator) when entering the room of a client who is known or suspected of having primary tuberculosis.

4. Susceptible people should not enter the room of a client who has rubella (measles) or varicella (chickenpox). If they must enter they should wear a respirator.

5. Limit movement of client outside the room to essential purposes. Place a surgical mask on the client if possible.

Droplet Precautions

Use the Tier One precautions as well as the following:

1. Place client in private room.

2. If a private room is not available, place client with another client who is infected with the same microorganism.

3. Wear a mask if working within 3 feet of the client.

4. Transport client outside of the room only when necessary and place a surgical mask on the client if possible.

Contact Precautions

Use the Tier One precautions as well as the following:

1. Place client in private room.

2. If a private room is not available, place client with another client who is infected with the same microorganism.

3. Wear gloves as described in Standard Precautions.

   a. Change gloves after contact with infectious material.

   b. Remove gloves before leaving client's room.

   c. Wash hands immediately after removing gloves. Use an antimicrobial agent.

   d. After handwashing do not touch possibly contaminated surfaces or items in the room.

4. Wear a gown (see Standard Precautions) when entering a room if there is a possibility of contact with infected surfaces or items, or if the client is incontinent, has diarrhea, a colostomy, or wound drainage not contained by a dressing.

   a. Remove gown in the client's room.

   b. Make sure uniform does not contact possible contaminated surfaces.

5. Limit movement of client outside the room.

6. Dedicate the use of noncritical client care equipment to a single client or to clients with the same infecting microorganisms.

Source: Adapted from JS Garner and the Hospital Infection Control Practices Advisory Committee (HICPAC), Guidelines for isolation precautions in hospitals, *Infection Control Hospital Epidemiology*, 1996, 17:53–80 and NCID Home Page, February 18, 1997, and *American Journal of Infection Control*, 1996, 24:24–52.